Daily Life
in
Louisiana
1815–1830

Daily Life
in Louisiana
1815–1830

Liliane Crété

Translated by Patrick Gregory

Louisiana State University Press
Baton Rouge and London

Originally published in 1978 as
La Vie quotidienne en Louisiane, 1815–1830
Copyright © 1978 by Hachette
Translation copyright © 1981 by
Louisiana State University Press

Designer: Albert Crochet
Typeface: VIP Trump Medieval
Typesetter: G & S Typesetters, Inc.
Printer and binder: Thomson-Shore, Inc.

LIBRARY OF CONGRESS CATALOGING IN PUBLICATION DATA

Crété, Liliane.
  Daily Life in Louisiana, 1815–1830.

  Translation of: La vie quotidienne en Louisiane, 1815–1830.
  Bibliography: p.
  Includes index.
  1. Louisiana—Social life and customs.
  2. Creoles—Social life and customs. I. Title.
F374.C7413   976.3'05   81-8315
ISBN 0-8071-0887-1   AACR2

Contents

Illustrations

Preface

If an historian wishes to describe the daily life of a given period of modern history in any meaningful detail, he must sharply limit the scope of his inquiry, for styles and customs, as well as physical surroundings, change with alarming rapidity. The years from 1815 to 1830 mark a watershed in the history of Louisiana, an era of tension and transition between the Old World and the New; between two opposing ways of life, the Creole and the American; and even, one might say, between two centuries—for the Creoles clung tenaciously to the customs and beliefs of the past and were reluctant to acknowledge the innovations heralded by the nineteenth century.

The War of 1812, that futile and misbegotten conflict, came to a formal end on December 14, 1814, with the signing of the Treaty of Ghent. News of the treaty did not, however, reach Louisiana in time to forestall the Battle of New Orleans, which took place two weeks later, on January 8, 1815. In this engagement, Americans and Creoles united in an effort to defeat the British and to assert their allegiance to the Union.

As the French historian André Maurois has remarked in his *History of the United States*, the Treaty of Ghent "coincides with the end of an epoch. In the United States, as in Europe, the nineteenth century began in the year 1815." In America, the war served to bring into view a latent nationalist enthusiasm. It also led to an upsurge in industrial production—the result of the country's need to manufacture products hitherto imported from Great Britain. The vitality of the young Republic suddenly made itself felt in all directions. In the East, the new spirit manifested itself in the burgeoning of new in-

dustries; in the South, in the proliferation of profitable cotton plantations; in the West, in the opening of vast new territories for settlement and exploitation.

There now began for Louisiana an era of unprecedented peace and
prosperity. The introduction of the steamboat in 1815 revolution-
ized Mississippi River travel, and almost overnight New Orleans became one of the most important ports in the Union, second only to
New York. Docks lined the riverbanks for miles upon miles, receiving and dispatching ships to and from every corner of the globe.

The Treaty of Ghent seemed to have effectively mended Anglo-
American relationships, and Great Britain resumed its role as chief
market for American cotton. The invention of the cotton gin at the
end of the eighteenth century, along with the extraordinary growth
of industrialization in England and the proliferation of factories
manufacturing cotton goods, contributed to the rapid development
of the new regions of the South: Alabama, Louisiana, Mississippi,
Arkansas. Louisiana was inundated with wave upon wave of settlers,
coming from all parts of the country and every walk of life. They
planted cotton and sugarcane wherever transportation was available
and the soil permitted. The western part of the state, however, was
given over to herds of livestock.

The year 1815 also saw the arrival in New Orleans of Bonapartist
refugees from the Bourbon Restoration, who added a new element to
the already heterogeneous population of the city. The Bonapartists
formed a distinct group of their own, apart from both the Creoles
and the Americans.

The upsurge in agricultural production led to an increased demand for field laborers and consequently reinforced the hold that
slavery already had on the South. This "peculiar institution" had become built into the region's economic structure and was essential to
the prosperous running of the large plantations. I have attempted to
integrate the story of the black people of Louisiana into my narrative
in a manner that stresses their importance and conceals nothing of
their plight.

Nothing can justify an institution that reduces human beings to
chattels and divides husband from wife, children from parents. Yet it

is only fair to point out that the careful study of innumerable documents, including contemporary letters, journals, diaries, and travel
accounts, seems to indicate that slaves in Louisiana were not, on the
whole, ill treated by the standards of the times—an era when flog-
ging was still a common mode of punishment in the British armed
services. During the Civil War, few slaves took the occasion to revolt
against their masters, and after the war a large number of them
chose to remain on their old estates. We should also bear in mind
that, from about 1820 on, the price of slaves rose steeply. Each slave,
then, represented a considerable investment to his or her master,
and the owner watched over the slave's well-being with a sense of
humanitarianism solidly reinforced by self-interest.

Our story comes to an end around the year 1830. Although the
daily life on the large estates and in the small villages would remain
relatively unchanged for years to come, New Orleans underwent a
transformation during the next decade. Its population leaped from
29,737 to 102,193; its character changed from a Franco-Hispanic
colonial outpost to a modern, bustling, go-ahead American metropolis. English became the language of the streets, and the Faubourg St.
Mary replaced the old French Quarter as the fashionable part of
town. The old-guard Creole aristocracy remained stubbornly fixed
in its ways, but its political and social influence was on the wane.
Many other groups and factions were simply absorbed into the new,
mixed population. Bonapartists, revolutionaries, and royalists ceased
to turn their hopes and aspirations toward France and came to consider themselves neither more nor less than native Louisianians.
New minorities entered the region, and the Irish and Italians formed
the basis for a social class previously unknown in the state: the white
proletariat.

The reader will notice that I have not only limited the time span
of this study, but have laid emphasis on the urban aspect of Louisiana—that is, on New Orleans. I hoped in so doing to bring into
focus the spectacle of a still vital and dominant Creole society as it
came into conflict with the far more vigorous and dynamic society
that was presently to supercede it. The Creoles, of course, were
eventually absorbed into the population. Only the Acadians, remote

from the rest of society in their backwater swamps and prairies, managed to resist the process of Americanization for another century.

Above all, I have sought to capture in these pages an image, however fleeting, of a society and way of life that even at its height was already marked for oblivion.

Acknowledgments

I wish to extend my warmest thanks to those people in the United States who helped me bring this work to completion, most particularly Mr. Colin B. Hamer, Jr., director of the Louisiana Division and City Archives Department of the New Orleans Public Library; and Mrs. Jean Jones, his assistant. I also wish to thank Mrs. Helen Burkes, curator of the Special Collections Division of the Howard-Tilton Library, Tulane University, for her innumerable kindnesses; and Natalia Easterly, who exerted herself so generously on my behalf.

Daily Life
in Louisiana
1815–1830

Introduction

More than a century after the discovery of the Mississippi by the Spaniard Hernando de Soto, the great river again received a visit from white men. These explorers were not rapacious soldiers in pursuit of a fairytale city of gold, but a merchant and a holy father who hoped to discover at long last the famous "Northwest Passage" opening into the China Sea.

According to Charlevoix, French settlers in Canada had long heard tales from the Indians about a great river to the West "called Mechasippi by some and Micissipi by others, which flowed neither North nor East." Their imaginations caught by such descriptions, they reasoned that the upper outlet of this river would afford a passage to China, while the lower outlet would open into the Gulf of Mexico.

The importance of such a route was fully appreciated by the governor of Canada, the comte de Frontenac, and by his colonial secretary Talon. In 1673, they commissioned a merchant from Québec named Louis Joliet and a Jesuit priest named Jacques Marquette to set out in search of this fabulous waterway. On May 17, 1673, the two men, accompanied by five Indians, left the mission of St. Ignace at Michilimakinac (Mackinac), which lay on the straits linking Lake Huron to the Lake of the Illinois (Lake Michigan) and struck out for the West. "Joyfully plying their oars," as Father Marquette later reported, the voyagers crossed the Lake of the Illinois and entered what is now known as Green Bay. They ascended the Fox River to its source, then continued down the Ouisconsing (Wisconsin) River, reaching the Mississippi on June 17.

Floating with the current, they descended as far as the mouth of the Arkansas River. The Indians they encountered on the way were

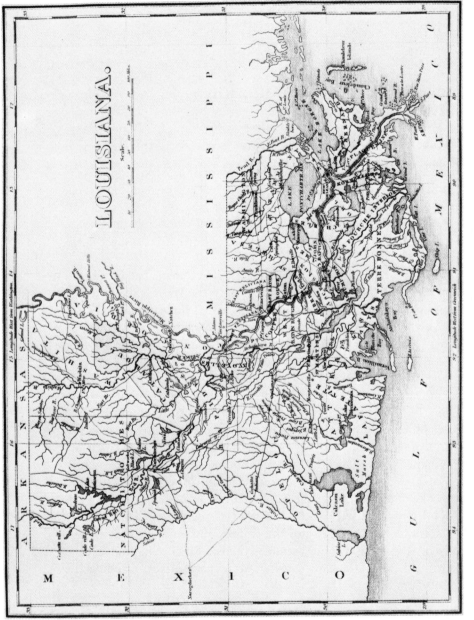

Louisiana, *ca.* 1827. Louisiana State University Department of Archives and Manuscripts

friendly and welcoming. Yet, according to Father Marquette, the explorers decided to push their luck no further—if they had only known it, they were a mere ten days' journey from the Gulf—for the "friendly savages" had warned them of hostile tribes further along the route who "blocked the passage to the sea."

Retracing their route, the two men parted ways at Green Bay. Father Marquette returned to his mission among the Indians; Louis Joliet, after passing the winter at Sault Ste. Marie, made his way back to Québec. News of the journey aroused great excitement in France, and the bells of Québec Cathedral were rung for an entire day to celebrate the discovery of the great river. But the Mississippi seemed too far away to be of any practical interest, and soon the memory of the discovery began to fade.

One man, however, remembered. René-Robert Cavalier de La Salle was the younger son of a prominent Rouen family who had come to the New World to seek his fortune. La Salle had already devoted several years to a firsthand study of the Indians; several times he had ventured into the wilderness, and he had even lived as a trapper among the Iroquois. At the time of Joliet's expedition, La Salle held the command of Fort Frontenac. He had previously secured trading privileges for the fort, and he immediately perceived the economic implications of Joliet's discovery. Leaving fort, land, and trading concessions behind and armed with letters of recommendation from the comte de Frontenac—a patron at once well disposed and highly influential—La Salle set sail for France. He hoped to obtain a royal charter permitting him to complete the exploration of the Mississippi and granting him rights over all the lands he should discover.

La Salle succeeded in his mission. He received a letter of patent on May 12, 1678; among the rights it accorded him was a monopoly on the sale of all buffalo hides within his domain.

While he was in France, La Salle made the acquaintance of the prince de Conti and enlisted his support. The prince put at his service the chevalier Henri de Tonti, who was to accompany La Salle on the expedition. In addition, friends and family contributed substantial sums of money. On his return to Fort Frontenac, La Salle set about making preparations for the trip, and after an initial false start, his expedition was launched in January, 1682.

The troupe consisted of twenty-three Frenchmen—including a royal notary and a Franciscan monk—eighteen braves, ten squaws, and three Indian children. They sailed down the Illinois, reaching the Mississippi toward the end of January. On February 6, they began their journey down the river, stopping from time to time to exchange gifts with the Indians living along the banks and to advise them of the benefits to be gained from the protection of the mighty king of France. On April 7, they reached the Gulf. "Monsieur de La Salle," the chevalier de Tonti recorded, "sent out boats to explore the channels. Some went to the left, some to the right; Monsieur de La Salle chose the center. In the evening each group gave his report: to wit, that the channels were very fine, being both wide and deep."

The expedition then withdrew a short way upstream. When they had found a sufficiently dry spot, they erected a stone marker bearing the French coat of arms and the inscription "Louis the Great, King of France and Navarre, April 9, 1682." They intoned the Te Deum and the Domine Salvum fac Regem. There was a shout of "Long live the King!" followed by musket salvos. La Salle then proclaimed:

By virtue of His Majesty's commission, which I have here to hand, I hereby lay claim and take possession, in the name of His Majesty and his successors, of this land of Louisiana: its waters, harbors, ports, bays, channels; its nations, peoples, provinces, cities, towns, villages; its mines, fish, streams, rivers—of everything within its confines extending, on the East, from the mouth of the St. Louis River, also known as the Ohio, Olighinsipou, or Chukgua. This I do with the consent of the Chabanons, Chikassas, and other tribes who dwell therein, with whom we have concluded alliances. I also lay claim to the length of the Colbert or Mississippi River and to all the rivers flowing into it, from its source beyond the land of the Sioux to its outflow into the Gulf of Mexico.

The members of the expedition then set up a cross, sang the Vexilia Regis, and buried a lead plaque bearing a Latin inscription that commemorated the event. The ceremony concluded with more shouts of "Long live the King!" The legal right of possession was ratified on the spot by Jacques de la Métairie, the royal notary.

The Realms of the Sun King

The following year, La Salle returned to France. He was received by the king without any sign of enthusiasm; evidently Louis XIV appreciated neither La Salle's hardships and heroism nor the value of the lands that the explorer had acquired for him. Nevertheless, the king concluded upon reflection that Louisiana was worth colonizing, and he entrusted La Salle with the command of another expedition.

La Salle set sail with a frigate and three smaller vessels. On board were five priests, twelve gentlemen, some hundred soldiers, and a complement of artisans and laborers, along with a full load of provisions and tools. Arrived at the Gulf of Mexico, the ships failed to locate the inlets of the Mississippi and finally dropped anchor in what is now known as Matagorda Bay, on the coast of Texas. For two years, La Salle and his party explored the region in search of the elusive Mississippi. At the end of that time, despair, sickness, and desertion had reduced his band to a miserable thirty-six men. With sixteen of that number, La Salle then headed north toward the country of the Illinois. A few eventually reached safety, but La Salle himself perished en route, murdered by one of his own men in the course of a mutiny.

Ten years passed before another expedition was launched. Louis XIV, at war with virtually all Europe, had almost forgotten his American domains when an energetic young officer of Canadian birth, Pierre le Moyne, sieur d'Iberville, reopened the question of their colonization to the king's ministers. Iberville was subsequently put in charge of a small flotilla, which entered the waters of the Mississippi on March 2, 1699.

Iberville penetrated far enough upstream to bring back reports of the beauty and lushness of the river's upper reaches, but he elected to found his own colony on the coast between the mouths of the Mississippi and Pensacola, where the Spaniards had lately established a fort. The site was called Biloxi (so named after the Indian nation that inhabited the region), and it was here that the colonization of Louisiana truly began.

The site was ill chosen, for the coastline was so low that heavy merchant ships could come no closer than four leagues from the shore, and even the lighter brigantines could approach no closer than two leagues. The soil was sandy, good neither for crops nor for livestock; and the climate was so hot that, by the beginning of April, the settlers had to limit their efforts to clear the terrain around the fort to two hours in the morning and two hours in the evening. To make matters worse, everyone came down with dysentery.

The colony had difficulty maintaining its population. A few families living around the fort eked out an existence on small crops of vegetables and food that they bought from the Indians. The rare reinforcements from France consisted for the most part of social misfits or delinquents of both sexes.

Louisiana, remote and inhospitable, seems to have been regarded as a land of penance and punishment, and the Sun King's policy of religious intolerance did nothing to further its colonization. When four hundred Protestant families who had fled to the Carolinas after the revocation of the Edict of Nantes sought permission to relocate in Louisiana, the comte de Pontchartrain, the king's representative, blandly informed them that "His Majesty had not chased the Protestants from his European domain in order for them to found a republic in his American colonies."

Eventually the inhabitants of Biloxi were transferred to a more salubrious site on the Mobile River, across from an island that provided a harbor to serve as a port for the new colony. The king undertook to send provisions, soldiers, a few laborers, some priests, two nuns, and twenty-three young women "of pious and virtuous upbringing" to serve as wives for the soldiers and other inhabitants of Mobile. For the moment, the colony enjoyed relative prosperity.

The prosperity was short lived. According to a report written by the colony's *commissaire-ordonnateur*,[1] one sieur de La Salle, in August, 1708, the inhabitants numbered "two hundred seventy-nine persons, of whom six are ailing; plus sixty itinerant Canadians inhabiting the Indian villages along the Mississippi without permission of the authorities, and whose libertine behavior with the native women sets at nought the efforts of the missionaries and others to instruct the Indians in the mysteries of religion." In 1710, the sieur

1. The *commissaire-ordonnateur* was the legal and financial officer of the French Louisiana colony and was entrusted with public expenditures, exercised certain judicial functions, and presided over the Superior Council. He shared the governmental administration of the colony with the governor, who was responsible for the military and general administration. For a detailed discussion of the history of this office, see Donald Jile Lemieux, "The Office of 'Commissaire Ordonnateur' in French Louisiana, 1731–1763: A Study in French Colonial Administration" (Ph.D. dissertation, Louisiana State University, 1972).—TRANS.

de Bienville, brother of le Moyne d'Iberville and governor of Louisiana, reported that food was so scarce that "most of his men depended on the Indians to supply them with nourishment."

But Louis XIV, preoccupied with problems at home, had little time or money to spare for his American possessions. France was debilitated by the long-drawn-out War of the Spanish Succession, and the king's ministers decided to turn over the management of the Louisiana colony to some entrepreneur. Antoine Crozat, a prosperous financier, applied for the Louisiana concession, and he received the charter at Fontainebleau on September 14, 1712. The colony at that time consisted of two infantry companies numbering fifty men apiece, seventy-five Canadians in the service of the king, twenty-eight families, and twenty Negroes. There were only five forts in the entire territory: flimsy structures hastily thrown together out of mud, logs, and sticks. The charter was valid for fifteen years; but at the end of five, Crozat renounced his rights to what had clearly proved an unprofitable venture.

JOHN LAW AND THE COMPANY OF THE WEST

Louisiana next came under the proprietorship of the Company of the West, which had been founded by the Scottish financier John Law. Law's monetary theories had beguiled the regent, Philippe of Orléans; he is credited with the introduction of paper money into France. The company's land agents touted Louisiana as a virtual paradise on earth. "The region," they proclaimed, "abounds in deposits of gold, silver, copper, and lead." On the basis of such reports, the company's stock soared, and a fair number of colonists—or rather, prospectors—booked passage for Louisiana.

The first of the ships arrived on February 9, 1718, bearing three companies of infantry and sixty-nine settlers. The month of June brought more soldiers, more settlers, and a number of convicted felons sentenced to transportation. Once again, the sieur de Bienville assumed the office of governor, and one of his first acts was to launch an expedition to determine a favorable site for establishing a permanent settlement. The site chosen was an Indian landing stage on the right bank of the Mississippi, but the place proved susceptible to flooding, so a levee was constructed to protect the new houses from the river's erratic waters. The town was named New Orleans in honor of Law's royal patron.

In order to encourage the development of agriculture, large concessions of land were granted to some of the richest and most influential of the king's subjects, who in return were expected to supply the manpower to operate the farms. Law populated his own "four square leagues" on the Arkansas River with Germans. (These hardy and industrious pioneers, finding themselves abandoned when the Scottish financier subsequently went bankrupt, made their way to New Orleans and were given a grant of land some twenty miles from the town.) Other large landowners imported French peasants to work their holdings. Many of these succumbed to the effects of the climate; those who survived, free from the scrutiny of their absentee landlords, fell prey to the temptations of idleness.

The company soon found itself turning to the slave trade to supplement the labor supply. Slaves were brought over from Guinea and soon became so numerous that Bienville, in 1724, issued in the name of the king a *Code Noir*, or Black Code, governing the importation of slaves and regulating foreign labor. This code, which remained on the books for over a hundred years, had as its first article the expulsion of all Jews from the colony.

At regular intervals, the company's vessels delivered fresh shipments of immigrants: landless peasants from France or the Palatinate, unemployed laborers from the cities, penniless younger sons of noble families, political exiles. All too often, the cargo also included felons who were being transported by force. The colonists were indignant at being forced to receive such guests; they protested to the king, who eventually decreed that "henceforth, no more vagabonds or criminals will be transported to Louisiana."

THE CASKET GIRLS

In order to meet the spiritual needs of the colony, the Company of the West dispatched to New Orleans a number of Jesuit priests and a delegation of Ursuline nuns. It also sent over a group of young orphan girls, each of whom was duly supplied, at the company's expense, with a casket containing a modest trousseau. These "casket girls," as they were called in Louisiana, were placed in the care of the nuns, who undertook to supply them with the rudiments of an education and with suitable husbands. To judge by the number of families who claim to be descended from these virtuous young ladies, they were a marvelously prolific lot. But the demand for marriageable girls was so overwhelming that the company was obliged to resort to less delicate means of recruitment and scoured the streets and alleys of Paris for readily exportable women.

The shortage of women led many young men to look to the Indian squaws to cook, clean, and satisfy their sexual needs. In many cases, these attachments culminated in marriage—especially in the Illinois Territory. But although these unions were blessed by the Jesuit missionaries, they were generally frowned on by the administrators. There was always an element in the colony that regarded frequenting prostitutes as preferable to intermarrying with the natives.

It was with reference to this same subject that the *commissaire-ordonnateur*, Jean-Baptiste du Bois Duclos, lodged an official complaint in 1713 about a shipment of twelve young women "so ugly and ill-favored" that the colonists and particularly, as he emphasized, the Canadians, found even the native women preferable to these "horrors." Duclos lamented the fact that some men would, when put to the test, choose a pretty face over a virtuous disposition.

The bankruptcy and subsequent flight from France of John Law in 1720 was a serious blow to the Company of the West, and its stock plummeted. It became increasingly difficult to recruit settlers for the colony as hopes of discovering gold or silver mines faded. The paper money that served as currency in Louisiana declined in value, and trade languished.

Moreover, the Indian nations, with whom the French had enjoyed generally friendly relations, were growing restless; some, indeed, were openly hostile. The English, who viewed the French colonial expansion with alarm, fomented Indian discontent. The French territories completely encircled the thirteen British colonies, blocking their expansion to the West; and now the two great powers began to play off one Indian tribe against another in order to improve their own strategic positions. For many years to come, France and England would take pride in the fact that the blood shed in these border skirmishes was seldom that of their own subjects. As Bienville recorded in 1723:

The Chactas [Choctaws], whom I aroused to activity this past winter, have just totally destroyed three villages of the cruel and bellicose Chickasaws, who were hampering trade on the river. They have brought back more than four hundred scalps and more than a hundred prisoners. It is a splendid achievement, the more so since the victory was obtained without the risk of a single French life, due to my care in setting one group of savages against the other.

On November 28, 1729, the Natchez, infuriated by repeated expropriations of their land, massacred two hundred Frenchmen. In order to recover the French women, children, and Negroes held captive by the Indians, a war party was launched against the tribe, consisting in part of two hundred Choctaws and a number of free blacks. The expedition was ill conceived and ill executed; only the blacks and the Indians fought bravely or to any purpose, and at the end of the operation the Natchez sought refuge with the Chickasaws. At New Orleans, a city wall was built to protect the citizens from future Indian incursions. Henceforth, the settlers had to deal with the combined forces of two enemy nations. "The war with the Natchez affected only the river traffic, that with the Chickasaws threatens the whole colony," wrote Monsieur de Beauchamps, the military commander of Mobile, to the government at home. He went on to complain of the fanaticism of the governor, Etienne Périer, whose sole ambition was "to slaughter natives" while totally disregarding the repercussions of such policies on the colony as a whole.

In 1731, the Company of the West, declaring total bankruptcy, ceded the colony back to the crown. Under the company's management, the seeds of permanence had been planted in Louisiana: New Orleans had been founded, as well as important establishments at Tchoupitoulas, Cannes-Brulées, Baton Rouge and Pointe Coupée.

Louis XV appropriated Louisiana for himself. The inventory, drawn up under the direction of the *commissaire-ordonnateur*, showed a net worth of two hundred sixty-three thousand livres. Blacks were assessed at seven hundred livres, horses at fifty-seven, and rice at three livres the hundredweight. For the third time, Monsieur de Bienville was appointed governor.

THE INDIAN WARS

The years passed; the colony languished. With the help of their black slaves, the colonists cultivated silkworms, indigo, tobacco, rice, cotton, and bayberries—all with only modest success. In 1741, the Jesuits experimented with growing sugarcane; the results were inconclusive. Severe tornadoes and prolonged draughts led to frequent crises of food and shelter; yellow fever epidemics ravaged the population, and the mortality rate of the livestock was terrible. The lack of laborers, carpenters, cabinetmakers, and shoemakers was sorely felt. Nevertheless, New Orleans could boast a dancing master—a Parisian by the name of Baby who had arrived with the household of the marquis de Vaudreuil—and so many cabarets that a police regulation of 1743 stipulated that "no more than six publicans can reside in the town."

In 1745, New Orleans had only eight hundred inhabitants, and it was entirely possible to encounter an alligator in the muddy streets when returning from church on a Sunday morning. But under the governorship of the marquis de Vaudreuil, a brave display of elegance was affected. Members of his entourage wore powdered wigs, jewels, and brocades. Brilliant balls were the order of the day, with fine wines and gilded furniture imported at great expense from the home country.

A chronic state of misunderstanding existed between the governors and the *commissaires-ordonnateurs*—the agents of the crown charged with overseeing the colony's expenses. Denunciatory and totally contradicting reports piled up at the ministry in Versailles, while in New Orleans factions and vendettas flourished. This administrative strife was far from beneficial to the colony.

Meanwhile, the Indian wars continued. The French still struggled to subdue the Chickasaws, while the Choctaws, dissatisfied with the subsidies they had received from the French, threatened to transfer their allegiance to the British. The soldiers sent by the king to defend the colony proved yet another source of anxiety. Governor

Bienville complained of having to assume command of a band of "stunted creatures four and a half feet tall, as corrupt as they are cowardly." Governor Périer affirmed that "it would be better to send our slaves into combat, if only they weren't so expensive to replace." And Governor Kerlerec, who succeeded the marquis de Vaudreuil, beseeched the king to send Swiss mercenaries, because the brutality of the French soldiers, he explained, had turned the colonists against them.

It should be noted, however, that some sixty soldiers displayed such meritorious behavior that they were honorably discharged from duty and married to "royal wards" sent over from France for that very purpose. Each couple was awarded a tract of land, along with a cow, a calf, a rooster, five hens, a rifle, an ax, and a spade. In addition, for the first three years they received food rations and small quantities of gunpowder, lead, and a variety of grains. The descendants of these exemplary men and women assured the colony's future.

Another element of stability were the Acadians, who began arriving in Louisiana in 1756. The Peace of Aix-la-Chapelle in 1748 put an end to the War of the Austrian Succession, but it failed to halt the rivalry between England and France. After several years of uneasy peace, the two nations found themselves again on the brink of war. The Scots, who had established themselves in Acadia shortly after France ceded this colony to England in 1713, distrusted the political and religious loyalty of the French settlers and decided to expel them. The French Acadians were herded onto ships and unceremoniously deposited at various points along the coasts of the other American colonies, in the hope that they would somehow be absorbed into the Protestant, Anglo-Saxon population. The emigrants were received in a few places with kindness and decency, but far more often they met with hostility and suspicion. Many sought to make their way to Louisiana, where they could hope to find the protection of their fellow countrymen and coreligionists.

The Acadians straggled into New Orleans in small groups after enduring grueling and often perilous journeys. Most of them settled in the Delta, a swampy region of alligators, snakes, mosquitoes, and towering cypresses hung with Spanish moss. The joy of being on French soil once more seemed to compensate, however, for the difficulties of the terrain, and the Acadians set to work with a will to tame the Delta.

But Louisiana was not fated to remain French soil for long. The combined force of two million English colonists was gradually brought to bear on the sparsely settled French frontiers, and incessant border skirmishes turned into open combat as Europe once again plunged into war. No help was forthcoming for Louisiana from the home country. "We are running short of everything," lamented the colonial administrators, "and the discontent of the Indians gives cause for deep concern." Their appeals fell on deaf ears. The ministers of Louis XV were preoccupied with troubles at home, and the nation as a whole had no interest in colonial affairs.

British supremacy soon made itself felt on land and sea, in America and the West Indies. Yet the war dragged on. At the instigation of the French, Spain entered the conflict as a French ally—and promptly lost Cuba. Louis XV, fearing that his new ally would be disheartened by this setback, decided to present Louisiana to his "esteemed and beloved cousin" Charles III, king of Spain. The documents certifying the transfer of the colony to Spain were signed at Fontainebleau on November 3, 1762, but were kept a state secret. It was not until 1764 that the governor of Louisiana was authorized to convey the news to the inhabitants of the colony.

"HURRAH FOR BORDEAUX WINE!"

The war was finally brought to an end with the treaty signed on February 10, 1763. Great Britain was ceded Canada and most of the eastern portion of the Louisiana Territory. Spain retained the other part, including New Orleans; while regaining Cuba, she yielded Florida to England. Those inhabitants of Louisiana who found it intolerable to live under English rule were given eighteen months to dispose of their property and relocate where they wished. For obscure reasons, Spain did not take official possession of Louisiana until 1769. A Spanish governor was dispatched, however, as early as 1766. When Don Antonio de Ulloa, a renowned scholar and world traveler, arrived in New Orleans, he was greeted with icy reserve by the inhabitants.

The political situation in the colony was confused: Spaniards,

Frenchmen, Indians, and Englishmen mingled freely but were uncertain of their rights and privileges within the territory. English ships plied the Mississippi between Manchac, Natchez, and Baton Rouge, carrying on a lively and more or less illicit trade with the inhabitants and importing a great many black slaves. French and Spanish officials functioned side by side; but although Spanish laws gradually replaced French ones and the Spanish treasury paid the colony's bills, although French soldiers and French administrators received their salaries from the Spanish governor Ulloa, the Spanish flag did not fly over New Orleans and there was still a segment of the population that steadfastly refused to recognize Spain's sovereignty. The territory was rife with intrigues and rebellions; in New Orleans, public meetings were held at which feelings ran dangerously high. "It is hardly pleasant to have to govern a colony given over to revolutions and which, for the past three years, no longer knows if it is Spanish or French," wrote Philippe Aubry, a French army officer who administered the territory jointly with Don Antonio de Ulloa.

At last a group of prominent citizens launched a bona fide rebellion. Armed men paraded through the streets of New Orleans shouting: "Hurrah for the King! Hurrah for Good King Louis! Hurrah for Bordeaux wine! To hell with Catalonian rotgut!" On the advice of Monsieur Aubry, Don Antonio fled the city with his family.

The king of Spain delegated General Alejandro O'Reilly to put a stop to this chaotic situation. In July, 1769, O'Reilly arrived on the Mississippi at the head of several regiments, and on August 18 he officially took possession of Louisiana. O'Reilly immediately ordered the arrest and trial of the leaders of the rebellion. Six were condemned to the gallows, another six to imprisonment in the fortress in Havana. For want of a hangman, those condemned to death were executed by firing squad. The rebellion was crushed and peace reigned once again, but O'Reilly earned an indelible reputation for cruelty.

The succeeding Spanish governors—Unzaga, Gálvez, Miro, Carondelet—proved capable and broad-minded. They realized that the colony's primary need was to attract new settlers; and although Protestants were not permitted the use of public churches, the authorities allowed them the private observance of their religion.

In the years following the War of Independence, innumerable American families settled in Louisiana. When the king of Spain misguidedly appointed Father Antonio de Sedella representative of the Holy Inquisition to oversee the spiritual well-being of the colony, the governor, Esteban Miro, had him detained and shipped to Cádiz. "The mere name of Inquisition uttered in New Orleans," wrote the governor to the Spanish authorities, "would be sufficient not only to check immigration . . . but would also be capable of driving out those who have recently come."

The governors were equally tolerant in their attitude toward commerce. A warm welcome was extended to French, English, and American merchants, and lucrative business connections were established not only along the Mississippi, but as far east as Philadelphia. The governors grew rapidly acclimatized to local customs: they learned to view with equanimity the widespread smuggling and the general disregard of official Spanish trade regulations.

The policy toward the Indians was designed to promote peaceful relations, not only between the Indians and the Spaniards but among the various Indian nations as well. As part of their effort at conciliation, the Spaniards actively sought alliances with the Indians and showered them with gifts. In 1784 Governor Miro presided at a gathering of representatives of several Indian nations; three years later he received thirty-six chiefs of the Choctaws and Chickasaws—these two nations being at last at peace—with enormous pomp in New Orleans. A ball was held in the Indians' honor, and some military parades were organized. According to the intendant Navarro, each Indian returned to his village "with a Spanish heart."

The relations between the French and Spanish populations, so stormy at the outset, now improved rapidly. Intermarriages between the two communities became common: the example was set by some of the leading Spaniards who, whether from political opportunism or personal inclination, allied themselves through marriage to the most prominent French families of Louisiana.

French remained the common language of the colony and the chief language of the schools. In New Orleans, enrollments in the French schools in 1788 totaled some four hundred students of both sexes, whereas the Spanish school—the first public school in Louisiana—had only about thirty. As Governor Miro remarked, "The introduction of the Spanish language into the colony has been a difficult task. . . . The best that we have been able to achieve to date is that the courtroom debates are conducted in Spanish."

It is hardly surprising, therefore, that the first newspaper to appear on a regular basis in the colony, beginning in 1794, was the French-language *Le Moniteur de France*. In spite of a recent influx of Spanish and Anglo-Saxon settlers, the French remained in the ascendancy; and two new waves of immigrants, both the results of political upheavals, further enhanced and enriched French influence: Royalists fleeing from the Revolutionary tribunals in France, and planters, often accompanied by their slaves, escaping from the turmoil in Santo Domingo.

In 1788 New Orleans was swept by fire. The rebuilding of the city was carried out at the expense of the Spanish government and with the aid of a generous *hidalgo*, Don Andrés Almonester y Rojas. New Orleans was now transformed from a provincial French town into a characteristically Spanish one. The houses of the wealthy boasted balconies and elaborate wrought-iron grillwork, through which one caught a glimpse of shady patios and sparkling fountains.

Meanwhile, the port flourished. New Orleans had become the receiving point for virtually all the goods from the area west of the Appalachians, which had recently opened up to colonization.

THE TREATY OF SAN ILDEFONSO

The Americans had come to regard the Mississippi as their birthright, a passage designed to link the newly settled western territories to the sea and to the whole world beyond. They resented the heavy export duties imposed by the Spanish and agitated continually for free navigation of the river all the way to the Gulf.

The Treaty of Versailles, signed in 1783, returned Florida to the Spanish but left the northern boundaries of the territory somewhat vague. Inevitably, these boundaries became a subject of dispute. On October 27, 1795, the United States and Spain concluded another treaty at Madrid, according to which Spain received a strip of territory east of the Mississippi, from the thirty-first parallel to the Gulf of Mexico, while the Americans gained the right to navigate freely on the river and to establish a depot at the port of New Orleans.

Although these terms were clearly favorable to the new nation, many Americans found them unsatisfactory. A sizable faction had hoped for nothing less than American possession of New Orleans; there were even those who demanded the annexation, pure and simple, of the entire Louisiana Territory.

From France, meanwhile, Napoleon Bonaparte was also casting a covetous eye on the territory. Eager to enlarge France's overseas empire, Napoleon entered into negotiations for Louisiana with Charles IV, the pusillanimous king of Spain. Bonaparte assured the king that "the restoration of Louisiana to France would provide a protective bulwark for Spain's Mexican territory, and serve as a guarantee of peace in the Gulf area." Charles was the more easily persuaded because the territory had proved a considerable drain on the Spanish treasury. Beside the upkeep of the military installations, the salaries to soldiers and administrators, and the annual payments in money and merchandise to the neighboring Indian nations, there had been sizable sums expended to encourage immigration: to the Isleños, brought from the Canary Islands at the government's expense, to the Acadians, and to others. Charles IV had few regrets in parting with a possession that had given him so much worry and so few rewards.

The Treaty of San Ildefonso, which was concluded on October 1, 1800, transferred all of Louisiana to France, with the understanding that if France ever wished to divest itself of the territory Spain would have the first claim. The treaty also stipulated that France would undertake to enlarge the Italian holdings of the Crown Prince of Parma, the king of Spain's son-in-law.

The treaty was kept secret for some time, for Napoleon feared that if the English learned of his acquiring the territory they would have no qualms about seizing it for themselves. But in 1802 he requested the Spanish government formally to transfer Louisiana to France, and the news of the treaty became known. In the United States, feelings ran high: it was felt that the aggressive French would be less desirable neighbors than the pacific Spanish. Just prior to the territory's transfer, American trading privileges in New Orleans had been curtailed—a development that was now seen as an "act of hostility" on the part of the new owners, who had clearly put pressure on the departing Spanish.

The United States Congress, indignant at the news, called for a show of force. "We must hasten to take possession of New Orleans whilst in the hands of the sluggish Spaniards, and not wait until it is in the iron grasp of the Caesar of modern times," thundered James Jackson, the senator from Georgia. President Jefferson preferred private negotiation to public bombast: he instructed Robert Livingston, his minister plenipotentiary in Paris, to initiate discussions with the French. Presently James Monroe, former governor of Virginia, was sent over to join Livingston in negotiating the purchase of the city of New Orleans.

By the time Monroe reached Paris, discussions between Livingston, François Barbé-Marbois, the minister of the treasury, and Talleyrand, the minister of foreign affairs, were well under way. The situation favored the American negotiating team. The expeditionary force sent by Bonaparte to quell the rebellion in Santo Domingo had been defeated, war with Britain seemed imminent, and, in short, the First Consul had lost interest in his American possession and resolved to renounce it. Although the transfer of Louisiana to a third nation was expressly forbidden by the Treaty of San Ildefonso, Napoleon showed no scruples: to the astonishment of the Americans, he had Talleyrand propose the cession not of New Orleans alone, but of the entire Louisiana Territory.

Jefferson was immediately apprised of the offer. Although he knew that a constitutional amendment was necessary to authorize the purchase, he too refused to stick to technicalities: the opportunity was simply too good to be lost. He gave his assent, and the negotiations were brought to a swift conclusion. On April 30, 1803, the treaty ceding Louisiana to the United States was signed by Livingston, Monroe, and Barbé-Marbois, the designated representative of the First Consul.

THE FIFTEEN-MILLION-DOLLAR PURCHASE

The territory acquired by Jefferson for the sum of fifteen million dollars more than doubled the size of the United States. The purchase converted the Mississippi River into an American waterway from its source to its outlet and opened a seemingly limitless expanse of virgin land to exploration and settlement. The United States was elevated overnight to the rank of a world power—much to the satisfaction of Napoleon Bonaparte. "The acquisition of these new lands," he declared, "firmly establishes the might of the United States; and by this sale I have bequeathed to England a naval rival that sooner or later will humble her pride."

On December 18, 1803, as the American troops under General James Wilkinson came within sight of New Orleans, the Spanish forces in the city embarked for Havana. Two days later, Louisiana was formally turned over to the American authorities by Pierre Clement de Laussat, the French colonial prefect who, in his brief tenure of office, found time to introduce several new laws, establish a fire brigade, and deliver two notable speeches. His first address, delivered the day after his arrival in New Orleans, celebrated France's reannexation of Louisiana: "Your separation from France marked one of the darkest moments in her history. It was concluded by a feeble and corrupt government as part of a disastrous peace following an ignominious war." In his second address, he spoke of the territory's sale to the United States: "Prudence and humanity, wedded to a far-seeing political vision—the hallmark of that genius who holds the destiny of nations in sway—have given new shape to France's glorious plans for Louisiana's future. In ceding Louisiana to the United States of America, France has designated you, the people of Louisiana, as a living pledge of that friendship which, with every passing day, binds the two republics ever closer, and which serves to promote their common peace and prosperity."

On December 20, 1803, the ceremony of transfer took place in the Place d'Armes in New Orleans. As ranks of New Orleans militia and American soldiers stood rigidly at attention, the French tricolor was ceremoniously lowered, while the Stars and Stripes was raised on an adjacent flagpole. When the two flags were both at half-mast, there was a momentary pause, and cannons boomed to salute the union of the two nations. The ceremonies culminated in a state banquet at which four toasts were drunk: the first, in madeira, to the United States and Jefferson; the second, in malaga, to Charles IV and Spain;

the third, in champagne, to the French Republic and Napoleon; and the fourth to the good fortune of the people of Louisiana.

The American, Spanish, and French representatives did their best to maintain harmonious relations among their constituencies, but discordant notes were soon heard. In 1804, Congress took it upon itself to divide the territory into two sections: the southern section, extending from the Gulf of Mexico to the thirty-third parallel, was designated the Territory of Orleans, while the northern section, with its capital at St. Louis, was called Louisiana. This partition aroused the ire of the population, as did the imposition of English as the official language of the territory. There was equal indignation at a regulation that forbade the importation of slaves into the region, except those belonging to American citizens who chose to settle there.

The Creoles were confused and angered by the course of events. Already disoriented by the change of nationality from Spanish to French, they looked on William C. C. Claiborne, the energetic young American governor, as an interloper. Claiborne was accused of awarding the most lucrative and influential administrative posts to his fellow Yankees, and of having little knowledge of the laws, customs, and social structure of the territory. The fact that he neither spoke nor understood Spanish or French increased the sense of alienation between the people of Louisiana and the new American administration.

"The government representatives here commit one blunder after another," wrote the former prefect de Laussat to the minister of the marine in Paris. The cultural rift extended to the most petty details: de Laussat qualified as "ridiculous" and "pretentious" the American efforts to supplant the waltz and the cotillion with the reel and the jig. A Creole beauty was heard to exclaim in the course of a ball, "The Spanish ruled over us for thirty years, yet they never forced us to do the fandango!" The new rulers were branded as cultural barbarians and roundly despised for their industry and enterprise. The Yankees, in turn, considered the Creoles lazy, decadent, snobbish, and immoral.

LOUISIANA ENTERS THE UNION

Such dissension was to have its consequences. Article III of the treaty of cession asserted hopefully that Louisiana's "incorporation into the Union would take place as soon as possible, following the procedures established by the Constitution." The Union, however, showed some reluctance to take Louisiana to its bosom. When Congress entertained the question, "Are the people of Louisiana ready for self-government?" the response was in the negative.

The Creoles were not unnaturally indignant, and their anti-American prejudices were reinforced. Yet two years later, New Orleans celebrated the Fourth of July with extraordinary exuberance. Festive dinners were arranged; a play, *Washington, or the Liberty of the New World*, was performed before a large and enthusiastic audience; a sumptuous ball was held at the City Hall; a high mass was celebrated and a Te Deum offered at the convent and the cathedral; and the New Orleans militia hosted a banquet at Bayou St. John.

It would be pleasant to take these joyous demonstrations as proof that the people of Louisiana, despite their bitterness at being judged "irresponsible" by Congress, had come to recognize the prosperity of the territory under American rule, to appreciate the social and economic advancement promised by the new laws and institutions—to realize, in short, that the merits and advantages of American dominion outweighed the inconveniences and irritations. But the safest interpretation of all this festivity would be that the Creoles were simply unwilling to pass up the opportunity to throw a party!

Agriculture and commerce were indeed flourishing. Cotton was becoming an important commodity, as was sugarcane: Etienne de Boré's discovery, in 1795, of a means of crystallizing the juice of the cane had made the crop attractive to the planters. All along the lower Mississippi, slaves were clearing land, building houses, planting and harvesting crops. The Indians, banished from their ancestral lands by a series of treaties, had disappeared into the interior.

New Orleans prospered and grew. The city's first bank was opened, to great fanfare; it was soon followed by a second. Schools were founded. New settlers arrived: the younger sons of well-to-do Virginia and Carolina planters; sturdy adventurers from the North and East; and emigrants by the thousands from Cuba—both French planters with their slaves and free blacks who had fled Santo Domingo several years before in the wake of the revolutionary upheaval and now had to flee once more because Napoleon's invasion of Spain had made any French presence in Cuba unwelcome.

The immigrants received a warm welcome from the Creole population and a cool one from the Americans, who resented this "invasion" of foreigners. Governor Claiborne attempted to stop the influx by rigidly enforcing the existing laws restricting the importation of blacks. All black males above the age of fifteen were denied entry into the territory—a regulation that, however, went quite unheeded.

In 1810, the census figures for the territory listed 76,476 inhabitants, with 24,552 living in New Orleans and its environs. The publication of these figures led to a reconsideration of the territory's status, and on January 4, 1811, the U.S. House of Representatives voted 77 to 36 to admit Louisiana to the Union. A month later, President Madison ratified the bill, and on April 30, 1812, the territory became a state and recovered its original name of Louisiana.

1

Geographical and Economic Background

> I will say again what I have said on numerous occasions: Louisiana is without doubt the most beautiful place on Earth, by virtue of its fine climate and superb location.
> All the plants native to Europe can successfully be grown there, as well as almost all those native to the American continent.
> —*A Historical and Political Account of Louisiana,*
> by M. de Vergennes (1802)

A visitor to Louisiana in the first quarter of the nineteenth century would have encountered a startlingly flat terrain covered with dense forests, wide prairies, and great stretches of marshland. The region was rich in water: in addition to the great river, there were innumerable streams, peaceful bayous, and limpid lakes. The territory abounded in fish and game, and its rich soil yielded abundant crops. To the dazzled eye of the visitor, the country might well have seemed an earthly paradise.

The Louisiana that was incorporated into the Union in 1812 was a small, boot-shaped state, bordered on the north by what was later to be Arkansas, on the west by Texas, on the east by the Mississippi Territory, and on the south by the Gulf of Mexico. Divided into twenty parishes (*i.e.*, counties), its population, as we have seen, exceeded 75,000. By 1830, it had 215,504 inhabitants and thirty-one parishes.

Louisiana is the flattest of the states: Mount Driskill, its highest point, is only some five hundred feet above sea level. It is also one of the wettest. Vast stretches lie below sea level, and the entire Delta region is crisscrossed with swamps, streamlets, lakes, and bayous.

The coastline from the Mississippi Sound to Vermilion Bay has been so ravaged by the waters as to resemble a torn piece of lace. From Vermilion Bay to the Texas frontier, by contrast, the shoreline is straight, one continuous series of swamps. Five passageways give access to the Mississippi: the North or Loutre Pass, the Northeast Pass, the Southeast Pass, the South or Grand Pass (the most heavily trafficked), and the Southwest Pass. The Balize, at the entrance to the Grand Pass, was a hamlet inhabited by a few fishermen and the chief pilot, who, according to Perrin du Lac, was "the only pilot who has the right to enter and leave the Mississippi." The customs station was also situated there.

It was a desolate spot. One early nineteenth-century voyager, A. Levasseur, found the view from his ship's deck "wondrous and terrifying." Thousands of fallen trees carried downstream by the river lay rotting along the muddy banks; among them slithered "enormous, shifty-eyed alligators."

From the Balize to New Orleans stretched "a flat and marshy plain, uninhabited and uninhabitable," overgrown with "moist rushes and trees, their trunks embedded in mud." Some seventy miles above the Balize, however, the landscape became less wild. Until that point, one saw only row upon row of cypresses, draped in Spanish moss; now other trees began to make an appearance: willows, green oaks, magnolias, pecans, sycamores. Farms and plantations lined the banks of the Mississippi, the farmhouses of the small landholders who raised rice and corn gradually giving way to the vast estates of the sugarcane planters, with the dark outline of the cypress forests looming in the distance.

THE DROWNED FORESTS

The drowned forests, one of the wonders of the South, were a haven for birds, otters, alligators, turtles, catfish, bullfrogs, assorted reptiles, and innumerable insects; only an occasional trapper's canoe troubled their solitude. The lowlands of Louisiana were entirely covered with cypresses; their towering trunks rose from the stagnant waters like "slender grey columns topped by capitals." A cathedral-like silence pervaded these forests, and the thin shafts of sunlight that penetrated their depths created a dramatic interplay of light and shadow. Here the full terror and majesty of nature seemed to converge. An early traveler, C. C. Robin, was deeply moved by the spectacle: "I thought myself in a vast temple where, rapt in contemplation, I remained a mute witness to divine mysteries. Yes, this was indeed a temple, the sacred habitation of Divine Nature who, remote from the profane gaze and destructive hands of man, performs innumerable miracles unbenownst to human kind."

At this era, the cypress forests extended from the outskirts of New Orleans to the shores of Lake Pontchartrain. This magnificent lake was connected by the Pass Chef Menteur to Lake Borgne, which in turn flowed into Chandeleur Sound. Thus, for ships coming from the East Coast, Europe, or the West Indies, the lake route was as readily accessible as the Mississippi. The Lake Pontchartrain region was noted for its year-round beauty and healthy climate. Even at the height of summer, a light breeze could be counted on to make the heat bearable.

Along the low-lying banks of the Mississippi, poplars and willows formed an attractive backdrop of pale green. A levee of compacted earth confined the capricious river within its banks and protected the sugarcane plantations that stretched up- and downstream from the capital. The Creoles had given names to different sections of the riverbank: the Tchoupitoulas Coast, the Coast of the Burnt Canes, the German Coast (described by Berquin-Duvallon at the beginning of the nineteenth century as "the most flourishing part of the colony"), the Acadian Coast, and finally Baton Rouge, the future capital, which in 1826 was a sleepy little town with a population of less than 1,200.

All the small towns in Louisiana bore a certain resemblance. The streets were unpaved, and the houses seldom more than one or two stories high, with broad, sloping roofs. The center of town usually contained a church, a post office, a few tradesmen's shops, a market; sometimes there was a bank, a courthouse, a newspaper office, or a school, occasionally a prison or a convent. Virtually every town had a tavern. The most prominent citizens were traditionally the mayor, the sheriff, the doctor, the banker, the justice of the peace, and the lawyer.

The German Coast was situated some twenty-five miles from New Orleans, on the right bank of the river. This prosperous region was divided into two parishes, the lower one named St. Charles, the upper St. John the Baptist. In 1820, the population of these two parishes totaled 7,716. There were no vast plantations here: the inhabitants of this coast, industrious descendants of the German settlers who had arrived in Louisiana in John Law's time, were for the most part market gardeners who brought their produce to town daily via canoe. They were not rich, but comfortably well off.

At the confluence of the Mississippi and the Bayou Lafourche—a long, picturesque waterway winding through fields and villages all the way to the Gulf—stood Donaldsonville. This small municipal center was the first relay station for the horses of the postal service that linked New Orleans with the Attakapas District, Opelousas, Rapides, and Natchitoches.

From Baton Rouge northward, the terrain slightly gained elevation, and sugarcane cultivation gave way to cotton. At this period, cotton was already the chief product of Louisiana, the mainstay of small and large landowners alike. The cotton fields were gradually invading both forests and prairies, not only in the region of Baton Rouge but along Bayou Lafourche and further north in Natchitoches and Ouachita Parish. In summer, the cotton fields burst into frothy white blossoms—a spectacle of dreamlike loveliness.

During the period from 1815 to 1830, a steady stream of immigrants flowed into the state, and much new land was cleared. Yet the region remained basically unchanged. Three quarters of the state were still covered with forests; vast stretches were devoid of human habitation. In the great swamplands of the South, where the land was virtually uncultivable, the only inhabitants were trappers and fishermen who lived with their families on the wooded hillocks that rose above the flooded terrain. The copper skins and high cheekbones of these rugged people bore evidence of their Indian ancestry. The islands of Barataria Bay still offered shelter to a motley collection of pirates, smugglers, cutthroats, and other adventurers. Along the banks of the Bayou Plaquemine, the Black River, and the Atchafalaya, the overhanging trees, choked with vines, created a stifling and claustrophobic atmosphere which oppressed the traveler canoeing on these waterways. Although the bison had now abandoned the prairielands of Louisiana, the forest regions still harbored bears, cougars, and Indians.

THE FERTILE PRAIRIES

A network of bayous and lakes bordered the Attakapas region, of which one enthusiastic traveler, C. C. Robin, wrote: "There is no spot on Earth that offers civilized man a happier prospect for passing his days." The Attakapas is a fertile plain watered by three bayous (the Teche, the Vermilion, and the Tortue), and the Atchafalaya River. The area is particularly well suited for raising livestock. Formerly, the region had a somewhat sinister reputation, for the Atakapas Indians were reputed to be cannibals—a rumor that may have had some foundation in fact, for the practice was not unknown among the Indians of the Southwest, and the Karankawa tribe in nearby Texas did, on occasion, feast on human flesh. But by the early nineteenth century these "man-eating savages" had become peaceful cattle raisers.

Beside the Indians, the region had about two thousand inhabitants of mixed origins: Acadians, Creoles, Spaniards, and Americans. They all raised cattle; some also grew cotton, indigo, and, more rarely, sugarcane. The crops were plentiful, and the landscape pleasing. Expanses of emerald green prairie were varied by groves and occasional small forests. Immense oaks, perhaps the most imposing tree of the region, were reflected in the calm waters of the bayous and rivers. Pines, magnolias, catalpas, sycamores, wax trees, hickories, laurels, beeches, and cypresses also proliferated. And the region was rich in fish and game.

To the traveler entering from the south, Louisiana offers one final visual surprise. Beyond the Attakapas, the land becomes rolling, rising in a series of gentle hills. This is the Opelousas region—a more varied landscape than the Attakapas, for here forests alternate with prairies. The trees in this area are even more varied; the rivers and bayous flow by at a quicker pace, their waters clearer and more sparkling. The grasslands, too, are greener and more luxuriant. According to William Darby, an early nineteenth-century witness: "All the plants and crops now cultivated in Louisiana were first introduced in the Opelousas region; and with the exception of sugar cane and oranges, the most desirable of them have all prospered. Cotton, indigo, and tobacco are grown there; the first being the chief cash crop."

In 1815, the Opelousas District was relatively well settled. The land was productive and the climate agreeable. Darby described it as follows:

Few spots on the globe of an equal extent exhibit more diversity of surface, or a greater variety of soil and vegetable production than does Opelousas. Every forest tree found in Southern Louisiana, except a few species, exist in Opelousas. Here are beheld all the changes of soil, from the deep fertile loam of Bayou Boeuf, to the sterile pine woods; from the broken hills of Bayou Crocodile, Calcasiu, and Sabine, to the Marsh Prairie on the gulph of Mexico; and from the deep and almost impervious woods along Atchafalaya, to the widely extended plains that open their vast area, upon the banks of the Mermentau and Calcasiu Rivers.

It was wonderful cattle country. Sleek, well-fed, long-horned cattle grazed everywhere—images of pastoral peace and plentitude. So vast were the prairies and so huge the herds that many settlers passed a full two years without having inspected all their cattle.

The Distant Provinces

Further north lay the parishes of Avoyelles, Rapides, and Natchitoches. The latter, which encompassed 6,784,000 acres, contained only 2,870 inhabitants in 1810. Ten years later, the population was 7,486, of whom 2,266 were slaves and 415 free blacks. The town of Natchitoches, one of the earliest settlements in Louisiana, was situated on the right bank of the Red River; William Darby described it as "a very thriving village consisting of about one hundred and fifty houses."

At the beginning of the nineteenth century, the Indians were an important element of the population in Natchitoches and Ouachita. Living in settlements in the forest, they carried on a lively trade in furs with their white neighbors. It was a region of oak forests, pine-covered hills, prairies dotted with wild flowers, and water everywhere: lakes, rivers, bayous. Natchitoches had long been famous for its tobacco; in recent years, its cotton had gained the reputation of being the best in Louisiana. In addition to these two profitable commodities, Natchitoches produced hides, beef, pork, lumber, and corn.

To the north, beyond the prairies and forests, lay the farthest outposts of Louisiana. Colonization had lagged in this wilderness region, largely because of its remoteness from the trading center of New Orleans and because, for the Spaniards, it lay outside the main overland route to the Texas territories. It was inhabited by Canadian backwoodsmen, drawn to the area by the quest for fortune or adventure. They had found the climate agreeable, the game abundant, the Indians friendly, the squaws compliant: many of them put down roots there. In time they were followed by farmers and planters of Anglo-Saxon stock. By the beginning of the nineteenth century, the settlers along the Ouachita River and Bayou Boeuf had begun to grow cotton and tobacco; the cattle raisers had taken over the prairies. The new wave of poorer settlers were relegated to the pine forests, where the soil was thin and sandy.

The landscape was extraordinarily colorful and varied. "It is among the most beautiful regions of lower Louisiana," asserted one French traveler, Perrin du Lac. The geographer William Darby remarked that the "Boeuf is by far the most beautiful stream that is found in Louisiana within the alluvial soil." Its current he found "constant," its waters "clear and pure." He went on to note that the land along its banks was well suited to the cultivation of cotton and well planted with "black oak, poplar, white oak, sweet gum, black walnut, red oak and ash."

From these descriptions, it is hard to see why Ouachita Parish remained so sparsely settled; but in the early nineteenth century many of the settlers lived several miles from their nearest neighbors, and in the autumn, when the Ouachita River reached its lowest level, river travel was limited to the lightest canoes and communications between the settlements, consequently, were not easy. In fact, communications between the remoter provinces and the capital were difficult at the best of times. In 1815 the round-trip journey between Natchitoches or Ouachita and New Orleans took thirty to forty days. Ten years later, due to the introduction of the steamboat, the time was reduced to three weeks—at least during the seasons when the rivers and bayous were navigable.

KING COTTON

The rapid growth of cotton production, together with improved means of transportation (the steamboat played a particularly important role) and the establishment of a stable political system, brought Louisiana unprecedented prosperity. Like its sister states of the South, Louisiana's economy was based on agriculture. The *Annals of Louisiana* record that in 1820, out of a total population of 153,406, 53,641 were engaged in farming, 6,251 in commerce, and 6,041 in industry.

Indigo, a leading product of colonial times, had given way to cotton, rice, and sugar, which were hardier and more reliable crops. In the 1820s, the records reveal a slight falling off in the cultivation of tobacco. Rice, though disdained by the large plantation owners, was popular with the farmers and small landowners of the Delta. Sugar seems to have been the prerogative of the leading Creole landowners, but cotton was grown by virtually everyone. Indeed, cotton had become the staple of the economy, bringing financial security to many and great wealth to some. In the western and northern parts of the state, a plutocracy of cotton growers was emerging, which was soon to join forces with the sugar-growing aristocracy in the South. The cotton dynasties ruled their domains like feudal lords; their members became the leading citizens of their home towns, their parishes, eventually the state. From 1830 on, King Cotton ruled supreme, governing both the economy and the politics of Louisiana.

Louisiana's best customer was England, which purchased about 70 percent of the cotton destined for export and about 50 percent of the total production. In the course of the ten years from 1815 to 1825, cotton exports progressed steadily, increasing from 46,000 bales (of three hundred pounds each) in 1815–16 to 186,471 bales in 1824–25. By way of comparison, the total cotton production of the United States was 700,000 bales in 1820, rising to 3,100,000 in 1851.

The price of cotton was subject to fluctuations in the world market or, more precisely, in the markets of Liverpool and Manchester.

It was English demand rather than American supply that determined the price structure—much to the annoyance of the French and other buyers. In 1821, the price per pound of first grade cotton was 17 to 18 cents. In 1822, it climbed to 20 cents, only to tumble to 12.5 cents in 1826. But King Cotton took such setbacks in his stride.

The fluctuations in the market, which were entirely beyond the control of the planters, allowed the cotton brokers the opportunity to make substantial "killings." One of the boldest speculators of the period was Vincent Otto Nolte, a German from Hamburg who became a well-known figure in New Orleans. Nolte, who described himself as a "merchant-commodity investor in cotton," had two firms in Liverpool and two in New York. He acted as agent for some of the largest European textile mills and boasted that even the English companies employed him to make their purchases. He was recognized in international circles as one of the shrewdest speculators ever known— but this reputation did not prevent him from going bankrupt.

Few plantation owners sold their crops directly to the mills: middlemen handled the great majority of the sales. Occasionally the cotton was sold through banks that had previously acquired proprietorship of the crops by means of loans. Every spring, local financiers, planters, agents of foreign firms and of northern millowners, and brokers converged on New Orleans—at the Maspero Exchange, or at the cotton-presses of the French Quarter and the upper town—and the bidding began.

Under the warm southern sun, the cotton industry prospered. The crop was rarely subject to blight, it was easy to pick, and the profits were substantial. A German traveler, Karl Anton Pöstl, informs us with typical Teutonic precision that in 1826 (the year of his sojourn in New Orleans) "one could set up a cotton plantation for $10,000." The cost of 1,500 to 2,000 acres of fertile land in the Red River Valley was, he informs us, $3,000; ten black field workers could be obtained for $5,000. The first year, one could count on producing thirty bales of cotton on twenty-five acres. The following year, more land could be cleared and the production doubled. The planter was thus almost assured of receiving an annual income of three hundred dollars for each slave that he owned.

Louisiana, Alabama, Tennessee, and Mississippi were all major producers of cotton, and all the cotton they produced was sent each autumn to New Orleans to be shipped to Europe or the Northeast. The city profited enormously from this trade and became one of the leading commercial centers of the nation, as well as a seaport of prime importance. The continued growth and prosperity of the city depended not only on the increased agricultural production of the southern states, but on the expanding patronage of the newly settled western states. In spite of the gradually improving land routes to the East, the western states continued to ship their cargoes down the Mississippi: wheat, grain, corn, lumber, salted beef, bacon, linseed oil, lead, buffalo hides, squirrel skins, even whiskey. The eastern states, by contrast, chose to send their manufactured goods overland to the West through the Alleghenies, even though steamboats now carried cargo up the Mississippi and the Ohio.

Such circuitous routing of produce and merchandise was an obstacle to the nation's economic expansion, and in 1817, at the instigation of De Witt Clinton, the governor of New York, work was begun on a series of canals designed to link Lake Erie to the Atlantic. The Erie Canal was finished in 1825. It was 363 miles long, linking Albany to Buffalo. As soon as it opened, the conveyance charges for cargo dropped from a hundred to fifteen dollars a ton, and the duration of the trip between the two points was reduced from twenty days to ten. The new route established once and for all the commercial supremacy of New York, leaving New Orleans to seek solace in its romantic past and in the fact that throughout the 1830s, until the financial crash of 1837, it had been the richest city in the United States.

Sugarcane and Tobacco

The opening of the Erie Canal was not immediately fatal to New Orleans. Until the Civil War, the city ranked second to New York among American seaports. The bulk of her business, however, was in exports: between 1821 and 1861 her export income increased by 1,500 percent, her import income by only 600 percent. Most of the profits came directly or indirectly from cotton or sugar, rather than from merchandise from the West.

Sugar was the second-ranking commodity. In 1830, Louisiana was supplying half of all the sugar consumed in the United States, and the sugarcane planters constituted the most prosperous group in the state. In those regions where sugarcane grew well, planters tended to sacrifice other crops—even tearing out cotton plants—to increase their yield of cane. In 1828, Louisiana had more than three hundred sugar plantations, employing 21,000 people; a few years later, there were seven hundred plantations, and sugar production had increased from 15,000 to 45,000 barrels.

It has been estimated that a sugarcane plantation brought its owner, good year or bad, a 6 to 11 percent yield on his capital. Pöstl, our German traveler, observes that "the harvest never fails," but that the planter can hope for no income his first year, for it takes eighteen months for the plants to come to maturity. The establishment of a plantation required a sizable investment: a terrain capable of producing 400,000 pounds of sugar per annum represented, in 1830, a capital investment of $170,000, with annual expenses reckoned at $10,700. Some sugar planters clearly overreached themselves: one hundred sixty-six plantations were wiped out in the crash of 1837. Louisiana owed its return to prosperity largely to the stability of the cotton growers.

Along with indigo, tobacco had been one of Louisiana's earliest cash crops. From 1825 on, there was a marked decline in its production, due to a sudden slump in foreign and East Coast demand. Between 1817 and 1825, the number of barrels of tobacco sold dropped from 36,000 to 14,413. At the same time, internal consumption increased to 10,000. By 1834, the exports had almost regained the level of 1817, but the figures suggest that the tobacco growers as a group never attained the degree of prosperity enjoyed by the owners of cotton and sugarcane plantations, and many of them had recourse to supplementary crops or livestock breeding, while a number of growers decided to replace their tobacco with cotton.

Even as commerce flourished, industry remained sluggish. To be sure, the major sugar plantations had their own refineries, and just outside New Orleans a vast refinery was established, capable of processing up to 200,000 pounds of sugar. In the vicinity of the capital, there were also factories manufacturing rope and hairpowder, and a dozen distilleries that produced tafia or molasses brandy. Brick factories were also scattered through the state. Strangely enough, Louisiana did not possess a single cotton mill. Shiploads of cotton left New Orleans daily, bound for Liverpool, Boston, and New York, to return in the form of sailcloth, nankeen, or Indian cloth. In the process, vast profits were pocketed by the Yankees and the British.

The inhabitants of Louisiana shared the South's general repugnance for industrial activities. The South had come to rely on its exports of cotton and tobacco to pay for the manufactured goods that it steadfastly refused to produce. Few southerners saw any reason to change this state of affairs, and they tried to demolish the protectionist policies adopted by Washington, which favored the industrial North at the expense of the agricultural South. The seeds of discord between North and South were sown when these policies went into effect in 1824. The growing specialization of the different regions of the country was to lead to grave conflicts of interest which, aggravated by the moral issue of slavery, culminated in the ruinous War of Secession.

At the time Louisiana entered the Union, however, her future seemed secure, and her citizens had little reason to doubt that New Orleans would soon assume the preeminent rank predicted for it by President Jefferson: "The position of New Orleans certainly destines it to be the greatest city the world has ever seen. . . . For beauty, pleasure, and convenience, it would certainly be eminent."

2

New Orleans

New Orleans, the wet grave, where the hopes of thousands are buried; for eighty years the wretched asylum for the outcasts of France and Spain, who could not venture one hundred paces beyond its gates without utterly sinking to the breast in mud, or being attacked by alligators; has become in the space of twenty-three years one of the most beautiful cities of the Union, inhabited by 40,000 persons who trade with half the world.

So wrote the German traveler Karl Anton Pöstl, who arrived in New Orleans by riverboat on a Sunday morning in the year 1826. From the deck, the city seemed to open out in a graceful crescent, revealing itself "in all its splendour." The view, he reported, "is splendid beyond description. . . . A single glance exhibits to view the harbour, the vessels at anchor, together with the city situated as it were at the feet of the passenger."

A contemporary, the architect B. H. Latrobe, was somewhat less enthusiastic, although he conceded that New Orleans displayed at first glance "a very imposing and handsome appearance, beyond any other city in the United States in which I have yet been." But Bernhard, Duke of Saxe-Weimar, was frankly disappointed. Approaching the city by the lake route, he observed: "The first view of the city was really not handsome because it was the old part, which consisted only of little one-story houses, with mud walls and wide projecting roofs."

It should be borne in mind that the duke had failed, on his arrival, to find a cab to take him into town and, rather than pay six dollars to a boatman to bring him to the city center by way of Bayou St. John and the Carondelet Canal, had chosen to make his way on foot. The long trek across the swamp, along a muddy footpath, may well have contributed to his disenchanted view of the city. But another visitor, Captain Basil Hall, who also arrived in New Orleans via Lake Pontchartrain, corroborates the duke's picture: "The city of New Orleans, which we reached before sunset, made no great show from its being built on a dead level." He admits, however, to being impressed by "the old, narrow streets, the high houses, ornamented with tasteful cornices; iron balconies and many other circumstances peculiar to towns in France and Spain."

Must we conclude from these conflicting statements that the beauty of New Orleans was purely in the eye of the beholder? On the contrary, what they make clear is that a visitor's initial impression of the city depended largely on his choice of route. New Orleans appeared at its best when approached by way of the river.

By perusing the travel reports of the period—sometimes contradictory, but often vividly detailed and always lively—by examining maps and documents in the city archives, and by scrutinizing *Paxton's Directory* (a commercial almanac issued by the easterner John Paxton in 1822), one can put together a reasonably clear picture of the physical appearance of the city during the years of its greatest prosperity. New Orleans was at this time divided into three sections. The old quarter, locally called the Vieux Carré, laid out by Adrien de Pauger in 1721, had become the bastion of the established Creole families. To it had been added the Faubourg Tremé, beyond Rampart Street; the Faubourg St. Mary further upstream, a burgeoning new American district; and, downstream from the Vieux Carré, the Faubourg Marigny, established by the prominent Creole Bernard de Marigny in an effort to rival the dynamic new American quarter.

The Faubourg Marigny

The Faubourg Marigny was one of the many monuments to the long rivalry between the American and Creole communities of New Orleans. The economic prosperity that followed Louisiana's entrance into the Union was accompanied by a surge in population. In a short time, the American sector grew overcrowded, and areas for expansion were sought. A stretch of land across from the Esplanade, on the banks of the Mississippi, was judged attractive for development because the river was sufficiently deep there to permit the construction of docks. The land belonged to Bernard de Marigny, a wealthy Creole.

The two men responsible for drawing up a development scheme were Samuel J. Peters, an American businessman, and James H. Caldwell, an English actor and theater manager. Their plans for the site were grandiose, including a theater, a grand hotel, a row of shops, cotton presses, a waterworks, and a gasworks. Blueprints in hand, they approached Marigny.

After long and difficult negotiations, the Creole finally agreed to the sale of the land—or what remained of it, for he had already disposed of parts of it elsewhere. Then, to the rage of the two developers, Marigny changed his mind. Peters and Caldwell now transferred their attention to the Faubourg St. Mary, and Marigny undertook to construct a modified version of the Peters-Caldwell plan on his own terrain. He laid out the streets himself, choosing the names with exuberant poetic license: Victory Street, Street of Love, Street of the Poets, Music Street, Street of Mystery. There was even a Champs-Elysées and a Craps Street, named after the dice game which, according to tradition, had been imported into Louisiana by the duc d'Orléans and his brothers during their visit to Marigny in 1798.

Bernard de Marigny had hoped to turn his new Creole quarter into the commercial center of New Orleans, but he discovered that the prosperous merchants, wealthy planters, and fashionable lawyers of the Vieux Carré were reluctant to move their offices to the other side of the Esplanade. The Faubourg Marigny, so ambitiously conceived, became the home of the less successful and less wealthy among the French and Creoles. The Americans, who by now were flocking into the city in great numbers, settled for the most part in the Faubourg St. Mary. Thus, although capital was pouring into New Orleans in the 1820s, it was largely absorbed by the uptown districts. The Creole dominance of the city was clearly on the wane.

By 1830, the Faubourg St. Mary, with its colonnaded mansions and its gardens fragrant with magnolias, orange blossoms, and camellias, easily outshone the Vieux Carré. A new city had sprung to life under the Creoles' very eyes, but few of them seemed to notice. In the Vieux Carré, the planters, lawyers, hoteliers, bankers, merchants, and shopowners went about their business, confident that New Orleans was where they were, that the vitality of the city depended on them.

Faubourg Marigny, *ca.* 1821. The large house in the right foreground is the home of Bernard de Marigny. From a lithograph by Félix Achille Beaupoil de Saint-Aulaire.

New Orleans had never been livelier, gayer, more attractive than during the 1820s. It was an era of hilarity and eloquence, of mortal duels and lighthearted pranks, of fabulous balls and memorable banquets. To be sure, every summer brought an epidemic of yellow fever, but the majority of the victims were mere visitors or recent settlers in New Orleans—the better Creole and American families made a point of retiring from the city during the dog days of summer. Some took up residence on their plantations, some along the salubrious shores of Lake Pontchartrain. When the heat abated, the fashionable families flocked back to the city, eager for conviviality and entertainment. New Orleans resumed its joyful, hectic rhythm.

The Vieux Carré

The original plan of New Orleans comprised eight streets: Orleans, Toulouse, Chartres, du Maine, Ste. Anne, St. Philippe, Bourbon, Bourgogne. As new streets were laid out, the original *carré* or square was transformed into a perfect rectangle framed by an outer wall. In time, the walls were dismantled; three great arteries, each bordered with sycamores, now defined the limits of the Creole city. Then as now, fifteen streets led from the river to Rampart Street, and seven from Canal Street to the Esplanade. At the center, facing the Mississippi, was the Place d'Armes. The square was girdled by a fence with intricate wrought-iron gates; inside, maple trees offered restful, green shade.

The streets were both straight and wide (thirty-six feet wide on the average), and bordered by brick sidewalks or *banquettes*, as they were called locally. Alongside the sidewalks were gutters that permitted the outflow of water from the river to the swamplands—for one of the peculiarities of New Orleans is that the city is set on land that lies below the level of the Mississippi and slopes gently in the direction of Lake Pontchartrain. During the rainy season, when the gutters were clogged, the unpaved streets turned into vast mud puddles.

One can scarcely overestimate the labor required of the first generations of settlers—or, more precisely, of their black slaves—to establish their city on this flat marshy plain, covered with forests, in-

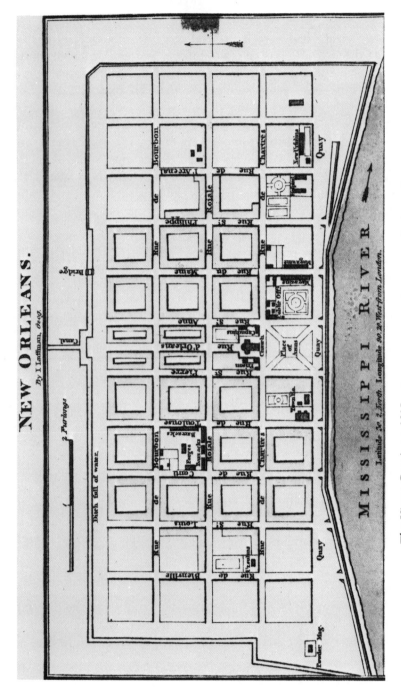

The Vieux Carré, *ca.* 1815.   Louisiana State University Department of Archives and Manuscripts

fested with mosquitoes and reptiles, and flooded some eight months a year by the Mississippi. Trees had to be felled, levees built, drainage ditches dug, a major landfill operation carried out. In fact, the drainage problem was never satisfactorily resolved. In the course of a century, through the toil of the slaves and the ingenuity of their masters, the squalid hamlet that had sheltered Bienville and his companions was transformed into a city that was the boast of the entire nation—but where it was impossible to keep one's feet dry.

Europeans accustomed to the splendors of Rome, London, and Paris may well have found the civic pride of the citizens somewhat extravagant. No great artists or architects had lavished their talents on New Orleans; there were no splendid palaces, no sumptuous mansions, no parks or public gardens conceived on a grand scale. The city was built exclusively of wood and brick, and the only gardens were small, private patios. Nevertheless, the city had a distinctive character. The decorative balconies and iron grillwork of the houses gave it a very special charm, and the three principal buildings—the cathedral, the city hall, and the presbytery, which formed the northeast side of the Place d'Armes—were truly memorable.

The architect Latrobe, who made so many valuable observations, remarked that "although in detail these buildings are as bad as they can be," yet the ensemble produced "an admirable effect when seen from the river or the levee." The three structures had been erected after the fire of 1788 from funds supplied by the generous Spaniard, Don Andrés Almonester y Rojas. When Latrobe viewed them in 1819, the cathedral was as yet without a steeple; that was added in 1824. Some visitors were disconcerted by the bright paintings that adorned the interior of the cathedral. As Karl Pöstl reported: "The catholics had the strange notion of painting the interior, taking for this purpose the most glaring colors that can be found—green and purple. The church is painted over in *fresco* with these colours, and presents at one view a curious taste of the creoles." The more sophisticated Saxe-Weimar commented that the cathedral "resembles a village church in Flanders."

The cathedral was flanked by the presbytery and the city hall, both praised by Latrobe for "their symmetry and the good proportion and strong relief of the facades." The northeastern and southeastern sides of the square were occupied by a hotel and a row "of shops with one story above a high ill-proportioned roof covered with Italian tiles."

To the southeast lies the levee. Since Louisiana had joined the Union, New Orleans had become the chief port of export for agricultural goods from the West. Merchant vessels from all corners of the earth crowded the docks for several miles, and the tourist who wished to visit the levee had to make his way through a maze of cotton bales and sugar barrels, elbowing and being elbowed by a boisterous and motley crowd of all occupations and all nations.

PRIVATF HOUSES

Between Levee and Bourbon streets lay one of the smartest commercial and residential districts in New Orleans. Here were found the most prosperous mercantile establishments, the most fashionable hotels, the best *pensions*, shops, and cafés. Here too were the handsome townhouses of the local merchants—brick structures one to three stories high, whose colored stucco facades added a note of exuberance to the neighborhood. Henry Castellanos, a late nineteenth-century New Orleans writer, described them thus:

No house of aristocratic pretentions was without its courtyard or *patio*, the centre of which was ornamented with a fountain and enlivened by tropical plants. The main entrance was through a wide gate or *porte cochère*, in the interior of which was kept the cumbersome family carriage; beyond, a wide staircase led to the upper apartment. The windows, those of Spanish construction, I mean, were very wide and always opened upon the patio. The sills were covered with pots of aromatic plants, chief of which was the fragrant rosemary. Iron balconies, objects of hygienic necessity in this hot climate, were attached to every building more than one story high, and became matters not only of comfort but of beauty.

One of the finest examples of New Orleans private architecture was built in 1823 for a wealthy merchant. It contained a magnificent patio, slave quarters, stables, a shelter for carriages, and even separate bachelor apartments for the sons of the family.

None of the houses, not even the more recently built ones, had cellars, for in New Orleans one had only to plunge a spade into the ground to strike water. However, the first floors of many houses were raised above street level, with the space between the ground and the first floor being used for storage.

In this same elegant district were the Calaboso—the former Spanish prison—on St. Peter Street, where felons, escaped slaves, and debtors were all herded indiscriminately together; the Governor's Palace on Levee Street, a somewhat run-down structure that served as the assembly hall for Louisiana's state representatives until it was destroyed by fire; the Ursuline Convent, an imposing edifice dating from 1733, its brick facade covered with grey stucco; Condé Hall, a long, unpretentious wooden building that enjoyed the distinction of being New Orleans' first dance hall; the St. Philip Theater, restored at a cost of $12,000 in 1810 and soon thereafter relegated to use as a ballroom; and an ambitious complex of buildings—a theater, a hotel, and Orleans Hall (a lavishly decorated gaming hall dating from 1827)—all built by John Davis, a refugee from Santo Domingo. Here also, at the corner of Chartres and St. Louis streets, was the Maspero Exchange, site of the city's most important auctions; the Café des Réfugiés on St. Philip Street, meeting place for the Santo Domingo exiles; and the Maritime Hotel, frequented by the members of Jean Laffite's pirate band.

Behind the cathedral a lovely, tree-shaded garden offered the citizens shelter from the summer sun. The peace of the garden was often disturbed, however, for the fast young set of Creole society had chosen this spot for their duels—an insidious pastime that was all too rapidly adopted by the Americans.

At Bourbon Street there was a marked change in architectural style. From there to Rampart Street, most of the houses were low structures of mixed brick and wood, with an intermingling of simple, plankwood cottages. Almost all of them had overhanging tile or shingle roofs that extended out over the broad sidewalks. By this device the houses themselves remained cool even in the heat of summer, while the pedestrians outside were sheltered from both sun and rain.

Latrobe reports that the floor plans of these dwellings were straightforward: "The two front rooms open into the street with French glass doors. Those on one side are the dining room and the drawing room; the others are chambers. The front rooms, when inhabited by Americans, are the family rooms, and the back rooms, the chambers."

Saxe-Weimar's travel journal leads us to believe that there still existed in 1826 a number of old buildings, remnants of the French colonial regime, constructed of cypress wood and a mixture of earth and Spanish moss—for how else can we interpret his reference to structures with "mud walls"?[1] But it is peculiar that no other writer, not even the conscientious Latrobe, saw fit to mention these buildings.

Many eyewitnesses, by contrast, commented on the excellence of the urban street lights, inaugurated in 1796 by Governor Carondelet. Oil lamps hung on chains at every street corner; they were lit at sundown and extinguished at dawn. The system was financed by an annual chimney tax of nine réales per chimney levied on each homeowner. Under the American administration, the tax was retained: now it was one dollar per annum per chimney. "Perhaps no city in the Union can boast of being better lighted than New Orleans," wrote John Paxton. Yet until 1840 the gentry never ventured out at night unless accompanied by a slave carrying a lantern.

THE CEMETERY

Rampart Street divided the upper from the lower town. At the very center, across from the Vieux Carré, was the Place du Cirque, commonly known as Congo Place, for it was here, John Paxton wrote, that "the Congo and other negroes dance, carouse and debauch on the Sabbath." On one side, the square bordered a large boat basin that linked up to Bayou St. John by a narrow channel running through the swamps. According to Paxton,

We frequently see in the Basin from 70 to 80 sail, of some 550 to 600 barrels, from the West Indies, Pensacola, Mobile, Covington and Madisonville. . . . By this Canal is brought cotton, tobacco, lumber, wood, lime, brick, tar, pitch, bark, sand, oysters, marketing, and a great variety of other articles. A great number of Indians come by this route to New Orleans with their furs and peltries.

---

1. The early French settlers constructed their houses of a heavy framework of timbers, with the spaces between the posts filled with *bousillage*—a mixture of grass or Spanish moss and clay. The exterior was then covered with plaster or siding. This type of structure was very common, and a few buildings of this type survive to this day.—TRANS.

St. Louis Cemetery. From a watercolor by John Latrobe, son of Benjamin Latrobe.

In the surrounding area, a conglomeration of inns, taverns, and cafés had sprung up.

Adjacent to the Basin was the St. Louis Cemetery, which dated back to the early days of the Spanish settlement. It had been originally reserved for Catholics, but a Protestant section had subsequently been added, and behind the Protestant section was an area for blacks. In 1823 it was decided to lay out another cemetery, also dedicated to St. Louis, a little farther from the city center. In the following year, an architectural engineer from Paris named Leriche was commissioned to erect sixty tombs, thirty for whites and thirty for blacks.

The inhabitants of New Orleans were obliged to give considerable thought to their burial arrangements, for one could scarcely break the surface of the soil without encountering water. Latrobe records a visit to the old St. Louis Cemetery: "There are two or three graves open and expecting their tenants; eight or nine inches below the surface, they are filled with water, and were not three feet deep." Which prompted this macabre reflection: "Those who could not afford a lead coffin had their dear ones' corpses devoured by crawfish."

Because interment was out of the question, the dead were "buried" above ground in brick mausoleums resembling small, windowless houses or in sepulchers encased in a wall: "In one corner of the Catholic burying ground are two sets of catacombs, of three stories each, roughly built and occupying much more room than is necessary." The epitaphs on the tombs ranged from the plain to the sententious. Latrobe was prompted to copy out the inscription on the tomb of a twenty-year-old girl: "Passerby, cast a respectful eye on this last resting place of a virtuous daughter." The Protestant cemetery, Latrobe reported, "has tombs of much the same construction, but a little varied in character." A few well-placed trees lent an air of romantic melancholy to the surroundings.

No-Man's-Land

Common Street leads into Canal Street. A map of the city dating from 1827 designates these two thoroughfares as a "projected navigation canal." Evidently the intention was to extend the Carondelet Canal beyond the Basin and to link Lake Pontchartrain to the Mis-

sissippi. The plan was never executed, but the citizens of New Orleans were left with an avenue that one enthusiastic traveler, Joseph
Holt Ingraham, described as "the broadest in New Orleans and destined to be the most magnificent." The area that had been reserved
for excavation served as a kind of "no-man's-land" between the Creoles and the American settlers. The line of demarcation was known
on one side as Canal Street, on the other as Rue du Canal. This spacious thoroughfare, more than one hundred fifty feet wide, testified
to the growth and prosperity of New Orleans during the forty years
before the Civil War. It also indicated the direction in which the city
was developing. Presently even Bernard de Marigny would have to
admit that the Faubourg St. Mary had become "the spoiled child of
the Mayor and Council, the object of their tender affection."

During the 1820s Canal Street was becoming the main business
artery of the city. It boasted solid office buildings, elegant townhouses, a variety of shops, and substantial hotels. (One such, the
Planters' and Merchants' Hotel, offered travelers "one hundred
twenty suites, sixty rooms with single beds, and a dining room able
to accommodate two hundred fifty guests.") Also on Canal Street
was the Charity Hospital, with beds for up to one hundred thirty patients. At the corner of Bourbon Street stood the first Protestant
church built in the city, Christ Church, which Latrobe described as
"a plain octagon without any architectural merit of design or execution," but notable for a "very good organ" and a marble monument
bearing the following inscription: "The citizens of New Orleans to
testify their respect for the virtues of W. C. C. Claiborne, late governor of the State of Louisiana, have erected this monument to his
memory, 1818." The homage was sincere, if somewhat late in coming; but then, it was said that the American governor had, by the
time of his death, shed his brusque American ways and become
thoroughly "creolized."

The streets of the Faubourg St. Mary, whether commercial or residential, were bordered by oaks, elms, and pecans. The houses were
charming cottages, graced with porches and small gardens. Brick
was the principal building material: Latrobe reports sadly that the
faubourg "already exhibits the flat, dull, dingy character of Market
Street in Philadelphia or Baltimore."

Under the energetic leadership of Samuel Peters and James Caldwell, the faubourg developed rapidly, acquiring a market, cotton presses, Masonic lodges, churches, hotels, depots, and a cemetery. It also had its own theater, erected on Camp Street by Caldwell in 1822—a magnificent structure that soon became a rival to John Davis' Orleans Theater. Caldwell's building featured two notable innovations: gas lighting inside and a paved sidewalk outside. The latter was much appreciated at a time when most of the sidewalks in town were of raised earth bordered by a drainage ditch.

Further upstream was a suburb "radiant with rural charms," as Reverend Clapp later described it. Here wealthy Americans were building the early Greek Revival mansions so admired by Latrobe. Snubbed by the Creoles of the Vieux Carré, the Americans had taken themselves elsewhere; they proceeded to build homes of a scale and magnificence unknown in the Creole quarter. In time, the Garden District, where the American aristocracy resided, became the showplace of New Orleans.

At first glance, the Faubourg St. Mary appeared prosperous and sedate, a bastion of Anglo-Saxon Protestantism. But paradoxically, it also harbored the most notorious and disreputable section of New Orleans. "The Swamp," located at the upper end of Girod Street, was the haunt of pimps, prostitutes, criminals, and derelicts. It also served as a pleasure spot for the Mississippi flatboatmen and keelboatmen, nicknamed "Kaintucks" by the Creoles, who associated all long-haired, boisterous rowdies from upriver with the state of Kentucky.

The buildings of the Swamp were made of rough planks or lumber salvaged from barges. Flimsily thrown together and jostling each other helter-skelter were saloons, brothels, gambling dens, and hotels. Occasionally all these functions were grouped under a single roof, so that the visiting boatman could find, for a relatively modest charge, drink, cards, a woman, and a place to sleep without having to venture out into the sinister streets of the district. The buildings were as bleak and squalid inside as outside. The bar often consisted of a plank of wood resting on two barrels, while the sole decoration of the brothels was red curtains at the windows and a lamp of the same color at the entrance. After nightfall, the police steered clear of the Swamp, and it was every man for himself.

Faubourg St. Mary, *ca.* 1821. From a lithograph by Félix-Achille Beaupoil de Saint-Aulaire.

The Historic New Orleans Collection

The Faubourg Marigny was far less picturesque. Still new, the district seems to have elicited little comment from travelers. With the exception of several handsome homes bordering the Esplanade and the elegant mansion of Bernard de Marigny, most of the houses were unpretentious wooden dwellings. New Orleans society stayed aloof from the district, and the faubourg languished. Even Bernard de Marigny took to spending most of his time at his magnificent plantation, Fontainebleau, on the north shore of Lake Pontchartrain.

Main Street of the World

For a stretch of several miles along the levee of the Mississippi, boats of all types and all nations rocked gently at moorage. They ranged from rustic flatboats—a sort of glorified raft shaped like a box, used exclusively for downstream traffic—to tall sailing ships with proud, lofty masts.

"The first object that presents itself is the dirty and uncouth backwoods flatboat," wrote Karl Pöstl. "Hams, ears of corn, apples, whiskey barrels, are strewed upon it or are fixed to poles to direct the attention of buyers." Then came the "more decent keelboats, with cotton, furs, whiskey, flour." Nearby were drawn up the "elegant" steamboats, which announced their comings and goings "by hissing and repeated sounds," while sending up "immense columns of black smoke." Further downstream could be found "the smaller merchant vessels, the sloops and schooners from Havannah, Vera Cruz, Tampico," and further still the great oceangoing ships from New York, Baltimore, and Europe. Opposite the Market was the landing stage for the steam ferryboat that plied between the banks of the Mississippi.

At this period it was not uncommon to see as many as thirty or even forty steamboats in port at the same time. More than seventy such craft were in operation in 1822, bringing into New Orleans cotton, tobacco, flour, coal, hemp, cordage, beef, pork, corn, lead, pelts, and other products from the rivers that empty into the Mississippi.

The flatboat was still the principal means of transporting merchandise to market, but the advent of the steamboat had spelled the doom of the keelboat. As steamboat traffic increased on the river, keelboats grew rarer and rarer. Many keelboat captains took employment with the steamboat companies, where their nautical expertise and intimate knowledge of the river were in great demand.

The natural advantages of the site made New Orleans preeminent among American ports. Even the largest vessels could approach close enough to shore for the cargoes to be unloaded by means of a rudimentary bridge of planks stretching from dock to shipboard—an enormous saving of time and effort.

When the Mississippi was at floodtide, the waters almost reached the top of the levee. Captain Basil Hall noted in his journal that one spring the river was "so like a bowl filled to the brim that it seemed as if the smallest shake or the least addition would send it over the edge and thus submerge the city." He added that "the footpath on the top of the levee was just nine inches above the level of the stream."

The levee, a long earthen dike bordered with magnificent shade trees, was a favorite promenade for visitors and townspeople alike. There the true international flavor of New Orleans made itself felt: people of every language and every nation mingled on the levee, while from the ships was unloaded merchandise from every corner of the earth. To some dazzled visitors the levee was "the main street of the world," "the world in miniature"; to others it was simply "one of the most marvelous places imaginable."

A flourishing trade was maintained with the East Coast, the Caribbean Islands, and Europe, as well as with the cities and hamlets that bordered the Mississippi. Visitors like Captain Hall were awed by the sheer abundance of the goods piled on the levee. Mounds of coal, "floated down in arks or flatboats all the way from Pittsburgh," were flanked by stacks of pavingstones from Liverpool. Heaped everywhere "without apparent order" were bales of cotton, barrels of tobacco and sugar, cases and casks of merchandise stretching "as far as the eye could see in both directions all along the river."

The levee was the liveliest part of town. And the noisiest: all day long, sailors from all corners of the world exchanged greetings, abuse, and ribald pleasantries with the Mississippi boatmen in a makeshift mixture of English, French, Spanish, Italian, Portuguese, Greek, Chinese, and Creole. Merchants and retailers hurried back and forth giving orders, while black longshoremen sang their plaintive songs in African dialects, "Negro-English," or Creole patois as they carried bales of cotton or rolled barrels along the levee. Black women balancing baskets of rice cakes and gingerbread on their heads made their way through the multitude, liltingly crying their wares.

Northerners found the scene marvelously exotic. While still on shipboard, Latrobe formed his first impressions of New Orleans from the "strange noises" emanating from the levee: "It is a more incessant, loud, rapid, and various gabble of tongues of all tones than was ever heard at Babel. It is more to be compared to the sounds that issue from an extensive marsh, the residence of a million or two of frogs." To Karl Pöstl, it seemed that "a kind of music, accompanied with human, or rather inhuman voices, resounded in almost every direction."

THE MARKETPLACE

Along the levee, just a few steps from the Place d'Armes, stood the market building, a long brick structure supposedly modeled after the Propylea in Athens. It too was frequented by a jostling horde of people speaking in a confusion of tongues. As Captain Basil Hall reported, "On entering the crowd my ears were struck with a curious mixture of language; the fishermen were talking Spanish while among the rest of the crowd there was a pretty equal distribution of French and English." One section of the market hall was reserved for meat, another for vegetables. At the far end of the vegetable section was the fish counter. "In the vegetable market," Hall recalled, "I saw peas, cabbages, beet-roots, artichokes, French beans, radishes, and a great variety of spotted seeds and carawansas; potatoes both of the sweet and irish kind; tomatoes, rice, Indian corn, ginger, blackberries, roses and violets, oranges, bananas, apples, fowls tied in three by the legs, quails, gingerbread, beer in bottles and salt fish."

Visitors were impressed by the sheer abundance of the produce, and by the intentness and knowledgeability of the milling crowd of buyers. With every purchase, the enterprising market people threw in a *lagniappe*—a little something extra: a bunch of radishes, a rose, a handful of matches.

Near the pillars of the market hall, Captain Hall observed, stood small makeshift stands offering refreshments. Black women sold coffee and hot chocolate and "distributed smoking dishes of rice, white as snow"—an especial favorite of visiting country folk—along with gumbo, a local specialty that most newcomers quickly learned to appreciate.

In his travel journals, Bernhard de Saxe-Weimar refers to small shops inside the market hall that sold coffee and oysters. And in the market, as on the levee, black women circulated through the crowd with baskets of delicacies, while pretty quadroons, their hair done up in an elegant *tignon*, offered "bouquets of Spanish jassamine, carnation and violets, as *boutonnières*, for the old beaux."

Latrobe found the market much to his taste: "The articles to be sold were not more various than the sellers. White men and women, and of all hues of brown, and all classes of faces, from round Yankees to grizzly and lean Spaniards, black negroes and negresses, filthy Indians half naked, mulattoes curly and straight haired; quadroons of all shades, long haired and frizzled, women dressed in the most flaring yellow and scarlet gowns, the men capped and hatted." He spent a "half hour or more" strolling along the levee. Near a pile of bricks he discovered a bookseller "whose stock of books, English and French, cut no mean appearance."

Americans and Creoles, rich and poor, white and black, slaves and free all met and mingled at the market. Some came to shop for themselves or their masters, others to take a quick lunch of a dozen oysters or relax over a cup of coffee; still others came simply to enjoy the spectacle. People from every walk of life repaired to the levee to replenish their stock of news and gossip, which would soon be expended around the kitchen table or on the patio.

According to tradition, the market occupied the site of an ancient Choctaw trading station. The Indians still brought their products there: hides, furs, herbs, and the legendary green powder, made of dried sassafras leaves, that was used to make *gumbo filé*. Day in and day out, they could be seen seated on the ground, silent and immobile and seemingly oblivious of the commotion around them. Occasionally one encountered a drunken Indian in the streets. A contemporary witness, Henry Castellanos, comments on the "tottering Choctaws" of the market, "reeling drunk in Father Adam's costume, well worn, diaphanous blanket being substituted for the historical fig leaf." Such figures were a far cry from the "noble savage" that had haunted the European imagination only a few decades before.

The Guardians of the Peace

At two o'clock in the morning, Corporal Marcel's patrol brought in a certain James Smith, charged with disturbing the peace. . . . At midnight and three quarters, the patrol brought in a sailor, arrested on the levee and accused of stealing a lady's dress. . . . At nine o'clock, the market police brought in, by order of its commander, Monsieur Monoit, a runaway slave, Louis by name, who was consigned to the police jail. At 9:15, Grimau, a regular policeman, brought in a small Negro, Pierre by name, belonging to Monsieur Baptiste, a free colored man, for setting off fireworks; he was consigned to the police jail. . . . Arrested on the Place d'Armes, a mulatto, Augustin, caught putting fireworks in the cannon; consigned to the police jail. . . . Monsieur Lévêque, jeweler, brought in a Negro named Henry Braoum, accused of threatening to kill his wife; consigned to the police jail. . . . At eight o'clock, the guard was called out to break up a group of Negroes in a cabaret. . . . Madame Fox asked the guard to bring in her Negro, Pat by name, who was consigned to the police jail. . . . At ten o'clock in the evening, the Faubourg St. Mary patrol brought in a young savage gone to drink, Noe James, found asleep at the corner of Carondelet and Canal streets; he was consigned to the police jail. . . . At one o'clock, the south patrol brought in John Schimin, drunk, found sleeping at the Basin. At midnight, the north patrol brought in a sailor divested of his trousers, found asleep by the herb market; consigned to the police jail. . . .

At six o'clock in the evening, the police of the central station, on duty at the Basin, saw three people bathing who refused to leave the water. . . . The mounted patrol found two cabarets open at 9:30 in the evening, one at the corner of Toulouse and Rampart streets, the other at the Basin. . . . The first north patrol brought in a certain Mr. John Kamp, found asleep in the boiler room of a steamboat. . . . A cart was driven by at full gallop. . . . The Faubourg St. Mary patrol picked up a wounded man on Girod Street. . . . A free Negro woman named Marie Casanova summoned the Faubourg Marigny guard to arrest the Negro Jean-Baptiste, belonging to Monsieur Nicaud, for stealing four madras handkerchiefs, six piastres, and a wallet. . . . The license numbers of carts speeding: 98, 30, 9, 159, 530.

That is a sample of the daily logbook of Captain Dutillet, guardian of the peace. In this era, the New Orleans police force consisted of a captain, two lieutenants, two sergeants, three corporals, and forty watchmen. Twenty-two men were assigned to the *carré* and the

Tremé district, sixteen to the Faubourg St. Mary, and eight to the Faubourg Marigny. The force was small, but, to judge from records such as the one quoted above, New Orleans was a fairly peaceable town. The principal activities of the police seemed to be rounding up runaway slaves, apprehending drunken sailors, and making sure that bars and cafés observed their licensing hours and that drivers of carriages and carts kept within the speed limit.

We find no mention of murder, housebreaking, or armed assault against the inhabitants. There are indeed a few references to cases of robbery and bodily injury, but these usually involved sailors and other less reputable elements of the population, and occurred in neighborhoods where respectable citizens had no business to be after nightfall.

The newspapers reinforce the impression of a decorous and law-abiding community, for there is virtually no mention of crime or violence in their pages. This is a surprising state of affairs for a city that had long enjoyed a reputation for easy-going, not to say loose, morals; whose population had quadrupled in the last twenty years, with the new inhabitants consisting largely of marginal and unstable drifters, fortune hunters, runaway slaves; which abounded in low dives and gambling dens; and where the neighborhood known as the Swamp served as a notorious refuge for pirates and other outlaws.

There is never any suggestion that the citizens of the residential parts of town showed any hesitation about venturing out at night. On the contrary, New Orleans was noted for its night life: its dinners, balls, operas, theaters, and other entertainments. Karl Pöstl remarks with evident satisfaction that "New Orleans, which less than fifteen years ago was the lurking hole of every assassin, is now in point of security not inferior to any other city." He attributes this improvement to the new police regulations, which, as he says, "deserve every praise."

In fact, Louis Philippe de Roffignac, the mayor of New Orleans, and his fourteen aldermen had drawn up a series of ordinances designed to assure public safety. A curfew was put into effect for slaves, sailors, and soldiers; it began at eight o'clock in the evening in winter, at nine o'clock in summer. Any such person found on the streets without written permission from his owner or commanding officer after the cannon had boomed from the town hall was forthwith conducted to the Calaboso or a police station. The same cannon signaled closing time for all bars and taverns in the city, "with the exception of a few respectable hotels and coffee-houses." It would, however, be rash to assume that these regulations were very strictly enforced.

"The city guards are generally idle all day and invisible during the night," complained a reporter in the *Louisiana Gazette* on October 5, 1825. Castellanos also had serious doubts about the efficiency of the watchmen: "Their occupation seemed to consist in loitering about town, in lounging around cabarets or in dozing away their time upon the benches of the guardhouse. The night watchmen were no better, although this branch of the service was occasionally supplemented by a citizen patrol." Saxe-Weimar, who witnessed a number of brawls at public dances, in some of which up to twenty people were injured, was amazed that the police never intervened.

The general failure of the press to report such occurrences may have a simple explanation. Herbert Asbury, himself a journalist and well acquainted with the seamier side of New Orleans life, asserts that robbery, armed assault, and arson were such commonplace occurrences during this period, and especially during the years 1827 and 1828, that the newspapers did not regard them as newsworthy. Priority seems to have been given to news from Washington or Paris, presumably on the theory that there was no point telling people what they already knew or could quickly discover for themselves at the market or in the midtown cafés. For example, the arrival of the first steamboat in New Orleans in January, 1812, received only a few lines of notice in the local press. In summary, we may perhaps conclude that violence was not indeed unknown to New Orleans, but that the city was no worse than many another American city on that score; and that in the better quarters of town the citizens felt safe and secure.

The Calaboso

The jail, clearly, was full to overflowing. But here again we must be cautious in drawing conclusions, for the building served as a combination prison and police headquarters. It provided accommodation not only for genuine criminals, murderers, and thieves from all over Louisiana, but also for debtors, for accused parties awaiting trial, and for a great many slaves charged with "desertion" or with petty crimes for which a white person would merely have paid a small fine.

The crowding was fearful, the sanitary conditions appalling. In 1820, a commission appointed to report of the facility found that prisoners sentenced to execution were confined, naked, in damp, cold cells. The proportion of sick prisoners was high, though deaths, surprisingly enough, were rare. There were frequent escapes and periodic riots.

Fortunately for themselves, the Indians were spared the horrors of the Calaboso. Old treaties were still respected in New Orleans, and Indians convicted of crimes were turned over to their tribal chiefs, who alone had the authority to inflict punishment on them. Such cases were rare, for the Indians, as Latrobe remarks, were "scrupulously honest." From time to time, a Choctaw might be escorted to the police station to sleep off his drunkenness, but it was generally agreed that the "savages" were the most peaceable and law-abiding element of the population.

The mayor was authorized to employ slaves and free blacks detained in prison, as well as convicts, both black and white, for public works projects. The prisoners were dressed in red jackets and trousers; on their red caps were heavy metal badges stamped with their prison number. Black and white prisoners were chained together until 1827, after which they were kept separate and dressed in different garb. The guards were permitted to use force to maintain discipline in the work gang, and prisoners were often chained to their wheelbarrows. Every day sixty to eighty chained blacks shuffled out of the prison yard, escorted by watchmen with whips in their hands and swords by their sides. The chain gang cleaned the sewers, swept the gutters, repaired the levee, and, on occasion, manned the fire pumps. Most of the prisoners were slaves, sentenced for petty misdemeanors. During their imprisonment, their masters received twenty-five cents a day in compensation for their lost services.

Fire, flooding, and mud were the chief preoccupations of the mayor and the aldermen. The last affliction was costly to cope with, for there were no paving stone quarries in Louisiana and stone had to be brought in from the East. Over the years, the citizens had acquired a somewhat philosophical attitude toward muddy streets, but presently a Paving Stone Committee was formed to deal with the matter once and for all. The committee solicited bids and eventually awarded contracts. It stipulated that two-thirds of the cost of paving the streets should be assumed by those property owners whose land abutted the public streets, while the remaining one-third, as well as the cost of paving the public squares, would be borne by the municipality. The task was a formidable one, and work proceeded slowly. It was ten years before pedestrians were able to make their way about the city without sinking in the mud.

The people of New Orleans were celebrated for their refined taste and elegant manners. Yet the fact that the mayor felt obliged to forbid the citizens to "throw into the gutters, streets, or canals, or onto the levee or river banks, or any place of public assembly, offal, fecal matter, or other such substances" seems to indicate that some of the inhabitants had no compunctions about emptying their garbage or chamber pots out the window. The law stipulated that the proper disposal of human waste matter was the responsibility of the individual citizen, and that such substances were not to be placed in the street-cleaning carts that made the rounds daily, including Sundays and holidays. This law was far from accomplishing its purpose, for it prompted certain impoverished or miserly souls to dump their refuse into the streets.

New Orleans possessed no underground sewer system, of course, and all waste water was emptied into the gutters, whence it flowed into the swamps. Each house had its outside toilet, a trench located in courtyard or garden, and the law stated that these trenches were to be emptied when they were filled to within a foot of ground level. It was further stipulated that this operation was to take place only between the hours of eleven at night and three o'clock in the morning.

WATER AND FIRE

The people of New Orleans did not as yet enjoy the convenience of running water in their houses. A waterworks had been under construction on the levee since 1810, but the project progressed slowly. (The architect Latrobe was engaged on it until he died of yellow fever.) In the meantime, the citizens used the local well water, which, according to John Paxton, was "clear and unsalted, but had an unpleasant taste, and could be used neither for drinking nor for washing clothes." Drinking water was drawn from the Mississippi and brought to town by wagon. The water was sold at the rate of 50 cents a barrel, or 6.15 cents for four buckets. This costly and cumbersome means of supplying drinking water continued through the 1820s.

The Mississippi water was transferred for domestic use to enormous glass jars, which the householder usually stored in the courtyard or garden. It was decanted in the sunlight, then filtered through alum, sand, or gravel. The water was reputed to possess exceptional qualities: for example, it was said to be largely responsible for the fertility of the local women.

Northern visitors were justifiably surprised that the municipal authorities had not seen fit to install a system of pumps, such as was in use in the city of New York at that time. Such a system would have permitted the distribution of water to individual households at a reasonable rate, facilitated street cleaning, and would also have been a great help in fighting fires, for the pumps could be readily moved from one place to another.

Fires were a constant source of anxiety. There had been two particularly devastating fires in living memory, one in 1788 and one in 1794, and the inhabitants of New Orleans were extremely fire-conscious. It was forbidden to construct new dwellings in the Vieux Carré in any material other than brick, and in recent years shingle roofs had increasingly been replaced by tile. Kitchens were often located in separate buildings to reduce fire hazards. New fire-fighting units had been established, new pumps imported from England, and a stock of ladders, buckets, grappling hooks, hoses, and axes laid by. Yet the menace of fire continued to haunt the city, for a majority of the houses were of wood, and the pumps were generally ineffective against a major blaze. In addition, the staff of fifty full-time firemen employed by the municipality was inadequate to deal with a serious emergency.

Attempts to recruit volunteer firemen initially met with little success. Then the mayor authorized the free blacks of the community to form two fire-fighting units of their own. In 1829, these were followed by a company of middle-class whites: merchants, administrators, and professional men. The volunteer fire brigades began to acquire distinctive personalities, along with an esprit de corps.

A sooty chimney, an overlooked candle, an act of negligence, or simply a clumsy gesture was enough to set a house ablaze. And there were innumerable cases of arson. Thieves used the confusion of a fire to make off with the householder's jewels and silver; ill-treated slaves set fire to their master's houses out of anger and despair.

A fire was everybody's business. At the first smell of smoke, the alarm bell was rung and neighbors, passersby, friends, and firemen all came running. Often the mayor himself joined in fighting the flames. A spirit of solidarity prevailed, and the citizenry could always be counted on to lend a hand in such emergencies—quelling the blaze, carrying out furniture and other valuables, comforting the victims, opening both their houses and their purses to those left homeless by the fire.

The firemen of 1820 had no proper uniforms but wore plain white hats, bought at their own expense, emblazoned with the number of their brigade. The hats of the captains and lieutenants bore the insignia of their ranks, and these officers also carried white batons and megaphones as symbols of authority.

Fire or the threat of it was a great social leveler. Under the direction of the fire chief, master and slave, rich man and poor, stood shoulder to shoulder to form a human chain, passing water buckets from hand to hand. The pumps were often inadequate, and all too many fires could only be contained when the flames had nothing left to devour.

The other danger was flooding. An abnormally heavy spring rainfall or a leak in the levee could produce devastating effects. In 1815, a large crack formed in the levee five miles upstream from the city, causing great damage to the outlying regions. The only defense against this sort of occurrence was constant patrolling of the levee over its entire length, many miles above and below New Orleans. Each landowner was responsible for the upkeep of that portion of the levee bordering his land, while the portion running through the city was maintained at public expense. During the many years in which the levee was in use, no major breaks occurred within the city limits—a silent testimony to the diligence and concern of private citizens and public officials alike.

STREET SCENES

In spite of its rapid growth, New Orleans seems to have been spared the usual afflictions of overpopulation. The city filled out gracefully, making good use of its spacious avenues and relatively wide streets. The sidewalks seem not to have been overcrowded; none of the contemporary chroniclers refers to traffic congestion. There was no housing crisis and no shanty towns. Dire poverty was virtually unknown, and there seem to have been employment opportunities for all. The city's economic expansion kept pace with its physical development. A man of modest means could rapidly establish a business by means of loans; he was generally able to pay off his debt in the course of three or four years. Of course, some men went bankrupt, but many more made sizable fortunes. The soaring price of slaves and the boom in construction were two indicators of the city's prosperity. Buildings were springing up everywhere, in the Vieux Carré as well as in the faubourgs. The construction was accompanied by two major municipal projects, the paving-stone project and the waterworks—all of which gave New Orleans the appearance of a gigantic construction site. Yet the city still retained its air of a provincial European town, and its distinctive charm seldom failed to surprise and captivate foreign visitors. The indomitable Mrs. Frances Trollope visited New Orleans in 1827 and recorded her impressions as follows: "The large proportion of blacks seen in the streets, all labour being performed by them; the grace and beauty of the elegant quadroons, the occasional groups of wild and savage looking Indians, unwonted aspect of the vegetation, the huge and turbid river . . . all help to afford that species of amusement which proceeds from looking at what we never saw before." She adds:

The town has much the appearance of a French Ville de Province, and is, in fact, an old French colony taken from Spain by France. The names of the streets are French, and the language about equally French and English. The market is handsome and well supplied, all produce being conveyed by

New Orleans and Its Suburbs, 1817. Based on a survey made in 1815 by Jacques Tanesse.

Louisiana Collection, LSU Library

the river. We were much pleased by the chant with which the Negro boatmen regulate and beguile their labour on the river; it consists of but very
notes, but they are sweetly harmonious, and the Negro voice is almost always rich and powerful.

Not all produce was conveyed by river. The Isleños of Bayou Terre-
aux-Boeufs still used their traditional mode of transport—large rustic carts drawn by cattle—to bring poultry and vegetables to market.
Meat also arrived by wagon, and a commendable concern for hygienic standards prompted the city council to issue the notice that "it is
strictly forbidden for butchers to sit on their meat while transporting said meat from the slaughterhouse to the butcher shop."

The council was also concerned with regulating city traffic. It forbade the galloping or trotting of horses in the streets and closed the
streets on Sundays and holidays to "wagons, drays, and other vehicles designed to carry goods, produce, or merchandise," with the exception of water wagons, street-cleaning carts, and vehicles bearing
essential goods. It also banned from the streets any vehicle whose
wheels were not properly greased.

The continual grinding and whining of wheels, so characteristic of
the city, was an inheritance from the days of Spanish rule. Faced with
an unceasing flow of contraband traffic emanating from the outlying
bayous and lakes and entering the city under cover of night, the Spanish authorities had forbidden the streets to vehicles with *greased*
wheels. A quiet vehicle immediately aroused suspicion, and any
trace of grease on the axles implied that the owner was up to no
good. Under American rule, the law was reversed, but many people,
out of ignorance or habit, continued to follow the old routine.

The streets of New Orleans emitted a cacophony all their own. Besides the bang, rattle, and squeak of horse-drawn vehicles, there was
the frequent tolling of church bells; the blare of trumpets, bugles, or
drums announcing an auction or the arrival of a shipload of oysters;
the murmur of a guitar wafting out the open door of a café; the whis-
tle of a steamboat about to depart; the songs of a chain gang punctu-
ated by the sharp, dry crack of the watchman's whip; and, all over
town and up to the very gates of the cemetery, the insistent drone of
the street vendors crying their wares.

New Orleans abounded in street vendors—a form of merchandising initiated by the Creoles and enthusiastically adopted by the Americans. In the month of January, 1823, thirty-two vending licenses were issued by the authorities. Only free males could procure the licenses, but the license-holders seldom did the actual selling. That task was generally reserved for black slaves: many plantation owners regularly sent their slaves into town to hawk surplus produce in the streets.

Most of these hawkers were women. Graceful and stately, they moved through the streets with heavy baskets balanced on their heads. "Strawberries, fresh and fine! *Bel pom patat, madam! Confiture, coco!*" The rhythmic chants verged on song. Passersby paused and craned their necks, shutters were flung open and housewives leaned out, inviting the vendors into the patio to display their wares and exchange the latest gossip. Two modern New Orleanians, Lyle Saxon and Robert Tallant, recalled that "each season had its special commodities. Early spring saw the arrival of strawberries, of Japanese plums; later, watermelons, dewberries, blackberries and figs appeared. Wild ducks, rice birds and other game were sold on the streets during winter."

These vendors often acquired a large clientele, and in order to protect the interests of the regular market merchants, an ordinance forbade the hawking of goods in the street during the hours when the market was open. Exception was made for the Indians and for slaves from nearby plantations who came to town on Sundays and holidays to sell the produce of their own small garden plots. Notions and articles of dress were also sold by the street vendors. In some cases, the items were of considerable value, such as the cashmere shawls that were all the rage at the time and sold for as much as fifty dollars.

Another characteristic street figure was the chimney sweep. At the first approaches of winter his cry could be heard throughout the town: "Sweep. . . . Chimney sweep. . . . Winter's a-coming. . . . Chimney sweep!"

The Houses

The residents of New Orleans relied exclusively on their fireplaces to heat their homes. The winters, then as now, were mild, with the temperature seldom falling below ten degrees Centigrade—though in 1823 there was a cold spell of unusual severity that blighted the oranges and severely damaged the crops. In general, however, the inhabitants were more concerned with the heat than with the cold. The ceilings and windows of the houses were high, allowing for free circulation of air. Patios, balconies, and open galleries served as sitting rooms in good weather.

Evening brought cooling breezes, but also a dense cloud of mosquitoes—a universal affliction for which there was no easy remedy. From early June to late October, the mosquitoes invaded the homes of rich and poor alike at sunset, dancing frenetically around the light fixtures and alighting with ferocious alacrity on any exposed surface of flesh. To shut the windows rendered the room intolerably close and hot. An alternative was to envelop oneself in fumigating smoke or to use mosquito netting. Latrobe reports: "Several of my friends, lawyers and other studious men, put up in their offices a kind of safe, or frame, covered with gauze, and write till late at night in perfect security."

Beds were invariably draped in netting, so the occupants passed the night bothered by nothing worse than the persistent buzzing of the ubiquitous pests. Sometimes, it seems, they even worked out of season, for Mrs. Trollope complains that in winter "the attacks of the mosquitoes were incessant, and most tormenting."

The houses were generally spacious and comfortable, but even the plantation owners' mansions were unlikely to strike the sophisticated visitor as overly sumptuous. The Creoles had inherited from their Spanish predecessors a certain austerity of taste, a revulsion from anything that smacked of the ostentatious. Their décors generally eschewed satin, damask, or gilt. No nymphs disported themselves on the ceilings, no shepherds and shepherdesses pursued their amours on the walls. The fireplaces were usually of brick rather than marble, the floors of cypress wood covered with straw matting in the summer and rugs in the winter. The historian Charles Gayarré recalls that in his grandfather's house the floor was of oak marquetry, "a rare thing in Louisiana, which I do not remember having seen in any other house." The furniture was solid but simple. The wealthiest Creoles had mahogany pieces, while the less wealthy contented themselves with cypress, cherry, or walnut. Those who could afford it ordered their furniture from France; others relied on local cabinet makers. The Empire style was in fashion in the Creole quarter, whereas the Anglo-Saxon districts of the city preferred Sheraton.

In the houses of the well-to-do Creoles, the drawing and sitting rooms were generally connected by large double doors. In the drawing room, one could expect to find the household's best furniture: an elegant crystal chandelier, a fancy mirror, a finely embroidered firescreen. Ancestral portraits hung on the wall; ensconced in one corner was an étagère that displayed the family's best china. Candles were preferred to oil lamps for lighting, and elegant candelabras were placed strategically around the room on tables and stands.

The drawing room was reserved for social occasions; the sitting room was where the members of the family gathered to talk, read, sew, or make music. This room generally contained a piano or spinet, a bookcase, a sofa and chairs, and more family portraits. Like the drawing room, it was crowded with furniture, but the pieces were more modest. One might well find on a side table palmetto fans stuck in sand-filled vases.

Each bedroom was furnished with a canopy bed and a large mirrored armoire. On the dressing table stood a pitcher and wash basin of flowered porcelain; the chamber pot was concealed inside the night table. Occasionally the room also contained a makeshift altar for private devotions: a table covered with blue satin on which were placed candles, a small vessel of holy water, and a figure of the Virgin or some favorite saint.

The dining room was enormous, on a scale commensurate with Creole hospitality. The silverware, china, and crystal, the table linen, the food and drink—all proclaimed the host's generosity and good taste. The table was usually fully extended, with all the leaves in place, ready to receive a full complement of relatives, friends, and any distinguished visitors who might happen by. When Lafayette visited New Orleans in 1825, Jean Ursin de Lavillebeuvre accommodated no less than fifty guests at his mahogany dining table.

The private wills of the period are of interest not only in revealing the relative importance that different articles of furniture possessed for an average Creole family, but also in underlining certain Creole

traits: their passion for gambling, for instance, and their disinclina-
tion for intellectual pursuits. The scarcity of books is as astounding
as the abundance of gaming tables. To be sure, the memoirs of de
Laussat inform us that the old marquis de Marigny possessed a considerable personal library, and there is no doubt that the Creole aristocracy counted among its members men and women of scholarly
achievement and general erudition; but on the whole the citizens of
New Orleans cared more for the pleasures of the flesh than the treasures of the mind.

3

Society

The social structure of New Orleans reflected the peculiar genius of the inhabitants. To an outsider, this structure might appear at first sight to be constituted by a rigid, precisely calibrated system. In reality, it had innumerable and ingenious variations. On initial investigation, the social hierarchy seems to divide itself into three general groups. At the summit were the whites: Creoles, Americans, and inhabitants of European origin. Next came the free blacks: emancipated slaves and their descendants, who were regarded as "half citizens." Lowest of all were the slaves, who enjoyed no civil rights and were relegated to the status of household property or chattel.

On further examination, however, the hierarchical system reveals itself as much more complex. For example, it was not always so easy to categorize a free black as occupying an intermediate position between the white elite and the black slave population. The whites never actually constituted a homogeneous social class; and if one were to rank the citizens of New Orleans according to wealth and cultural attainments, it would soon become clear that many blacks not only occupied the same position as whites but even surpassed them on the social scale. To be sure, both law and custom erected insurmountable racial barriers, and an individual of African blood, no matter how wealthy he might be or how pale his skin, could not be admitted to white society. But nothing prevented him from engaging in commerce, owning slaves, taking on a white business associate, or employing whites as laborers. Some blacks even became planters—a profession that held the highest rank in the social hierarchy.

The 1820 census listed the population of New Orleans at 29,000. (Undoubtedly this figure is inaccurate, for the census was conducted during the summer months, when a great many families had made their annual exodus from the city to escape the fierce heat and the threat of yellow fever.) The population is further broken down into 13,908 whites, 1,500 foreigners, 6,237 free people of color, and 7,355 slaves. For the parish of Orleans, the figures are 5,827 whites, 49 foreigners, 924 free people of color, and 7,591 slaves, for a total of 14,391 inhabitants.

Inexact as these figures are, they are instructive. They indicate that, in the overall area of New Orleans, the black population exceeded the white, and that the great majority of blacks lived in the city itself.

THE CREOLES

The Creoles made up the majority of the white population, although their numerical dominance was rapidly diminishing. In 1803 there were seven Creoles to every American; in 1812 the ratio was three to one; by 1830 it had shrunk to two to one. In the face of continuing American encroachments, the Creoles remained faithful to their own culture and way of life; they refused to adapt themselves either to the new spirit of egalitarianism or to the drive for economic expansion that the Americans brought in their wake. The deep-rooted Creole conservatism prevented them from acknowledging the emergence of a new class that had risen to prosperity on the economic boom. The space of a few years saw the establishment of two distinct white elites, one based on birth and the other on money.

The concept of caste was fundamental to the Creoles, and their own social organization was extraordinarily complex. Over the course of the past centuries, the French community had assimilated a number of foreign groups, eliminating virtually all traces of their national origins. Family names were Gallicized so that the German Sweig was changed to Labranche, the German Weber to Fabre. The Creoles also incorporated some Irish and a good many Spaniards. In fact, the very word *Creole* derives from the Spanish *criollo*, which originally designated white children born in the Caribbean. Little by little, the term came to designate the entire French-speaking population of Louisiana; by extension one referred to a Creole cow, a Creole slave, a Creole house, as opposed to an American cow, an American slave, an American house.

Of course, this generic use of the term was studiously avoided by the "first families" of New Orleans, who traced their lineage back to aristocratic ancestors in France or Spain and reserved the term *Creole* for themselves alone. Lesser families were classified as "Chacas," "Catchoupines," "Chaks," "Chacalatas," "Cachumas," "Bambaras," or "Bitacaux." The precise meaning of most of these terms is now lost, but we can assume that they all carried a generally pejorative connotation. According to New Orleans writer Robert Tallant, "Chacas" were tradesmen, "Chacalatas" country folk or peasants, and "Cachumas" anyone with a drop of African blood in his veins. Each stratum of Creole society looked down on the strata below it—and all had nothing but contempt for the American settlers. Even Creole slaves made a point of snubbing their American counterparts.

The Creole disdain of the Americans was without any real justification. Although it is true that the freebooting "Kaintucks" who roamed the city hardly represented the American character at its best, there were also many substantial citizens from Maryland, Virginia, and New England living in the city, whose family trees were fully the equal of the best Creole families. Among the members of the Creole community, Bernard de Marigny was virtually alone in espousing the American cause. After the Louisiana Purchase, he became a member of the Democratic-Republican party, became involved in politics, married an American wife, and except for his dispute with Caldwell managed to maintain friendly relations with the people of the "other" faubourg. Despite his preeminent social standing among the Creoles, his example was not followed.

However, individuals from both groups often came together in joint business ventures, for wherever money was to be made, the Americans were on hand to make it. Of the Americans, Latrobe comments: "Their business is to make money. . . . Their limbs, their hands, and their hearts move to that sole object. Cotton and tobacco, buying and selling, and all the rest of the occupation of a money-making community, fill their time and give the habit of their minds."

It would be scarcely appropriate to speak of economic competition between the Creoles and the Americans, for the Americans enjoyed an undisputed superiority in business affairs, and the more they prospered, the more the Creole economy languished and waned.

To be sure, there were only a limited number of professions that a Creole could follow without loss of status. Planter, banker, broker in rice, cotton, or sugar—these were all permissible occupations. He could also earn his living as a legislator, magistrate, or lawyer, or—a last resort—as a doctor. But retail business of any kind was considered beneath the dignity of a Creole gentleman, and to run a shop or sell anything over a counter was to descend to the level of a "Chaca." For the young man without means, it was far more honorable to marry for money than to accept employment outside his class. The Creoles attached no moral stigma to idleness, and virtually every respectable Creole family numbered a few layabouts and parasites among its household.

We must realize that, for the Creoles, idleness was by no means synonymous with inactivity. The idle Creole was always busy— hunting, riding, playing cards, putting in long hours with his mistress or at the cafés, making a call on his tailor or bootmaker, paying his respects to the society ladies at their weekly "at homes," or else, quite simply, strolling on the levee. Under the circumstances, the idle Creole had little time to spare for what the vulgar called "work."

Americans, especially New Englanders, were scandalized by the "eat, drink, and be merry" spirit of the Creoles, which struck them as outrageously pagan. The austere ornithologist John James Audubon confided to his journal that the Gallic exuberance of the city's inhabitants "really sickened" him. Robert Tallant recalls another visitor who recorded: "New Orleans is a dreadful place in the eyes of a New England man. They keep Sunday as we in Boston keep the fourth of July." Even the French regarded their Creole cousins with a certain reserve. "They display," wrote Perrin du Lac, "an excessive devotion to pleasure. The delights of the table, the boudoir, and the gaming board absorb all their time—the latter perhaps dominating all the others. Whole nights are spent at gambling, and whole fortunes squandered." Another French commentator, Pierre de Laussat, reproaches the Louisianians for their "snobbery of race and birth." He adds that the Creoles are "low in energy, fractious in temperament, and utterly lacking in civic spirit," and that they "bend to the will of others, while saving their complaints for the privacy of their own fireside or balcony." He also accuses the urban Creoles of being improvident and remarks that it is rare to find one who is "unfettered by debts."

Beside these critics we must set the other observers who succumbed to the romantic allure of Creole society, to its refinement and its aristocratic traditions. An American writer of the period, William Sparks, was full of enthusiasm for the Creole way of life: "In this population, if nowhere else in America, is seen a contented and happy people—a people whose pursuit is happiness and not the almighty dollar. Unambitious of that distinction which only wealth bestows, they are content with an abundance for all their comforts, and for the comfort of those who, as friends or neighbors, come to share it with them."

In general, however, Creole attitudes and behavior baffled the Americans, who were a hard-working, sober-minded folk, with a firm belief in Progress, unlimited ambition, and a profound respect for the sanctity of the dollar. To their eyes, the Creoles were lacking in industry, morality, and enterprise. "Many of the leading gentlemen," reports Latrobe, "when not talking of tobacco or cotton, find it very amusing to abuse and ridicule French morals, French manners, and French houses." Certain Creole habits, such as the kiss on both cheeks that the men used in greeting, struck the Americans as ludicrous.

Americans and Creoles were separated by their manners, customs, and political outlooks, but more formidably by language and religion. The fact that their children attended different schools and churches stood in the way of any fusion of the two groups. Yet the day would come when English would be universally accepted as the lingua franca of New Orleans.

By the time that day arrived, however, the Americans themselves had undergone fundamental changes. In adapting to the climate and to their Creole neighbors, they had, quite inadvertently, "gone native," absorbing certain characteristically Creole tastes and traits.

The Creole legacy to the Americans was an indolence and a joie de vivre; a rare and marvelous tolerance; hospitality, love of fine cooking, delight in festivities; a highly refined sense of caste and status; and an exuberant sensuality. Indeed, it was impossible to remain a Puritan in a city where the warm nights were heavy with the scent of jasmine, orange blossoms, and magnolia; where lovely quadroon women openly solicited well-to-do "protectors"; and where more heed was paid to the satisfaction of carnal appetites than to the salvation of the soul.

THE POPULATION

While many historians have chronicled the colorful lives of New Orleans' wealthy and aristocratic citizens, the humbler inhabitants of the city have received scant attention. The vast majority occupied that ill-defined and uneasy frontier between the middle and lower-middle classes. They included Creoles and Americans, white and black, second-generation immigrants and new arrivals from abroad.

Most of the new immigrants were from France. The vicissitudes of French political life had always exerted an important influence on the composition of Louisiana's population. Having served under French rule as a dumping ground for social rejects, under the Americans Louisiana became a land of hope and promise for Frenchmen. The last influx of French immigrants were Bonapartists, chased from their homeland by the Bourbon Restoration.

The Bonapartists constituted a large and vociferous group within the French émigré community. They were continually holding meetings, forming organizations, hatching plots, reminiscing about past glories, and dreaming of future triumphs. In imitation of the local volunteer militias, they assembled their own brass band and paraded through the streets on the anniversaries of Napoleon's most notable victories. They even conceived a daring plan for freeing their leader from his captivity on St. Helena. A schooner had been chartered, an expedition outfitted, and a mansion purchased on Chartres Street to house the Emperor on his arrival in New Orleans when, on September 10, 1821, news was received of his death. The Bonapartists of New Orleans remained loyal to Napoleon's memory, and when, thirteen years later, his doctor set up practice on Royal Street, his arrival prompted an outburst of fervent emotion. In response, the doctor presented the city with a bronze death mask of the Emperor, which was graciously accepted by the civic authorities.

We possess two contemporary accounts of the French colony at New Orleans. The Baron Montlezun, writing in 1816, reports:

The French inhabitants are rabid Bonapartists. There are hardly a dozen royalists among them. The Bonapartists await the arrival here of Grouchy, Lefevre-Desnouettes, l'Allemand [sic], Clausel, and other great men of that ilk; and to compensate themselves for the general scorn of the citizenry, they seek the approbation of pirates, buccaneers, democrats, terrorists, Septembrists, Robespierrists, Maratists, Brutusists, Scévolists, sans-culottes, regicides, levelers, and champions of liberty, equality, the inviolability of the Republic, fraternity . . . and death!

Karl Pöstl is more temperate but scarcely more approving:

The French are of all men the least valuable acquisition of a new state. Of a lavish and wanton temper, they spend their time in trifles which are of no importance to any but themselves. Dancing, fighting and riding are the daily occupation of these people. . . . With neither religion, morality or even education, they pretend to be the leaders of the *bon ton* because they come from Paris, and they in general succeed.

The rest of the foreign population, according to Pöstl, was composed of Germans, English, Irish, Spaniards, and several "very respectable" Italian families.

The Irish had long since made a place for themselves in New Orleans and could be found on all rungs of the social ladder. Some were prosperous merchants and exporters; others were bankers, doctors, dentists, schoolmasters, shopowners; still others were tavernkeepers or café owners. Those newly arrived from Ireland following the famine of 1822 were simple farmhands who could only earn their living by manual labor.

These hard-drinking, mercurial sons of the bog were viewed with alarm by the established population, and many whites preferred to employ slaves or free blacks, whose tempers were felt to be more reliable. However, the high price of slaves made them too precious to use for every task, so the humblest, most backbreaking jobs were usually reserved for the Irish. The construction of the New Basin

Canal, linking the Faubourg St. Mary to Lake Pontchartrain, and of the Pontchartrain railway was largely the work of Irish laborers. During the 1820s, the Irish were not numerous enough to constitute a white proletariat, but they were surely the forerunners of such a class.

There seems to have been no friction among the classes. The city's economic vitality made itself felt at all levels, and the chance of improving one's fortunes was open to all. The accumulation of riches was not, however, the ultimate social distinction—which is why some men who had made a killing in commerce or real estate then reinvested their money in slaves and land and devoted themselves henceforth to agriculture. Doctors were known to abandon lucrative practices almost overnight in order to become planters.

The sugar planters were at the top of the social hierarchy. Their beautiful, well-established plantations—virtually feudal estates—lay along the Mississippi, not far from New Orleans. Most of these properties belonged to the Creole aristocracy, and a newcomer had little chance of coming into one of them unless a bankruptcy occurred or an owner died without heirs. But Louisiana was rich in territory, and there were many other areas in which to establish a new domain. Cotton, here as elsewhere in the South, had become a favorite crop, and cotton plantations of all sizes were springing up wherever the soil was suitable. Indeed, cotton was to become the economic bulwark of the new plantation dynasties, and along the levee at New Orleans it was the price of cotton that was the main topic of conversation.

All the large plantation owners maintained a pied-à-terre in New Orleans. During the social season, they moved into town with their families and servants, leaving their country estates in the hands of managers. By this means, the gentlemen planters maintained their ascendancy on the social scene and set the tone for New Orleans society.

The Free People of Color

Neg' porté maïs dan so lapoche pou volé poules;
milâte porté cordon dan so lapoche pou volé choual;
n'homme blanc porté larzan dan so lapoche pou trompé fille.

Nigger carries corn in his pocket to steal chickens;
mulatto carries a rope in his pocket to steal a horse;
white man carries money in his pocket to seduce a girl.

—Edward Laroque Tinker, *Creole City*

This little Creole ditty offers us more insight into the blacks' role in New Orleans life than many a longer discourse on the subject. In a society whose laws and traditions pertained exclusively to whites and slaves, the free blacks formed a world apart. Like the whites, they had their social hierarchy, but here rank was determined more by skin color than by personal fortune. The full-blooded black was looked down upon by the griffe, who had one-quarter white blood. He in turn was snubbed by the mulatto, who was regarded with condescension by the quadroon. (In New Orleans, the term *quadroon* applied to those who were three-quarters white, as well as to those who had only an eighth or a sixth of black blood in their ancestry.)

The free status of some black families dated back several generations. The registry of St. Louis Cathedral records a marriage celebrated in 1724 between Jean-Baptiste Raphael and Marie Gaspar, both described as "free Negroes." In 1739, a military company consisting of fifty free Negroes was formed to fight the Chickasaws.

Many slaves were granted freedom in recognition of their bravery during the Indian wars. Others were freed from a sense of humanity. For instance, Pierre Caresse, on the point of being executed by General O'Reilly's firing squad in 1769, publicly granted freedom to his slave Cupidon, who had volunteered to share his master's fate. There were also personal reasons for freeing a slave: a master who had fathered children on one of his slave women generally intended, in his later years, to free both children and mother. Some slaves, finally, had their freedom purchased for them by more fortunate relatives or even managed to buy their own freedom with money earned by doing supplementary work for their masters or for other whites. A slave was automatically granted his freedom "in reward for public service" for giving warning of a nascent conspiracy or insurrection. The large proportion of mulattos among the free black population suggests that most slaves were granted freedom as a result of interbreeding. Among the emancipated blacks, there were very few full-blooded Africans, or "Congos" as they were called locally.

According to the French Code Noir of 1724, a master aged twenty-five or older could free a slave of his own volition, either during his lifetime or by the terms of his will. The Spanish regulations were more liberal: the master's age was lowered to twenty, and a slave could be freed either by written testimony in a will or by simply notifying the slave of his manumission in the presence of five witnesses. Moreover, a slave could request the court to determine his own monetary value, and if he happened to be in possession of the specified sum he could purchase his freedom on the spot, with or without his master's permission. In fact, the Spaniards proved themselves surprisingly lenient masters, and under their rule the free blacks in Louisiana enjoyed benefits that they were to lose under the Americans.

The American attitude toward the blacks was inspired by fear. The free blacks of Louisiana enjoyed the rights of free movement and free assembly and were able to bear firearms. Many of them were literate, and many came from Santo Domingo, where they had, the Americans felt sure, been contaminated by advanced ideas. Recent slave insurrections in the Caribbean, the abolition of slavery within the French possessions, and the success of the Revolution in France had combined to arouse the deep anxiety of both the civil authorities and the general public of Louisiana. Governor Miro and his successor Baron de Carondelet had both deemed it expedient to forbid the entry of slaves and free blacks from Santo Domingo, and, as we have seen, Governor Claiborne too had made a spasmodic attempt to stop the influx of blacks. The people of Louisiana, like other southerners, were haunted by the specter of an organized slave rebellion. Above all, they feared that the free blacks might someday join forces with their enslaved brothers—in which case the whites in certain areas would be vastly outnumbered and their annihilation virtually assured.

THE FREE BLACKS

The free black was made constantly aware of the precariousness of his position in a society that at best merely tolerated his existence. In general, he seems to have been determined to make the best of his lot, to enjoy the privileges accorded him as a "free" man, and to demonstrate his loyalty to the country in which he had made his home. The free blacks had no desire to rock the boat; they had little sympathy for revolutionary sentiments, and their influence did more to suppress such tendencies among the slaves than to encourage them. In fact, there seems to have been little solidarity between the enslaved and the free blacks. In times of peace, the main occupation of the free black militiamen was to patrol the swamps in search of runaway slaves. Free blacks frequently sought employment as overseers on white-owned plantations, and free blacks who owned slaves themselves were reputed for their brutality. In speaking of a wicked man of any color, slaves often used the phrase, "as bad as a free nigger."

Nevertheless, the Americans continued to eye the phenomenon of free blacks with suspicion, and eventually they enacted legislation designed to curtail its growth. A minimum age of thirty was stipulated before which a black could not be granted freedom; his conduct, moreover, had to be certified as having been above reproach for the four years prior to his manumission. (A slave who had saved the life of his master, mistress, or their children was exempted from these restrictions.)

In order to free one of his slaves, the owner made a deposition in court, explaining his reasons for taking such a step. This document had to be accompanied by a certificate of good conduct drawn up by an official of the court or by a justice of the peace, and another certificate, authorized by the Office of Mortgages, which guaranteed that the slave did not form part of any property mortgaged by the owner. On receipt of these papers, the court then ordered the posting of a notice informing the inhabitants of the community of the owner's intention to free the slave and requesting "all persons having any legal objections to this action to present themselves before the court of this parish within forty days of the date hereby affixed."

If nobody presented himself to oppose the action, the judge then drew up the papers of emancipation, but the former master still had to guarantee that the newly freed slave would not become a burden to the state on account of old age, physical or mental illness, or any other cause. After 1830, the legislation was again modified, and it became even more difficult for a slave to obtain his freedom. But the law of 1807, which fixed the minimum age for emancipation at thirty, had already done much to slow down the process and to cause untold hardships. For example, it frequently occurred that a slave-owner died before being able to free his children, who, by virtue of being born of a slave mother, were slaves in terms of the Code Noir. If a black man owned a slave woman and had children by her before freeing her, the children of this union were de jure his slaves and, in case of bankruptcy, liable to be auctioned off with the rest of his goods and belongings. Such cases underlined the cruelty of an institution that many in America were coming to view with horror and indignation.

The freedom accorded the emancipated slave and his descendants was hedged round with restrictions. The free black could take an oath before the court, make a will, acquire goods and property, or amass a fortune, but he could not vote, hold public office, or become a member of the bar. On every official document—will, business agreement, notarized affidavit—he was obliged to add the phrase "colored man" or "colored woman" after his signature. Governor Claiborne had with great reluctance permitted the free blacks to retain their own militia, but he had limited the force to four companies and placed strict controls on their use of arms.

A multitiered system of segregation was already in effect. By city ordinance, blacks were not permitted to occupy theater seats reserved for whites, and whites were prohibited from attending masques or dress balls organized by blacks. Gambling between whites and blacks was forbidden in the cabarets. And slaves were not allowed to attend the balls and festivities of the free blacks.

Such measures show that great care was taken to assure minimum public contact between blacks and whites. Undoubtedly these measures were due to racial prejudice, but they also reflect a conscious effort to avoid friction and maintain the status quo. Cabaret brawls were frequent, and tension between blacks and whites could be reduced by the gambling regulation. In refusing slaves and free blacks the right to assemble at a ball, the authorities were hoping to diminish any chance of collusion between the two groups. Moreover, slaves were too precious a commodity to risk having them injured in any racial brawls.

In fact, all the evidence indicates that the free blacks were trustworthy and upstanding citizens, who could always be counted on to cooperate with the authorities. They were frequently called on to "police the cabarets and other public places," where, according to a city ordinance, they were enjoined to keep order and empowered to arrest all persons disturbing the peace.

THE OUTCASTS

Whether fighting under the French, Spanish, or American flag, the blacks had proven themselves disciplined and courageous soldiers. Their valor during the Battle of New Orleans in 1815 won them the warm praise of General Andrew Jackson: "I knew that you loved the land of your nativity, and that, like ourselves, you had to defend all that is most dear to man; but you surpass my hopes. . . . Soldiers! The President of the United States shall be informed of your conduct on the present occasion, and the voice of the Representatives of the American Nation shall applaud your valor as your General now praises your ardor."

If many Creoles and Americans thought "Old Hickory's" praise a bit excessive, there is no doubt that the words gave great pleasure to the audience to whom they were addressed—not least because General Jackson had implied that the black soldiers' patriotism was fully comparable to that of the whites.

From his birth, the black was encouraged by his master, and by society at large, to mimic the manners and behavior of the whites. He was simultaneously informed that the black race was inferior to the white and that, although he should strive to emulate white standards, he could not, of course, ever hope to attain them. He had only to look around him to see that he lived in a society divided between the outcasts and the elect. Any possible doubt about that fact had been banished by a piece of legislation passed in 1806 that forbade blacks "to ever consider themselves the equal of whites" and imposed a fine or prison term on any black who took it into his head to strike or insult any white.

The Americans retained an old Spanish edict, dating back to the days of Governor Miro, that forbade free black women to wear their hair in any other style than the *tignon* or "madras"—a bureaucratic overreaction to the elaborate coiffures that the quadroon women had sometimes displayed at the theater. These lovely women captured the admiring gazes of all the males in the audience—much to the rage of the ladies of good society, who determined to teach the hussies a lesson. It is said that Madame Miro herself assumed leadership of the campaign and brought formidable pressure to bear on her husband, who eventually capitulated. Thus it came about that the black women of New Orleans were ordered by law to abandon their elegant coiffures in favor of a simple kerchief tied around the head "in the style worn by their Negress mothers." But virtue's triumph was to be short-lived, for a brilliant silk kerchief, artfully knotted and perhaps enhanced with a jewel, proved a wonderfully attractive adornment—an enhancement, even, to a lovely woman's charms!

Racial prejudice was not the sole force at play in this affair of the *tignon*. Sexual rivalry also played a role, for these black women were resented not only for their color but because they were the concubines of the elite of white society: the fathers, husbands, brothers, sons, and fiancés of the respectable white women.

In the beginning, the lack of white women had encouraged interbreeding; with time, it became customary. While the German Karl Pöstl attributes the great number of mulattoes in Louisiana to a "climate where sensuous passions are . . . easily excited," the Frenchman Perrin du Lac cynically remarks that the Creole preference for black women is due to the fact that such women are generally less demanding. "Many men would rather live in concubinage with a woman than marry. In that way they enjoy the advantage of being well cared for, along with the option of dismissing the woman if she proves unsatisfactory or unfaithful."

THE LADIES OF RAMPART STREET

It was not only bachelors who enjoyed the benefits of such relationships. Liaisons between married men and free black women were common in New Orleans; though hardly looked upon with favor, they were tacitly condoned. In a Latin society where the man has all the rights and the woman is required to respect the authority of her lord and master, no wife is expected to raise an outcry over an adulterous husband. The wives were supposed to maintain a dignified silence and to avert their eyes from their husband's indiscretions. But when their rivals chose to parade themselves before their very eyes, displaying the lavish wardrobes supplied by their husbands—then the wives' patience was taxed to the limit.

Such arrangements scandalized American visitors, and it is easy to understand why the Yankees were accustomed to refer to New Orleans as a "city of sin," while Boston preachers fulminated against it as the new Sodom. For many easterners, the Creoles were quite simply papists and libertines. And yet the Anglo-Saxon settlers, in spite of their scruples, quickly adapted to the local customs and set up their own pretty quadroon mistresses in cottages on Rampart Street. For a man, such a mistress constituted a prestige item, rather like a handsome horse and carriage.

Because marriage between blacks and whites was forbidden, these informal relationships were the sole possible for the two partners. In many cases, however, the black women seem to have preferred such liaisons to marriage with men of their own race, and often they were supported in this preference by their mothers. The English traveler Harriet Martineau reports:

The quadroons of New Orleans are raised by their mothers to be what they once were themselves. Some of the young male quadroons are sent to France, some to the far-flung plantations within the State, and others are sold as slaves. Often they marry women of darker skin than themselves, and the quadroon women then brand them as "disgusting." The girls are raised with great care, at least externally, and it would be hard to find women more attractive to look at or more accomplished.

This judgment is confirmed. by another Englishwoman, Frances Trollope, who writes that the young women were "educated with all refinements of style and accomplishments," and were "exquisitely beautiful, graceful, gentle, and amiable."

It would be a mistake to think of these women as prostitutes or, in twentieth-century terms, as call girls. All the contemporary witnesses give us to believe that it was rare for a woman to have more than one lover and that the ladies of Rampart Street were, in fact, noted for their fidelity and virtue. Among themselves, they referred not to being "kept," but to being "placed," and among their fellow blacks they enjoyed a definite social prestige.

Although Miss Martineau asserts that "some committed suicide, and many died of remorse" when their lovers left them, all the evidence indicates that "placement" was essentially a business transaction. There are, of course, a number of touching love stories concerning white men and black women, but although some of these affairs did indeed end in heartbreak and anguish, most of them had their termination in a handsome financial settlement. The men were expected to leave their mistresses in comfortable circumstances and to look after any children that had been born of the liaison. In most cases, the women were left their cottage, as well as a sum of money that had been decided on by the woman's mother preliminary to her daughter's "placement."

Many quadroons subsequently married black husbands of the same background as themselves. Some used their settlements to set themselves up in business; many invested their earnings in slaves, whose services they let out for hire.

Of course, these women constituted only a tiny percentage of the female free black population, and included only those who were good-looking, well-educated, and light of skin. Nonetheless, they left such a mark on the era and so captured the popular imagination that one tends to forget that the vast majority of free black women spent their lives as nurses, midwives, hairdressers, dressmakers, laundresses, street vendors, prostitutes, madams, or—most common of all—housewives.

In New Orleans of the 1820s, those black women who were not obliged to earn their livings stayed home. The poorer ones were occupied with household chores; the wealthier ones, who had slaves to do the domestic work, whiled away their days in the same manner as comparable wealthy white women.

The situation was different for the men. The leisure-class gentleman who lived wholly off his income was not to be found among the free blacks. Black men worked as skilled artisans or as simple laborers; a number of them could be found in business and in the professions. No less than seven hundred fifty blacks are listed as slave owners in 1830—a sure sign of their prosperity. Skilled blacks were much sought after for the quality of their work; they possessed a near monopoly on certain professions, and almost all the shoe-makers, draymen, and bartenders in New Orleans were free blacks. This circumstance inevitably brought them into rivalry with the poorer whites, who attempted to compete with them in the job market.

Like the whites, the blacks had their haves and their have-nots. Like the whites again, they took every opportunity to improve their standard of living and to advance themselves in the social scale. As a group, they played an important role in the economic life of the city and strove to assure their future security through hard work. Yet it is clear that many free blacks owed their prosperity to inheritances from a white father or grandfather that had permitted them to gain educations and to establish their own businesses. The lighter a man's skin in New Orleans, the higher his rank on the social and economic scale.

THE SLAVES

It was the slaves who constituted the hard-core working class. The economy of Louisiana, as of all the southern states, rested ultimately on their shoulders. Slaves had no civil rights; they belonged wholly to their masters. And like their masters' other belongings, they could be seized against nonpayment of debts. A bankruptcy in their master's household meant that they were sent to the Maspero Exchange to be auctioned off along with the horses, wagons, plows, and other remnants of the estate. Slaves were passed on to heirs or divided among them; they were the choice items in any inheritance and were avidly fought over by the interested relatives.

A cook, seamstress, or laundress was often worth $1,000 on the market; a young woman qualified for general housework, along with her two children, could fetch as much as $1,400. A ten-year-old girl was worth $350, a twelve-year-old girl, $600, a wagoner or laborer, $1,200, and a carpenter, $1,400. It is true that many estate inventories contained some blacks who were offered very cheap or listed as of "no value" because of old age, illness, some physical disability, or an addiction to drink. But for every "Barnaby, near-sighted, field laborer: $70" or "Marie-Louise, seventy years old: no value," there were many Eléonores at $900 a head, and Etiennes at $1,100!

A slave's monetary value guaranteed that he would be reasonably well treated. And without adhering to the self-serving fallacy promulgated by such proslavery apologists as R. Q. Mallard that "no laboring population in the world was better off than the Southern slaves," we should recognize that on the whole they were decently treated and subjected to fewer physical hardships than many European workers of the same era. They were seldom without food or shelter, their masters looked after them when they were sick and, as Pierre de Laussat noted, their masters limited their worst punishments to "a few strokes of the whip, or a few days' confinement without rations" for fear of losing them.

When Louisiana was still under Spanish rule, Berquin-Duvallon had noted that the blacks were not treated with "great severity"; an instance of theft, for example, that in Europe would have "brought its author to the galleys or even to the gallows" was punished "with a whipping and the attachment of an iron collar" when committed by a slave. The time when a slave had his ears cut off and his leg muscles slashed was long past. Today we regard whipping as an act of extreme brutality, but in the early nineteenth century it was considered a reasonable form of punishment and was regularly resorted to in the English armed services as a means of maintaining discipline.

PUNISHMENT

If a master desired his slave to be punished but lacked the strength or the inclination to punish him himself, he could take him to the local jail to be disciplined. The jailer, by city ordinance, was not permitted "to inflict or to have inflicted on the slave more than twenty-five lashes, nor to punish the same slave more than twice in a single week." For performance of this service, the jailer received the sum of twenty-five cents.

The whip was the most common form of punishment for slaves: ten lashes for setting off firecrackers in the street; ten to twenty-five lashes for dancing after nightfall in the public places set aside for

their use; ten to twenty-five lashes for participating in public gatherings other than funerals; fifteen lashes for attending a ball reserved
for free blacks; twenty-five lashes for owning a dog. City ordinances
prescribed that whippings could also be administered for being disrespectful to a white person, quarrelling with another slave, making
noise, disturbing the peace, singing obscene songs, or "playing quoits,
dice or other games in the street, on the levee, in the road and other
places."

Another common form of punishment for minor crimes was the
pillory. The victim was seated on a low platform opposite the Cabildo, with a placard around his neck proclaiming his name and the nature of his offense. The place was generally thronged with people,
and the wretched captive was exposed from dawn to dusk to the
jeers of the crowd. This degrading form of punishment was abol-
ished for whites in 1827, but continued for blacks until 1847.

Sometimes the masters intervened to save their slaves from arrest, preferring to pay a fine rather than to subject their slaves to the
jailer's lashes. After all, the slaves were their prize possessions, and
it would have been folly to risk their being injured. Sound business
reasoning, as well as a basis of humanitarian sentiment, generally
kept the Creoles and the Americans from mistreating their slaves. It
is no defense of the abominable institution to note that *Gone With
the Wind* gives a somewhat more accurate picture of slave life in the
South than *Uncle Tom's Cabin*.

Some masters found that disgrace was preferable to the whip as a
means of punishment. Sending a cook, coachman, or chambermaid
to work in the fields was the worst sort of punishment for a slave
accustomed to the privileges and prestige of domestic service. On
the plantations, it was sometimes possible to appeal to the pride and
solidarity of the field hands to maintain order. The master could also
threaten a disobedient slave with being put up to auction—a prospect that seldom failed to awaken acute anxiety, for the slave's habits were deeply set and a sense of security his most precious possession. That may be why many runaway slaves, after spending a few
days in the swamps, returned home to their masters. If plantation
life meant hard work, it also offered food and shelter. The overseer's
or driver's whip whistled above many heads, but few actually suf-

fered its bite. All things considered, it seemed better to face the wrath of the master than to spend any more nights in the swamps, where the will-o'-the-wisps seemed like evil spirits enticing their victims to a watery grave. The returned fugitive was often cooly received by his fellow slaves; he was generally viewed as a delinquent rather than as a hero, especially if the master was regarded as a lenient one.

Although all slaves were subject to the degradation of servitude, their individual conditions varied greatly depending on the character of their master and the nature of their work. The household servants were infinitely better off than those who worked in the fields or in the boiler room of a steamboat, and on the whole the slaves who lived in town were happier than those on the plantations. In New Orleans, many slaves enjoyed a comparative degree of freedom; it often happened that a planter would leave his townhouse wholly in the charge of a few faithful servants when he returned to his estate at the end of each social season. Charles Gayarré recalled with deep affection the two aged black women, Agathe and Marie, who looked after his grandfather's house in the old man's absence. Sometimes, too, slaves were left in charge of their master's business affairs: they both kept the accounts and carried on the day-to-day activities of the enterprise.

Many slaves were skilled artisans with established reputations; others were barbers, typographers, wagoners, smiths, stableboys, masons, carpenters, painters, shoemakers. Among the slaves of New Orleans we also find midwives and musicians. Sometimes the slave worked for someone other than his master; in fact, slaves were often rented out by the month or year. The master received pay for his slave's services, but the slave was permitted to earn something for himself by working additional hours. Occasionally, as we have mentioned, a slave could earn money in his free time—though always with his master's consent.

Skilled slaves were generally treated like any other employee by their masters or bosses, and their mode of living, at least on the surface, scarcely differed from that of the free blacks who worked at the same jobs. The domestic staff enjoyed the greatest prestige among the slaves; foremost among them were the cook, the nurse, and the coachman. These servants were often regarded by their masters with an affection and treated with a lack of reserve that northerners like Benjamin Latrobe found disconcerting:

Servants who are slaves are always treated with more familiarity than hirelings; probably because if you indulge and behave familiarly to a hireling you cannot, if he presumes upon it, correct him as you can a slave, and make him feel his inferiority by corporal punishment. Therefore we find cruelty and confidence, cowhiding and caressing, perfectly in accord with one another among the creoles of this place and their slaves.

The servants were regarded as members of the household, and a master returning from a journey would bring back presents for them as well as for his wife and children. Hundreds of black nannies were cherished in their old age and sincerely mourned in death by successive generations of their charges.

There were, then, at least a few slaves whose lives were relatively serene. We may note in passing the comments of the fervent abolitionist Frances Trollope:

I left England with feelings so strongly opposed to slavery, that it was not without pain that I witnessed its effects around me. At the sight of every Negro man, woman, and child that passed, my fancy wove some little romance of misery, as belonging to each of them; since I have known more on the subject, and become better acquainted with their real situation in America, I have often smiled at recalling what I then felt.

Work

The average white family owned at least two or three slaves. Even the notoriously tightfisted Judge François-Xavier Martin had a household of three: a valet-coachman named Tom, who accompanied him everywhere, and an old cook and her husband to whom he announced, on introducing them to his establishment:

I intend to be a generous master; I'll permit you a room but you must feed yourselves and supply my table with decent fare, besides cleaning the house in which we all reside, and which is yours as well as mine. This is all I require of you. The rest of your time is yours, and whatever money you may make and save after having nourished me and kept my clothes in a good state of repair is your absolute property.

Needless to say, the judge's fare was far from lavish, and his clothes were invariably threadbare and soiled. No chance for slaves to get rich while working for that kind of master! Nonetheless, they enjoyed a considerable amount of liberty and authority in his household. Tom treated his master, who was old and almost blind, as a nursemaid might treat a fractious child. If the Judge took the initiative to rise from his chair, Tom immediately inquired: "Where are you going, sir?" "I am going to take a walk." "What! Without consulting me? Don't you know it's raining?" And he obliged the old man to be seated. Tom was proud of the influence that he exerted on his master, though he acknowledged that the Judge was his superior

Judge François-Xavier Martin. From a lithograph by Jules Lion.

Louisiana State University Department of Archives and Manuscripts when it came to the law: "I can rule the old man as my master, but as judge, it's no go."

Well-to-do families had large domestic staffs. The cook and the gardener had two or three helpers each; the butler commanded a squad of chambermaids, valets, laundresses, wardrobe mistresses, dressmakers; the coachman was assisted by a groom. In some grand families, each child had a personal servant, and small black boys were sometimes employed exclusively to swat flies.

This battalion of slaves required the close supervision of the mistress of the house, for with the exception of the mammy, who would allow no one else to take charge of her nursery, and the cook, who was too conscious of her own value to trust the preparation of her delectable gumbos and exquisite pastries to anyone else, the rest of the staff had a tendency to delegate the tasks they had fought to obtain to subordinates, whom they often treated with disdain. This practice was widespread among the blacks, especially among the mulattoes, who aped the manners of whites in all respects and were also notoriously vain. There is an old Creole proverb that goes: "Mount a mulatto on horseback and he will deny that his mother was a negress."

The Creole upper classes were generally given credit for their kindness and fair-mindedness toward their slaves, but the Americans were regarded as the better masters: their slaves were usually better treated, better fed, and better dressed. The rare cases of cruelty toward slaves reported in this period involved Creoles, in particular Creole women.

The architect Latrobe was so struck by the reports of sadistic brutality among the Creole women that he derived no pleasure from attending balls: "I fancied that I saw a cowskin in every pretty hand gracefully waved in the dance." Bernhard de Saxe-Weimar was horrified by the ferocity with which his Creole landlady whipped one of her slave girls. The worst case on record is that of Madame Lalaurie, who savagely tortured her slaves. Her atrocious conduct was exposed by accident, following a fire that destroyed her home in 1834. Public indignation was such that Madame Lalaurie had to flee the city in fear of her life.

If mistreated, slaves had the right to appeal to the courts for justice. American law stipulated that "slaves who could prove to have been cruelly treated would be removed from their masters and sold at auction to the benefit of the state." The Code Noir contained certain provisions designed to ameliorate the plight of slave families: it was forbidden to separate a mother from her children if they were less than ten years of age or to import a slave child under ten years old without his mother, provided the mother was still alive. The Code also decreed that a master was obligated to look after his elderly slaves and that "those who were sick were to have all kinds of temporal and spiritual assistance which their situation might require." It was illegal to abandon a slave because of old age, sickness, or infirmity. If the case necessitated, a slave could be taken to the hospital, and the master was responsible for his upkeep there.

Of course, the masters had every reason to watch over the health and well-being of their slaves. The sugar planter Valcourt Aime is frequently cited as an example of a master who not only treated his slaves kindly, but risked his own health for them when they came down with contagious diseases. When one of his laborers grew too old for work in the fields, he found light chores for him in the garden, and women and children on his estate were never assigned tasks beyond their capabilities.

Foreign observers, while pitying the lot of the slaves, left no very flattering portrait of them. Pöstl writes: "There is no doubt that a malignant and cruel disposition characterises more or less this black race." Perrin du Lac describes the slaves as "devious, lazy, dishonest and cruel"; de Laussat calls them "slothful and untruthful."

If the slaves often behaved with the fecklessness of children, we must seek the explanation in the institution of slavery itself. As Alexis de Tocqueville explained:

The Negro enters upon slavery as soon as he is born; nay, he may have been purchased in the womb, and have begun his slavery before he began his existence. Equally devoid of wants and of enjoyment, and useless to himself, he learns, with his first notions of existence, that he is the property of another, who has an interest in preserving his life, and that the care of it does not devolve upon himself; even the power of thought appears to him as a useless gift of Providence, and he quietly enjoys all the privileges of his debasement.

PLEASURES

Among the pleasures not explicitly proscribed to the slaves were dancing, lovemaking, and an occasional glass of tafia or whiskey. The particular effects of music on the black spirit had been noted with approval by white masters since early colonial days: music seemed to alleviate the burden of captivity and relieve the slave's feelings of frustration and anger. When a royal edict was issued from Madrid in 1789, forbidding slaves to travel to another plantation on Sundays and holidays to attend a dance, the governor hastily wrote back in protest. The measure, he declared, would be unenforceable except on the largest, most populous plantations: "Where there are only three or four slaves . . . [they would] grow desperate when hearing the distant sounds of dancing and music, without being able to join in the festival."

Under the Americans, the tradition of the *gran bambousses* on Saturday night at the plantations and on Sunday afternoon in New Orleans was maintained. Sometimes the masters were in attendance to cast an indulgent eye on their slaves as they disported themselves to the rhythm of the drums.

As for lovemaking, it was not so much tolerated as actively encouraged. A slave's value depended to some degree on his or her procreative ability. At the slave market, blacks were closely scrutinized with this fact in mind. "Even a Creole lady pays close attention to all parts of the male's anatomy before concluding her purchase," wrote the scandalized chronicler C. C. Robin. "The female slaves are examined with equal attentiveness by all the prospective buyers." Everything was done to encourage mating between the slaves, "which would produce children, a source of riches for the master."

Marriage between slaves was not legally binding, since by reason of their servitude slaves had no civil rights. However, they could, with the consent of their master, have a marriage ceremony performed. When the two slaves belonged to the same master, the matter was easily resolved. Usually the master performed the ceremony himself, unless he preferred to call in a priest or pastor to marry the couple. In the case of household servants, the ceremony took place in the master's house and was followed by elaborate festivities. A responsible master respected the solemnity of these unions and did his best to assure that husband and wife would not be separated.

When slaves belonging to different masters wished to marry, matters became more complicated. Often the male slave's master was reluctant to solemnize the union, for the marriage would not work to his advantage. He would have to grant the slave time to make regular visits to his wife, and any children born of the marriage would belong to their mother's owner.

Contemporary witnesses agree that marriages between slaves were rare, but that many blacks both on and off the plantations lived together as husband and wife. These unions, however, were fragile. Domesticity was not a conspicuous virtue among black males. Furthermore, changes in the lives of their masters could cause their sale and dispersion.

The Slave Market

Slaves were often exchanged among friends and neighbors, for the buyer then had some assurance as to the quality of his purchase, and the seller some knowledge of the household to which he was sending his former charge. The newspapers of the time regularly carried advertisements, not unlike our own "Employment Wanted" notices, which a slave's merits and liabilities were forthrightly presented: "Adelaide, griffonne,[1] housemaid, saleswoman, and general housework"; "Pluton, black, about fifty, cowherd and footman"; "Eugène, general worker"; "Philippe, one-eyed, sailor"; "Azor, black, fifty-seven years old, carpenter, clapboard maker and daily help, afflicted with hernia and sometimes drunk." Occasionally group sales were announced: "Thirty horses, broken in, and forty blacks, almost all of Creole origin and with families"; "In four lots: a black woman named Betsy, a cart with three wheels and harness, three modeling tables." If slaves found no buyers through such ads, they were put on display at the slave market and sold at public auction.

Sometimes a man chose to pay off his creditors in slaves; thus on February 27, 1821, one Monsieur Lavergne wrote the planter and phi-

---

1. That is, a female griffe—a person of three quarters African ancestry and one quarter white.—TRANS.

lanthropist John McDonogh that, "wishing to fulfill his obligation," he was sending him, in lieu of a debt of five hundred piastres, his "good black woman Violette, eighteen years old," whom McDonogh could dispose of "however he wished." Lavergne advised him, however, to sell the woman, adding that her market value was eight hundred piastres.

Generally slaves sold for more before the harvest season than after it, when their labor was in less demand. But a healthy slave with useful skills was sure to fetch a good price at New Orleans, in season or out. In fact, few buyers had the cash to pay for a slave outright, and they often purchased him in two or three installments. If for some reason the buyer could not meet his payments, the slave was "repossessed" by the seller and put back on the market.

A slave auction was held daily at the Maspero Exchange from noon to three. It was a celebrated event, and people came from all over, not just to buy, but to exchange gossip and take in the spectacle. The Exchange offered the widest selection of slaves in the United States: "raw" African blacks, smuggled into Louisiana in defiance of the law; local blacks, victims of the financial misfortunes of their owners; blacks from Virginia whose magnificent physiques were the pride of the state "stud farms," which specialized in the rearing of slaves; blacks from Maryland and the Carolinas, shipped down to New Orleans because slaves fetched the best market price there. Also for sale were a good many stolen slaves, as well as kidnapped free blacks being passed off as slaves, unclaimed runaways, and a collection of drunkards, vagabonds, and layabouts who were offered by the city in an effort to save the cost of their incarceration.

Every age and degree were represented at the Exchange: field workers straight from Africa, unable to speak more than a handful of words in either English or Creole French; children with or without their mothers; attractive quadroons whose "usefulness" to their masters was only too readily discernible; tall, sturdy mulatto coachmen; mammies from Maryland, cooks from Creole Louisiana; laundresses and seamstresses; masons and cartwrights; boatmen and valets. And all the others as well: the sick and the crippled, the discarded and the ignored—all of whom cried out in supplication: "Buy me, buy me! I can do anything, buy me!"

Many visitors were appalled at the spectacle. Saxe-Weimar, for instance, records: "In Chartres Street, where we dwelt, there were two establishments which constantly revolted my feelings, to wit: shops in which negroes were purchased and sold. These unfortunate beings, of both sexes, stood or sat the whole day, in these shops, or in front of them, to exhibit themselves, and wait for purchasers."

Far from downplaying its slave market, however, New Orleans took great pride in its commercial leadership in this shameful industry. Where else could one hope to find so many buyers and sellers and such a vast selection of slaves: a footman fluent in three languages, a cook who could put the best French chefs to shame, a drayman who also played the fiddle? In this area as in many others, New Orleans was confident that it deserved its title of "Queen of the South."

4

⁊

The Creole Family

At the center of Creole life was the family, a family dominated by the figure of the father. His word was law, his judgment final and without appeal. Yet the Creole paterfamilias was far from abusing his privileges: he was notoriously an affectionate and indulgent parent and a generous and loving husband, though not always a scrupulously faithful one. The Creole families of the early nineteenth century did not believe in rigid discipline; and although they did not encourage the more extravagant whims and eccentricities of their members, they did little to curtail them. In modern parlance, they were permissive.

When matters were carried to extremes and a member of the family caused a public scandal, the paternal wrath was terrible to behold. It was rare, however, for an erring child to be actually banished from the family. Generally, the father did his best to smooth things over, and the family presented a united front to the world.

The closeness and solidarity of family life gave the Creole an exceptional sense of security. When things went wrong, he knew that he could rely on his family for support, sympathy, and a loyalty that extended to the farthest ramifications of the clan. There were few Creole families that did not harbor under their wing some disreputable uncle or decrepit aunt, some orphaned cousins, or a couple of relatives permanently down on their luck and gracefully resigned to receiving free room and board in perpetuity.

Creole hospitality was virtually limitless. Every weekend the plantations near New Orleans overflowed with guests, who occupied their time with hunting, cards, dining, and dancing. Nor was it unusual for the party to prolong itself: weekend visitors sometimes lingered on for a couple of months without the hosts displaying the least sign that they had overstayed their welcome.

Hospitality was a cult in Louisiana, and the guest was treated like a sacred object. After the Battle of New Orleans, Etienne de Boré opened his house for several weeks to Generals John Coffee and William Carroll, who commanded the Tennessee detachments, as well as to a number of their field staff. The latter were courteous and well-bred, although several of the more eccentric members of the staff had the disconcerting habit of putting their feet on the table while imbibing their after-dinner brandies. The aristocratic host was obviously nonplussed by this breach of etiquette, but when members of his family broached the subject to him he merely replied, "But what can you expect? It is the custom of their country."

The wealthy Creole planter ruled his estate like an absolute monarch; his subjects, the slaves, were expected to minister to his slightest desire. His style of living was a mirror of his prosperity: the large house, large family, great expanse of cotton or sugarcane, orchard and vegetable garden to supply his table, and ornamental garden laid out on a grand scale, bright with rare and beautiful flowers. His highest ambition for his children was that they might emulate his own style of living. He considered that all change was for the worse and contemplated the past with more pleasure than the future. Although he had lived under American rule for almost a quarter of a century, his imagination still turned toward Europe: he retained a deep nostalgia for the mother country and continued to cultivate French manners, customs, and tastes.

At a time when Americans placed little store in outward appearances and fine manners, the wealthy Creole never appeared in public without gloves, hat, and cravat; never spat or chewed tobacco; and made a habit of kissing ladies' hands. In short, he behaved like a perfect gentleman. And although some may have reproached him for his haughty bearing, his pride, and his indifference to those outside his class, he was commended for his good breeding and for the lavish hospitality that C. C. Robin said "was a credit to humanity."

Good manners figured more importantly in the education of Creole children than geography or Latin grammar, and however indulgent the Creole father might be in other matters, he tolerated no breach of social etiquette. The Creole style, though strict in the observance, was characteristically tempered by a certain gentleness of manner. William Sparks noted:

All who have ever entered a French Creole family have observed the gentle and respectful bearing of the children, their strict yet unconstrained observance of all the properties of their position, and also the affectionate intercourse between these and their parents, and toward each other—never an improper word; never an improper action; never riotous; never disobedient. They approach you with confidence, yet with modesty, and are respectful even in the mirth of childish play.

Such a passage suggests that Creole children were models of deportment. However, many witnesses agree that the children were frequently spoiled; and though the girls generally matured into charming young ladies, the boys all too often remained insufferable brats.

The Pursuit of Love

In Creole society as in other Latin cultures, a double moral standard prevailed. Women were expected to be virtuous, and men were expected to be men. In fact, with the exception of a few notoriously straightlaced families, young men of good breeding were actively encouraged to sow a few wild oats. A proper masculine education included some practical lessons in the art of love, and the proud father rewarded his diligent son with a mistress all his own.

On the plantations, the sons of the family were assigned shortly after puberty to bachelor quarters—small, octagonal structures two stories high, close enough to the main house to remain within the family orbit, but sufficiently removed to allow for privacy. It was there that the young men entertained their friends and had their first amatory adventures. Often it was their father who supplied them with young mulatto women, carefully selected from among the slaves on the basis of looks and health.

In town the arrangements were different. Although most of the townhouses possessed separate slave quarters, few of them had bachelor quarters. The young men usually lived at home and sometimes continued to do so even after marriage. But New Orleans was rich in resources, and there were a number of so-called *pensions* where white men could make the acquaintance of young black women. There was also the famous Blue Ribbon dance hall, whence came young quadroons, chaperoned by their mothers, in search of a serious "protector." With his father's blessing, his money, and sometimes even his personal assistance, the young Creole gentleman paused between a polka and a quadrille to enter into negotiations with the mother of the young woman of his choice. Once the terms had been agreed on, the young woman was installed in a small house on the edge of the Vieux Carré.

These liaisons lasted a year, two years, ten—or a lifetime. Some men willingly renounced marriage in order to remain with their mistresses. Others married but continued their liaison. The majority, however, terminated the arrangement when they married—which did not prevent them from taking a new mistress when the joys of connubial love began to wear thin. So it was that the Creole gentleman often found himself supporting two domestic establishments simultaneously and distributing his paternal affection between two sets of offspring.

The widespread infidelity of Creole husbands can be linked to a number of factors: the slave system and its contingent abuses; a tradition of promiscuity long honored in Latin cultures; and, perhaps most importantly, the fact that most marriages were arranged as a matter of business rather than affection. Men and women married to found a family with someone of compatible social rank. The romantic, impetuous, and passionate young Creole husband could have little sympathy for the young bride, timid, ignorant, and reserved, who was ushered into the bridal chamber by her mother like a lamb being led to the slaughter.

Yet the Creole husband demanded a wife who was both innocent and sexually passive. Women had early been placed on a pedestal, and they were expected to stay there. Robert Tallant cites the case of a man who abandoned his wife on their wedding night because she responded to his lovemaking with ardor. The story goes far to explain why many Creole men looked outside of marriage for an outlet for their sexual appetites. For them, the word *love* had two quite different meanings when it referred to a wife and when it referred to a mistress.

THE DEFENSE OF HONOR

For a Creole gentleman, the pursuit of love gave way to the defense of honor. The cult of honor was virtually unchallenged in male Creole society, and many a hot-blooded young man sacrificed his life on its altar.

A breech of etiquette, a hint of irregularity in business affairs, a careless word, a misinterpreted gesture—anything could become a pretext for demanding satisfaction, especially if the combatants were rivals for a young lady's affections. The Creole gentleman never fought with his fists; that would have been demeaning. He preferred to use the saber, the rapier, and most particularly the sword. The combat generally came to a halt with the first drawing of blood; but when the Americans took up the custom, dueling became even more risky than before, for the Americans, ill at ease with swords, opted to fight with pistols. Moreover, Americans tended to forget that what mattered most in a duel was the preservation of honor, not the extent of punishment inflicted on one's opponent.

A duel often required several days' preparation: witnesses were summoned, a suitable locale picked out, a doctor chosen in advance. Sometimes, however, duels were fought on the spur of the moment. The peaceful garden of St. Antoine, a few steps from the Blue Ribbon dance hall, was a frequent site of these moonlight encounters, for the Creoles were more sensitive to the slights paid their mistresses than those offered their wives, fiancées, or daughters.

Bernard de Marigny, a kind of early nineteenth-century playboy, was as famous for his duels as for his puns, his supper parties, and his losses at the gaming table. It is said that for several years he made a point of dueling regularly once a week, and he invariably emerged the victor. Marigny's exploits were the talk of the town, and some of them passed into legend.

His first duel arose from a political dispute with the representative of Catahoula Parish, a towering ex-blacksmith from Georgia named Humble. Marigny, who had taken offense at some remark of Humble's, sent his seconds around to demand satisfaction. The Georgian would not listen to them: "I know nothing of this dueling business," he told his friends. "I will not fight him." "You must," said his friends, "no gentleman would refuse." "I am not a gentleman," replied the honest Humble. "I am only a blacksmith." But his friends insisted: "You have the choice of weapons and can manage things so as to give yourself an equal chance against him." This suggestion gave Humble pause, and in the end he dispatched a note to Marigny: "I accept, and in the exercise of my privilege stipulate that the duel shall take place in Lake Pontchartrain in six feet of water, sledge hammers to be used as weapons." Bernard de Marigny measured five feet eight inches, while Humble was a huge man, almost a giant, nearly seven feet tall. The marquis gracefully acknowledged that his adversary had outwitted him and declared himself satisfied. The duel was called off.

The second Marigny anecdote concerns a duel and its aftermath. In the course of a duel, Marigny had wounded his adversary, a lawyer named Grailhe, quite badly. The man recovered but was unable to hold his head and shoulders straight. Months passed; an abcess formed on the wound. From time to time, the wretched lawyer could be seen dragging his bent and emaciated form through the streets. Clearly his days were numbered. And then he had another quarrel with Marigny, which once again brought the two men out "under the oak trees." (The phrase, a favorite New Orleans expression, refers to another favorite dueling spot, the oak-shaded plantation of Louis Allard near Bayou St. John.) Grailhe, who could no longer wield a sword, chose pistols for weapons. According to the legend, as recounted by New Orleans writer Grace King, Bernard turned to his seconds before he discharged his weapon and said, "This time I will try to straighten him out." The ball struck the lawyer in the precise location of the old wound, bursting the abcess. Curiously enough, Grailhe recovered his health and was henceforth able to walk upright, though his head continued to tilt at a curious angle. The story may well be apocryphal, but it serves to underscore the provocative and insouciant behavior that frequently accompanied dueling.

Still another dueling story, this one reported by Edward Laroque

Tinker, involves a young Creole officer and a veteran of Napoleon's army who commanded the New Orleans militia; it displays the more romantic aspects of the institution. Captain Buisson had called out the entire militia for full-dress maneuvers in the Place du Cirque. Sentinels had been placed at the four corners of the square, with strict orders to challenge anyone attempting to enter the area. To be sure, this was not Austerlitz, but Captain Buisson, as an old campaigner, took such exercises seriously. Thus he was furious to learn that one of his young Creole officers had responded to the challenge of the guard by drawing his sword, striking the rifle from the guard's hands, and entering the square without giving the password. Buisson called the young officer to him and demanded to know whether the report was true. "Yes, indeed, Captain," was the casual reply—whereupon Buisson, beside himself with rage, slapped the young officer across the face. The next morning at dawn, the two men assembled with their seconds "under the oaks." The captain had the first pistol shot and missed. Then it was the young Creole's turn, and he fired into the air. Trembling with anger, the captain called out to his adversary, "Are you insulting me again, Monsieur?" "Not at all, Captain Buisson," was the reply. "I was in the wrong to start with; realizing that, I would consider myself dishonored forever if I harmed so much as a hair of your head."

The custom of dueling was a cause of irreparable harm. It set up false standards of conduct; it caused mutilations and a good many deaths. Originally confined to the upper class, it gradually penetrated the middle classes. Men no longer fought exclusively to preserve their "honor," but out of a thirst for excitement, out of boredom, and even out of fear. According to an angry article that appeared in *L'Abeille* on January 22, 1828, it was the fear of ridicule that forced men onto the dueling ground. "A man who would be sure enough in his conscience to laugh off the boastings of a scoundrel or scorn the insults of a bully is overcome by fear at the thought of public ridicule."

For the Creole gentleman, in any case, death was preferable to dishonor, and he would have felt himself dishonored if he ever failed to accept a challenge. He kept himself in shape for any duels that might arise by regular visits to one of the city's many fencing masters.

Fencing lessons were part of a gentleman's routine, along with horseback riding, dancing, cards, and flirting with the ladies. The Creole male, even if he was a landed proprietor, spent little time at home. Certainly he was not studious: he read little and spent the minimum time possible over his accounts. A judge, banker, broker, or businessman went regularly to his office every morning but still managed to find plenty of time to allot to pleasure. A horseback ride along the Esplanade, a stroll on the levee, a game of tric-trac at Hewlet's or one of the other fashionable cafés—these provided agreeable interludes of relaxation in the course of a busy workday.

THE PATERFAMILIAS

There were no men's clubs at this period in New Orleans, but Creoles and Americans alike regularly repaired to their favorite cafés to discuss business or politics, play chess or dominoes, or simply relax in an exclusively masculine environment. The only difference between the Creoles and the Americans was that the former could be found in the cafés at any time of day, whereas the latter only put in an appearance after working hours.

The Creole was not, however, a heavy drinker. During the day he limited himself to frequent cups of strong, black coffee. In the evening, he might indulge in a glass or two of sherry or madeira, but never whisky, which he regarded as vulgar. Even the young Creole swells who spent their days lounging around the cafés respected the dictum that a gentleman never gets drunk; if someone appeared in public drunk with any regularity, he soon found himself excluded from polite society. "He drinks" was a fatal phrase that effectively closed all doors to him. This temperance was much to the credit of the Creole husband, and if their wives had much to complain of on other accounts, at least they did not have to contend with the clamorous importunities of a drunken spouse.

The infidelities of the Creole husband seldom seemed to undermine his family spirit. He was deeply attached to his children and adored by them, and he even passed for a good husband. Although he had commitments elsewhere, he always took his meals with the family and accompanied his wife to the theater, the balls, and the other social events that crowded the schedule of the well-to-do Creole family. The Creole husband was attentive to his wife's every wish, and many witnesses have remarked on the aura of domestic harmony that pervaded the Creole households. Under the circumstances, this fact may seem surprising, and one may exclaim, with Harriet Martineau:

What secure hope can there be for purity or for domestic peace in a household where the husband has two liaisons, one open, one secret; where every man has two families, each of which is supposed to be unconscious of the other's existence; where conjugal relations begin in duplicity, and every husband must keep a shameful secret locked within his heart?

But we must keep in mind that most Creole marriages were for convenience only, and that most women preferred an unfaithful husband to no husband at all. On the whole, the husbands adjusted easily to their double lives: the Creole's famous broad-mindedness often extended to a tolerance of his own vices.

One wonders how conscious the wives were of their husbands' infidelities. Surely most husbands must have had the delicacy not to flaunt their outside attachments—the exception being Bernard de Marigny, who used to arrive home carrying baskets of culinary delicacies, which he openly presented to his wife as the gift of Titine, Toucoutou, Zabette, or whoever his current mistress might be. But Marigny, the "mad Midas" of the Creoles, was noted for his eccentricities—he was once seen lighting his cigar with a ten-dollar bill—and besides, his marriage was known to be unhappy. After the death of a sweet-tempered American wife, he married a sharp-tongued Spanish woman who, to believe contemporary reports, would have sent even the most virtuous of husbands fleeing to the arms of the first available mistress.

Bernard de Marigny has struck many as the quintessence of the Creole spirit. Certainly with his pride, his impetuousness, his swagger, boastfulness, and bombast, he incorporated all the classic flaws, as well as some of the traditional charm and virtues, of the Creoles—and he also, clearly, served as a model to many generations of imitators. But equally representative, if less flashy, was the planter Etienne de Boré, who on his deathbed addressed his grandson, the writer Charles Gayarré, as follows: "Let no temptation ever betray you out of the path of honor and virtue. Keep your conscience always free from self-reproach, so that your death may be as calm as mine. . . . Farewell, let your motto in this world ever be: '*Sans peur et sans reproche.*'" De Boré left instructions that his funeral and funeral monument be kept as simple as decency allowed, and that a thousand dollars of the money normally reserved for burial expenses should be given to the Charity Hospital of New Orleans.

This high-minded aristocrat presents a happy contrast to the reckless Bernard de Marigny. Undoubtedly Marigny's upbringing had much to do with setting the pattern for his future life. Orphaned at fifteen, he entered into possession of a vast fortune at an age when most boys would have been content with a modest monthly allowance. Creole fathers were notoriously indulgent to their sons, encouraging them in habits of self-gratification rather than discipline or economy. How could one expect young Marigny, brought up in the Creole tradition of high living and deprived even of the minimal restraints that a father might have offered, to curb himself in his spending? In his time, Bernard was the most eligible bachelor in all Louisiana, possessing as he did an illustrious name, enormous tracts of land, an army of slaves, an immense fortune, and an agreeable appearance. When he finally took as his bride the young daughter of the American consul in New Orleans, the sense of disappointment among Creole mothers and daughters must have been acute.

Fortune alone did not make a suitable son-in-law. Money counted, of course, but less than the good name of the young man in question; and if a suitor was poor but well born he had every right to lay claim to a lady's hand—especially if she was no longer in the first bloom of youth. Under such circumstances, the father-in-law undertook not only to provide his daughter with a generous dowry, but also to find a job in the family business for his son-in-law. The family house was generally at the disposal of the young couple, who were free to live there at the father-in-law's expense.

THE PURSUIT OF A HUSBAND

A young woman without a dowry, no matter how charming she might be, had little chance of procuring a husband. Even if her dowry was sizable, her chances of marriage diminished after she had passed the age of twenty-five—though she might still settle for a widower with children or a penniless young man. Spinsterhood carried no personal stigma, but it was considered a mild disgrace for the family. That is why parents, despite the affection they had for their daughters, tended to marry them off to the first eligible suitor, without giving any serious consideration to how the bride herself might regard the match.

For the young Creole woman, it was the pursuit of a husband, not the pursuit of love, that became her chief preoccupation. Her goal was to found a family of her own, and in the excitement and exhilaration of the wedding preparations she may seldom have had time to ask herself whether she loved the man who was about to become her husband.

Sixteen was the conventional age of consent, but many girls married even earlier. From the cradle, the young girl was prepared for marriage, first by her parents, then by the Ursuline nuns who were entrusted with her upbringing and education until her formal entrance into adult society. Her "coming out" was usually marked by an evening at the Théâtre d'Orléans: a momentous event, for it marked the opening round in the search for a husband. No expense was spared to make the occasion a propitious one: wealthy parents ordered their daughter's gown from Paris, and those with lesser fortunes had the latest Paris fashions reproduced by local seamstresses. On the appointed day, the family hairdresser arrived to dress the abundant curls of both mother and daughter. The family then repaired solemnly to the theater, where their box became the focal point of the assembly, their appearance and their prospects the universal topic of conversation.

The young men in the audience discreetly eyed the debutante, and if they were suitably impressed by her beauty, grace, and fortune they dropped by her box at intermission to pay their respects. If the first encounter proved satisfactory and one of the young men wished to improve his acquaintance with the young woman, he could, using a friend as intermediary, request the father's permission to call on her at home.

The first formal visit was invariably of brief duration; by overstaying his time, the young man risked spoiling his chances as a suitor. The young people were not, of course, left alone: the girl's mother was on hand to chaperone, often accompanied by several relatives. The girl herself was expected to be bashful; she scarcely uttered a word, but her retinue took the occasion to ply the young man with discreet questions concerning his family background and financial prospects.

Creoles generally married their own, and parents, of course, preferred their sons- and daughters-in-law to come from families well known to them. Creoles were conscious of belonging to a superior race and were eager to protect their genealogies. And only by marrying into a family whose lineage was known to them could they avoid the risk of introducing a strain of mixed blood into their own line. In Louisiana, there were probably a number of families that passed for white, although their origins were in fact interracial. When an unknown suitor appeared on the scene, therefore, his origins were subjected to the closest scrutiny.

After four home visits, the father usually felt justified in requesting the young man to declare his intentions. If his answer seemed in any way equivocal, he was requested politely but firmly to take his suit elsewhere. Creole fathers had no patience for young men who didn't know their own minds and who caused their daughters to waste precious time.

Creole ladies were inveterate matchmakers and took a passionate interest in the progress of other people's courtships. If a young man hoped to win the heart of a girl or the good opinion of her father, he did well to enlist the aid of the womenfolk. Whenever two or three women gathered, their talk centered around marriageable young ladies they knew and their prospects for finding husbands. In New Orleans, it was usually a question of selecting the proper husband from a pool of candidates. But in certain remote regions of Louisiana, there were no proper candidates to be found. In that case, the mothers had to go the rounds of relatives and friends, inquiring whether they knew of any rich bachelor of good family. Immediately the wheels of matchmaking began to turn. If a suitable bachelor was driven to earth, the young lady was promptly dispatched to meet him, on the invitation of one of the accommodating women of his household, who could be counted on to help matters along. The visit might last several weeks or several months, depending on the elusiveness of the game. Sometimes, unfortunately, the wily creature managed to escape.

If worst came to worst, the provincial family could always resort to the New Orleans marriage market, which held certain attractions for mother and daughter alike. The mothers welcomed a chance to spend a season in town and usually made a point of chaperoning their daughters themselves in New Orleans, rather than delegating the task to some devoted aunt. Mother and daughter took up residence with friends or relatives and prepared to lay siege to the capital for the entire winter season.

A young lady could not expect to land a husband during her first year out and was free to examine the field and test her luck, as it were, for three or even four years. But after that she would have to move quickly to avoid becoming a spinster, for Creole men favored very young brides. It was common for middle-aged men to marry girls scarcely into their teens, and no one seemed to find anything objectionable in such unions. Don Andrés de Almonester, grandee of Spain and benefactor of New Orleans, was sixty years old when he married sixteen-year-old Louise de la Ronde. Thus, if a daughter proved indecisive or overly particular in choosing a husband, her parents usually felt obliged to select one for her or risk seeing her passed by.

ENGAGEMENT AND MARRIAGE

The suitor once accepted, the two fathers got together to negotiate the dowry (which could be as much as $40,000 in some cases) and to discuss the young man's assets. When these financial questions had been settled, the arrangements for the marriage could proceed. A notary was called in to inscribe a list of the young couple's possessions—furniture, slaves, cash—and to draw up the marriage contract. In Louisiana, the contract usually stipulated joint ownership of goods, and the furniture, silverware, and linen were traditionally supplied by the wife. After the marriage contract had been signed, the engagement was officially announced.

A grand dinner was laid on at the home of the young woman, in the course of which the young man ceremoniously presented his fiancée with a ring. In his new position as fiancé, he could call on his future bride as often as he liked, escort her to dances, and take her for walks on the levee. But no matter how long the engagement lasted, he was never permitted to be alone with her. Wherever the young couple went, her mother or some other female relative went with them. If the young man spent an evening at home with his fiancée, the most he could hope for in the way of entertainment was a lively game of dominoes or tric-trac with his future father-in-law.

A few days prior to the marriage, the young man offered his bride-to-be the traditional wedding basket, which generally contained lacework—handkerchiefs, a mantilla, a fan—as well as a cashmere shawl, gloves, and some jewels. She was not permitted to wear the jewels before her marriage, and custom also decreed that she remain at home for the three days preceding the wedding.

In New Orleans, the favored days for weddings were Mondays and Tuesdays. Saturday was considered vulgar and scrupulously avoided; as was Friday, the day set aside for public executions and referred to by the English-speaking population as "hangman's day."

The ceremony took place at St. Louis Cathedral, in late afternoon. The choirboys, candles, incense, organ—everything contributed to the solemnity of the occasion. The bride usually wore a silk dress embroidered with pearls and decorated with lace. Her veil, often a family heirloom handed down over several generations, was held in place by a crown of orange blossoms. She carried a bouquet of the same orange blossoms, which she would later place at the tomb of some beloved relative, dispatch to the convent where she had gone to school, or simply leave behind her in the church. The wedding ring was of two interlaced bands of gold, inscribed with her initials and those of her husband, and the date of the ceremony. Solemn and deeply moved, the bride knelt before the priest and prayed God to make her marriage happy and fruitful.

After the ceremony, the members of the family signed the register—a rather lengthy formality when there were more than fifty signatories—and then proceeded to the bride's home, where a sumptuous banquet had been prepared. On these occasions, Creole hospitality outdid itself. The food, the wine, the flowers, the music—everything was superb, reaching and even surpassing the standards of the finest European hospitality.

For the cook, the reception was an opportunity to display all his or her creative genius, and the wedding cake, rising tier upon tier at the center of the dining room table, was the center of all eyes. The bride cut the cake herself and distributed slices to all the unmarried girls present, who wrapped them carefully and put them under their pillows that night, along with a slip of paper on which they had written the names of three unattached young men.

After the dancing had begun, the bride quietly withdrew and followed her mother to the bridal chamber. Her mother helped her out of her wedding gown and into a delicate nightgown with matching negligee, tied up her long hair with a ribbon, tucked her into bed, and after a tearful embrace hurried from the room. Sitting bolt upright in the vast four-poster, her fingers clutching the bedclothes, her pale face reflecting mingled fear and resignation, the young bride seemed the very image of a virgin about to be sacrificed to a stern and implacable god. One imagines her listening for her husband's footsteps and fighting off the waves of panic that threatened to dissolve her courage and send her rushing headlong into her mother's arms—or, more likely, to her devoted black mammy, who at that very moment was imploring the Virgin Mary and a whole pantheon of voodoo gods to bring comfort, happiness, and domestic peace to her young mistress. Perhaps, too, the mammy had already taken the precaution of hiding some scraps of red cloth under the nuptial mattress or pillow to attract the *miché agoussou,* the Creole demon of love.

What did the young bride know about the physical aspects of love? In all probability, nothing whatsoever. The subject was taboo, and even at this critical moment the mother and daughter would hardly have found any terms in which to discuss it. By way of last-minute advice, the mother may have conveyed to her daughter that what was about to happen was an integral part of the wedding rite, and that the bride should submit with good grace and under no circumstances call for help. It scarcely mattered whether or not she was in love with her husband, for up to now she would have had virtually no physical contact with him—if her chaperones had been conscientious, not even a fleeting kiss. The man who was in a moment to slip in beside her was, therefore, almost a total stranger. Although some love-struck young girls experienced a commingling of rapture and fear, for most brides their wedding night was a painful ordeal to be endured with a pride and dignity worthy of their upbringing.

At this period, newlyweds did not depart on wedding trips. The honeymoon was usually spent under the bride's parental roof. The young couple was expected to remain confined to the bedroom for five days or more, with all meals being brought to the door by servants. If, as sometimes happened, the honeymoon was spent at the house of the groom's parents, the bride could not visit her mother until a prescribed amount of time had elapsed, and her parents were not permitted to visit the young couple for at least two weeks after the wedding. But once that stage of transition had passed, the two families became for all practical purposes one. As a French observer remarked, "to marry a Creole girl is to marry the girl plus five hundred relatives."

A Paragon of Virtue

Whether the marriage was for love or for convenience, it had the effect of transforming the inexperienced young girl into a woman of irreproachable virtue—at least if we are to believe the contemporary witnesses. As Karl Pöstl remarked: "As wives and mothers, they are entitled to every praise; they are more moderate in their expenses than the northern ladies and, though always neat and elegantly dressed, they are the inseparable assistants and companions of their husbands." William Sparks's comment was just as approving: "The high-bred Creole lady is a model of refinement—modest, yet free in her manners; chaste in her thoughts and deportment; generous in her opinions, and full of charity."

On the beauty of the young Creole wives, the commentators seem to compete in the extravagance of their praise. Their deep, luminous eyes, their delicate complexions, their white teeth, their graceful manners are lovingly attested by all. In the midst of this universal hymn of praise, a discordant note occasionally sounds: Pöstl, for instance, remarks that the ladies display a certain *embonpoint* and regrets that they do not "exhibit any waist." John James Audubon confides to his journal that he encountered "no handsome woman" in New Orleans, and that "the citron hue of almost all is very disgusting to one who likes the rosy Yankee or English cheeks."

As far as the learning of the ladies is concerned, the concensus is less flattering. "Never count on their intellectual resources or conversational talents," warns de Laussat. Pöstl declares categorically that "nothing can be more tiresome than a literary *tête-à-tête* with a creole lady." And Saxe-Weimar notes that the cultural attainments of the Creole society lady seem limited to "dancing and some instruction in music."

From all this evidence, it seems clear that the Creole ladies were indeed paragons of virtue. Their fidelity was above reproach, even though, as Karl Pöstl points out, they had ample cause to deceive their husbands. They were also models of propriety, blushing at the slightest hint of indelicacy and carrying their own sense of personal decorum to such lengths that some could assert that even after years of marriage they had never allowed their husbands to see them in the nude. But one cannot help speculating whether such excesses of virtue did not ultimately promote a certain rigidity of character, whether such exaggerated modesty did not shade into neurosis. Nor does it seem surprising that the husbands tired of these wives—especially since their intellectual formation was so deficient. It was not that the Creole woman was inherently less intelligent than her northern counterpart, it was simply that her taste for letters and literature had never been developed. Indeed, any attempt at formal study, whether the subject was Latin, history, science, or philosophy, was actively discouraged as a betrayal of one's sex. New Orleans did have some learned ladies whose company was much sought after by the intellectuals of the community—Mrs. Trollope makes mention of a bonnet maker who, standing amidst her ribbons and veils, dazzled her interlocutors with metaphysical speculations—but such women were Anglo-Saxons and would never be encountered in proper Creole society.

A Creole woman was expected to devote herself solely to her functions as wife and mother, which in general she performed to perfection. Creole women began their childbearing early and continued late. Eight or ten children in a family was by no means rare, and it often happened that a mother and daughter were pregnant at the same time.

The houses were spacious, the domestic staffs large, and there was always room for another child, whose arrival was greeted with joy. If the mother's milk was in short supply, there was always a black woman with an infant of her own who could serve as wet nurse. Every white household had one or more black mammies to care for the children. It was they who taught the children to speak in the mellifluous Creole dialect, they who told the children marvelous tales of Bouki the rabbit and taught them songs, often African in origin. The relationship between the black mammies and their white charges was built on mutual trust and affection. It endured, and the mammies constituted an integral part of the domestic scene.

Waited on hand and foot by servants, dispensing with any exercise, whether physical or mental, the Creole lady may seem to have passed her life in languor, in a dream of childbearing. The truth is, however, that her air of indolence was largely a sham.

Creole women were diligent housewives and kept a close watch on the daily running of the house. They were thrifty, well organized, and industrious. The wife watched not only over her family's needs, but also those of her slaves. She made sure that their living quarters were kept in good repair, that their clothes were clean and mended; she tended them when they fell ill and arbitrated their disputes. Her skill in training butlers, cooks, and washerwomen was such that Creole domestic servants always brought a high price on the slave market. She was renowned for her well-spread table and provided sumptuous and varied fare not only for guests, but for her own family. Under her tutelage, an inexperienced black cook was transformed into a culinary artist, capable not only of reproducing the mistress' recipes but of adding improvements of her own, so that the dishes became original creations whose ingredients were a jealously guarded secret.

CINDERELLA

The mistress of the house was often assisted in her household chores by a sister who had been less fortunate than herself in her quest for a husband. The customs of the times forbade a woman of good family either to earn her own living or, if unmarried, to live alone, so she was often obliged to seek shelter under her brother-in-law's roof. In many Creole households, these spinsters were a regular feature of the domestic landscape, immediately recognizable at social gatherings by their discreet and capable interventions, their zeal in interjecting a word of encouragement, congratulation, or commiseration, and their occasional lapses into pensiveness as they surveyed the animated scene around them. The typical spinster aunt was resigned to her solitary lot and built her happiness on the joys of others. Her emotional attachment to her nephews and nieces could scarcely have been more intense if they had been her own children. She was a bosom companion to her sister, a loyal ally to her sister's husband. Her position might well remain unchanged for life. But it sometimes happened that her monotonous existence was transformed by a Prince Charming, appearing in the familiar shape of her own brother-in-law. He came not as a vile seducer but as a bereft widower. Having lost his wife, he found it convenient to marry her sister—she was familiar, after all, with his quirks and habits, beloved by his children, respected by his servants, and thoroughly known and tested by himself. Though the circumstances of the courtship were inevitably tinged with melancholy, the Cinderella sister invariably accepted the proposal with alacrity. She knew full well that if she refused the offer her brother-in-law would seek a replacement for his wife elsewhere, and her position in the family would then be put in jeopardy.

There were few inconsolable widowers among the Creoles; nor, for that matter, were there inconsolable widows, though it was rare for widows to remarry unless they were exceptionally youthful or wealthy. But the lot of the widow was quite different from that of the spinster. As a woman of experience, she enjoyed both freedom of movement and a certain social prestige. She controlled her own property, and nothing prevented her from running a plantation, traveling abroad, receiving visitors, and paying calls. In fact, she could lead a very agreeable life unencumbered by a husband, always provided that the temptations of the flesh did not intervene. We must remember that at this period no Creole woman, even if free of conjugal bonds, could take a lover without causing a scandal that would compromise her family and force her to quit the region. A Creole woman did not lightly abandon the training of a lifetime to hurl herself into an affair that would entail loss of honor, dignity, and social position.

THE ART OF BEAUTY

Fortunately the Creole lady's austere morality did not extend to her mode of dress. She had a flair for clothing and self-adornment and spent long hours before her mirror perfecting her gift. She eschewed dark materials in favor of flowing, diaphanous garments in bright colors or soft pastels. During the day, she wore gowns of cotton or muslin, but for evening she indulged her taste for silk and satin. Her hair was the object of special attention. No prim chignons for her—her long black or chestnut hair was brushed ceremoniously every night, washed often, and done up in elegant coiffures. When the first white hairs appeared, she is said to have dyed them with coffee extract. Skin creams and herbal balms were applied to preserve the freshness of her complexion; and in order to maintain the fashionable pallor much admired by visitors, she never ventured outdoors in daylight, especially in summer, without covering her face with a thick veil. In part such precautions had their origins in the ever-present Creole racial obsessions: the women believed that a pale skin would testify to the purity of their breeding.

Nature and art combined to produce the much-touted beauty of the Creole women. They were not, of course, universally lovely. Frequent pregnancies, lack of exercise, and a penchant for fine food tended to make them overweight, and many acquired more than a hint of a moustache as they approached middle age. These defects were outweighed, however, by their dark eyes, glossy and abundant hair, and erect carriage. Visitors usually encountered them not in the cruel light of day but at night, by candlelight, at dinner, the theater, or at a ball—all backgrounds designed to display them at their best. The generous décolletage of their evening gowns set off their plump shoulders, their hair was adorned with jewels or flowers, and they handled their fans with a grace that could not but impress an admiring onlooker.

The fan was an indispensable part of feminine attire. In the practiced hand of a coquette, the fan—whether made of feathers, lace, or ivory, encrusted with mother-of-pearl, or fashioned out of simple palm leaves—became a delicate instrument for directing or concealing her glances, a weapon for tapping the fingers of an overbold admirer in the course of a tête-à-tête. It had its practical uses as well, for New Orleans was insufferably hot for three seasons of the year. The Creole ladies, who seem to have been particularly susceptible to the heat, relied on their fans as simple and efficacious restoratives.

Despite their languorous airs, the ladies displayed extraordinary energy on the dance floor. Condemned by custom and tradition to a passivity of manner that extended even to the nuptial bed, they found in dancing a liberation from the constraints of their daily existence. "They love dancing to the point of madness," writes Perrin du Lac, "and abandon themselves to it whenever the occasion presents itself." "They are the best dancers in the United States," attests Karl Pöstl. "They do great honor to their French teachers," adds Saxe-Weimar. And Latrobe remarks, "The dancing of the ladies was what is to be expected of French women; that of the gentlemen, what Lord Chesterfield would have called too good for gentlemen."

Waltzes, quadrilles, polkas, and cotillions were as popular among the mothers as among the daughters. Ever since the days of the marquis de Vaudreuil, the French governor of Louisiana, it had been the custom to turn both boys and girls of good family over to a dancing master for instruction. Girls were also taught to play the piano and to sing, and were instructed in solfeggio and drawing. But according to the memoirs of Audubon, who attempted to earn a living in New Orleans by giving drawing lessons and painting portraits, the citizens of the city cared as little for the visual arts as they did for literature. Berquin-Duvallon, another early nineteenth-century visitor, warned: "If you love scholarship and belles-lettres, Louisiana is no place for you! The atmosphere there is fatal to the Muses." Contributing to this intellectual apathy was the poor local standard of education, as well as the woeful negligence of Creole parents with regard to the intellectual formation of their children.

5

Education, Literature, and Cultural Patterns

The citizens of Louisiana were not unconscious of the inadequacies of their educational system. The *Courrier de la Louisiane* of April 5, 1828, complained:

There is not one institution of learning which by its organization and the number of its professors may deserve that name . . . there are indeed a few elementary schools, but nothing like what is called a college. In order to acquire that education they should send their children to Bardstown or to Baltimore, to France or to England. The education which best suits a man is that which he receives in the country where he is destined to live. . . . A man ought to be educated in Louisiana. But in Louisiana, that country so wealthy, so fertile, so liberal in its principles, so adverse to all kinds of aristocracy, save that of virtue and talents, what has been done?

In fact, the schools of Louisiana, according to the reliable testimony of Karl Pöstl, were notably inferior to those of other comparable American cities. The only school of any academic merit that Pöstl encountered was the one directed by Mr. Shute, rector of the Episcopalian church and "an enlightened and clever man."

It had not always been so. Yet as soon as William C. C. Claiborne became governor, he turned his attention to the problem of education in the Louisiana Territory. In 1805, Claiborne, with the assistance of his council, drew up a formal plan for primary and secondary instruction. Provision was made for public education for girls—a truly innovative step—and for the establishment of public libraries in every parish. Unfortunately, the legislature failed to allocate funds for implementing these measures. Instead, the directors of the various schools were authorized to hold lotteries to underwrite their expenses; and since many other institutions—churches, lodges, charitable foundations, parishes, even the state itself—used the same method for raising funds, it is not surprising that the public response was tepid. The Louisianians' general indifference to intellectual concerns added to the difficulty. In the end, Governor Claiborne was obliged to admit to the legislature: "I have to inform you that the law passed by the legislative council, 'An act to establish an university in the Territory of Orleans,' does not promise to advance the interest of literature with the rapidity which was contemplated." He reaffirmed his support of public education and proposed a new tax, such as already existed in several other states, to be assessed according to the taxpayer's ability to pay and devoted to the establishment and maintenance of the educational system.

Lotteries and Subsidies

Governor Claiborne's suggestions seem to have borne fruit. On April 9, 1811, the legislature granted the sum of $39,000 to the University of Orleans to finance a secondary school and several primary schools in the region. The secondary school, the Collège d'Orléans, would of course charge tuition, but in a commendable effort at democratization it was stipulated that fifty poor children should be admitted free of charge as day students and that $3,000 be set aside annually toward the school's upkeep. Provincial academies would receive an annual subsidy of $500 each.

This legislation was a real step forward. But the subsidies proved inadequate, and two years later the university again had to rely on a lottery to meet an immediate need for an additional $50,000. In 1819 the state raised its annual subsidy for the Collège d'Orléans to $4,000, in 1821 to $5,000. In 1823 the school was once more in financial difficulties, and the city resorted to gambling, a favorite pastime of the citizens, to relieve the cause of culture. An annual tax of $5,000 was levied on each of the six licensed gaming establishments in New Orleans. Of the $30,000 thus collected, three-fourths went to the Charity Hospital and the remaining one-fourth, or $7,500, was turned over to the Collège d'Orléans.

The school had been saved, but only temporarily. The next year, the state's subsidy dropped to $7,000, the year after to $3,000. In that same year, 1825, a new school called Louisiana College was founded in the town of Jackson, in East Feliciana Parish. The government had high hopes for this institution, which was to be a day school costing between thirty and sixty dollars a year per student, with meals provided for two dollars a week. The teachers appear to have been carefully selected—one of them had even taught at Harvard—but by 1830 the school had attracted no more than sixty students.

In the meantime, the Collège d'Orléans had closed for want of students and funds. Henceforth, the state subsidies were distributed among the two primary schools and a new secondary school that had just opened in New Orleans. In the primary school, instruction was limited to reading, writing, arithmetic, and the rudiments of English and French grammar. The secondary school took pride in its syllabus: "French, English, Latin, Literature, Mathematics, etc." At least fifty impoverished students between the ages of seven and fourteen were admitted to the three institutions free of charge. Funding, however, remained problematical. It was difficult to finance the existing institutions, not to speak of the public schools projected for each parish.

It was not that the state's coffers were empty: in 1825, after all, the not-inconsiderable sum of $15,000 had been set aside for the city of New Orleans to celebrate General Lafayette's arrival in a style "worthy of the patriotic warrior whom the American people delight to honor." But the development of an educational system seemed a far less pressing concern, and the governor's report of 1831 reveals that at that time many parishes had no form of public education at all.

With a few exceptions—the landowner Julian Poydras, for instance, who contributed $30,000 to found a school for the indigent orphans of his own district, Pointe Coupée—the well-to-do held to the belief that most working-class children, as well as all girls, would be wasting their time in the classroom. These children's parents appear to have felt the same. In the countryside, illiteracy was almost universal; among the urban lower classes, it was only the tradesmen who wished their children to learn to read, write, and perform basic mathematical calculations. On the whole, the ordinary folk in Louisiana seem to have looked on education as the profitless pastime of the idle rich.

Yet even among the idle rich, particularly the Creoles, there was little interest in intellectual pursuits. If they did not actively oppose the spread of the public school system, they did virtually nothing to encourage it. They lent no support to the establishment of a first-rate academy that would have profited their own children and made no effort to foster a cultural milieu in New Orleans itself that might have stimulated the intellectual proclivities of the young.

Such indifference cannot be attributed solely to inherent anti-intellectualism. More important, perhaps, was the bitter and deep-rooted rivalry between the American community and the French-speaking peoples of Louisiana. The Americans, naturally enough, wished instruction to be offered in English, whereas the Creoles remained loyal to their own history and traditions and refused to accept English as the official language. Both sides remained adamant and sent their children out of state for their education. The sons of the wealthy American families attended colleges in Georgia, Virginia, South Carolina, and New England, while the Creole elite traveled to Paris, Bordeaux, or Montpellier. What Louisiana needed but never found was some unifying cultural figure, some enlightened patron of the arts who might have quelled the wrangling and helped to forge an intellectual community to match the city's economic preeminence.

For want of such a patron, the schools depended on the gambling halls and the theaters for their support. Restrictions on the number of gambling establishments were now lifted, and the income from their licenses, along with an annual tax of $1,500 on each of the city's theaters, was allocated to the maintenance of the three new schools. In imposing the theater tax, the legislators made the curious argument that it would not only support public education, but also encourage the establishment of places of entertainment "both entertaining and instructive." The entrepreneurs Caldwell and Davis, whose theater was experiencing difficult times, must have wondered at this logic.

Apparently the schools found favor with the common folk, for the next year the number of students to be admitted free of charge was raised to one hundred for each of the three establishments. A report informed the legislature that the full curriculum was now in effect and that in the secondary school "two respectable professors were, in addition, giving lessons in Spanish and drawing." Yet there was no great clamor for admission: in 1828 the student body numbered two hundred and fifty students; in 1831, two hundred and forty-five. Almost all qualified for free tuition.

Well-to-do parents did not wish their children to mingle with the common herd; and because the middle class refused to participate, the academic standards in these institutions, especially in the secondary school designed to replace the Collège d'Orléans, declined rapidly. Before long, the schools were offering an abbreviated program of study designed for children who would need to earn their livings at an early age. No longer was there any question of providing an education suitable for future lawyers and doctors, but of supplying a bare minimum for young laborers. The schools never provided a level of education that would have matched the city's economic stature, and many came to remember with nostalgia the old Collège d'Orléans, which had at least enjoyed the prestige of its aspirations. During the fifteen years of its existence, the Collège, situated at the corner of St. Claude Street and Bayou Road, was responsible for educating many Creoles of future eminence in the community. In its last years, its principal was one of the best-known educators of the time, the French émigré Joseph Lakanal.

Despite his undoubted intelligence and administrative competence, Lakanal was largely responsible for the school's demise. In France, he had been one of the architects of the national educational system. He was also, however, a defrocked priest and regicide who had been forced to flee his country at the Bourbon Restoration. The more conservative of the New Orleans parents feared his influence on their impressionable offspring and agitated for his dismissal. The school board stood firm in his support, and, one by one, the parents withdrew their children from the school. In 1825, Lakanal submitted his resignation, but the damage had been done. The following year, the Collège closed its doors. Its enrollment had sunk to twenty students.

THE COLLÈGE D'ORLÉANS

The historian Charles Gayarré, who entered the Collège at the age of nine, has left us some charming vignettes of his teachers. There was the school's first principal, a Creole from Santo Domingo named Jules Davezac; the children gave him the affectionate nickname of Titus, "for if Titus was the delight of mankind, Davezac was the delight of his juvenile subjects." Then there was Rochefort, nicknamed "Tyrtaeus," also from Santo Domingo and also, in time, the school's principal. Professor of literature and Latin, he composed excellent translations of Horace, "which he delighted to read to his pupils." There was Selles, the drawing master, who loved to declaim Corneille and Racine, and the mathematics professor Teinturier, who was also an accomplished gardener and piano tuner—talents that proved useful for supplementing his meager salary.

Outside his areas of expertise—ancient history, Latin language and literature, French history—Rochefort was woefully uninformed. Moreover, he "was a monomaniac in his aversion to mathematics." If the subject was ever broached in his presence, reports Gayarré, he became edgy and irritable. "It was like offering water to a mad dog." According to legend, some students had once come across the professor puzzling over a piece of paper on which was written the sum of two plus two; only "after repeated efforts" did he extract the correct answer. Rochefort was a bachelor and inhabited the third floor of a building that also contained several classrooms. The unoccupied rooms on the floor he turned over to his favorites among the upperclassmen. Rochefort also organized outings for this select group—evenings at the theater, dinner parties at which he recited his own poetry. Because his salary was insufficient for such entertainments, the boys' parents were expected to foot the bill. These favored students escaped the usual school discipline and in consequence enjoyed vast prestige among their less fortunate schoolmates.

Teinturier, the professor of mathematics, was also a bachelor. He had a large garden on the outskirts of the city, where he grew vegetables and flowers. Sometimes, when the moon was full, he worked in his garden all night long; and during the dog days of summer he did his weeding and hoeing stark naked to demonstrate "that the white man could, in July and August, brave the canicular rays with impunity." He was a passionate naturalist. "Whenever we were not prepared for our lessons," writes Gayarré, "we used, in entering the class, to present to him in the most artless manner we could assume a string of insects about which he would descant most learnedly—at such length that the hour passed before he was aware of it. But if Teinturier loved the natural sciences, he detested poetry. A student would sometimes tease him by reciting some lines of French verse, and Teinturier would predictably explode with anger: "What! Boys! What do I hear! What nonsense is this? In my presence, too! This is positively disrespectful! Poetry! Pish! Pshaw! What is there in that thing called poetry? What does it *prove?*"

A boy had only to repeat some comment of Monsieur Rochefort to provoke another outburst: "Mr. Rochefort! Ha!ha! a mere coiner of rhymes, a manufacturer of jingling sentences. A fine authority, truly! A man who could not go through one of the simplest operations of the multiplication table! And you quote *him*, and to my face, too! You, who under my tuition are every day discovering and appropriating some of the celestial beauties and secrets of mathematics." Rochefort judged his colleague no less harshly: "Euclid! Euclid! Who is he? Oh, I see! Some of Teinturier's nonsense. Good God, that some of my best pupils should be exposed to be spoiled by that man, their imagination chilled, and their poetic fire extinguished just as it begins to rage." Gayarré himself concludes: "I do not believe that there ever was so restricted a spot on earth where so many oddities were assembled as within the learned precincts of this college."

Whatever its limitations, the Collège d'Orléans made an earnest attempt to turn out graduates who were gentlemen in the best sense and to equip them with a solid educational background. To judge from the rigorous schedule inflicted on the students, the Collège did more to stock the intellect than to develop it and may, indeed, have inspired many of its graduates with a lasting distaste for study. The students were expected to be up before dawn, even in winter. Breakfast consisted of a slice of bread, dispensed to each student as his name was called from a kind of service window. The period from seven-thirty to noon was devoted to lessons and recitation. There followed an hour for lunch and recreation, but at one o'clock the students returned to their lessons and continued without a break until seven in the evening. After dinner they could relax until bedtime. There was no school on Thursdays, and many of the students spent the day fishing in Bayou St. John. On Sundays the students attended mass at eight in the morning but were free to spend the rest of the day as they wished.

In Gayarré's day, there were about one hundred students at the school. There were only a few day students, most of them from families who could not afford to pay the boarding fees. Some of the day students paid only half of their fees, and some nothing at all. The Collège offered tuition to a small group of carefully selected children from poor families, who cannot have had an easy time of it among their well-to-do classmates. Gayarré reports that the scholarship students, because they paid no fees, were known as the "orphans."

Although at its founding the Collège had been hopefully referred to as a "university," it was in reality only a secondary school that limited its instruction to Latin, French, Spanish, English, literature, and mathematics. No Greek was offered, though lessons were available in music, dancing, and fencing—a curriculum that reveals the intentions of the school's governors to turn out "accomplished young gentlemen."

FEMALE EDUCATION

The goal of most private educational establishments in New Orleans at this period was to teach manners and produce young gentlemen and ladies. According to John Paxton, in 1821 there were sixty schools, both Creole and American, in the capital; a small number were reserved for the children of free blacks. Some of these schools were "respectable academies" serving up to two hundred students; others, more modest, taught as few as a dozen. The instructors were often drawn from the ranks of the French émigrés, who turned to schoolteaching to make a living. Those with no resources of their own became governesses or tutors; those fortunate enough to possess a little capital rented rooms for their classes and then placed a notice in the newspapers announcing the opening of a new educational institution. Thus we read in *L'Argus* that Messieurs Dufour and Roux have just opened a school in the Rue Dauphine, offering "reading, writing and arithmetic for three dollars; mythology, French, Latin, Italian, geography and history for five dollars; and mathematics for eight dollars." Dancing masters and music teachers also resorted to the newspapers to advertise for trade. One such instructor, so as not to overlook any possible client, offered to conduct lessons in either French, English, or Spanish!

Music, dancing, domestic arts, and embroidery played a major role in the education of girls and young women. The lower-class women seem to have been generally illiterate (it is disconcerting to discover that many young brides of the period signed their names with a cross), and those of the upper class were scarcely more learned. In the provinces, a number of female academies were founded to alleviate the situation. The *Gazette des Opelousas* informs us of a boarding school in Grand Coteau, established by the "widow of Mr. Charles Smith," which offered a program of study "previously unavailable in the region." From the same source we learn that the nuns of the Sacred Heart ran "an excellent school for young ladies." The school numbered many non-Catholics among its students, evidence that "the teachers held to their promises to avoid influencing the students on the subject of religion." Board and tuition at the Sacred Heart Academy was "thirty-five dollars a quarter, payable in advance." Apparently young ladies from Rapides, Bayou Boeuf, St. Martin, Lafayette, and even New Orleans came to Grand Coteau "on account of the particularly healthy climate of the region."

New Orleans' best-known school for girls was run by the Ursuline nuns—"an invaluable institution," as one French tourist, Baudry des Lozières, described it, "that has produced young ladies of unassailable virtue and mothers of exemplary excellence." The nuns offered instruction in reading and writing, French and English grammar, geography and history, sewing, domestic arts, and the catechism. Although the school, in John Paxton's assessment, provided "the most accomplished education, with the exception of dancing," the curriculum seems modest enough by modern standards and was scarcely calculated to instill a spirit of intellectual arrogance in the graduates. Nevertheless, it was superior to the other female academies in the region. Of necessity, girls from well-to-do American families were sent away to finishing schools in the East.

The Ursulines did not confine themselves to the education of young ladies of society, but also took under their care a number of orphans who were lodged "in a separate apartment" at the school. The nuns offered free tuition to poor students and conducted special classes for black girls. The free blacks of New Orleans, though separated from the whites by insurmountable barriers, at least had the chance to acquire an education that was neither better nor worse than what was available to white students. The children of wealthy blacks, like their Creole contemporaries, often went to France to complete their studies, returning imbued with French culture and ideas. And the blacks, like the whites, had their own French-language poets, equally prolific and equally execrable.

THE BATTLE OF THE LANGUAGES

The Creole population fought hard and long to defend its language and culture against American encroachments. The children were required to speak French at home and were sent to schools where English, if it figured in the curriculum at all, was taught only as a foreign language. As we have seen, those families who could afford it frequently sent their sons and daughters to France to acquire a patina of French manners and ideas. Few Creole families were willing to acknowledge that the days of French dominance in Louisiana were numbered and that the future of their state lay not with Europe but with America. The parents of Charles Gayarré were an exception: they chose to send their son to Philadelphia to be trained as a lawyer and to acquire a first-hand knowledge of American law and customs.

It is hard to blame the Creoles for clinging to their ancestral traditions, but the fact remains that they used their French heritage less as a source of spiritual strength than as a stick with which to beat the Americans. The vast majority of Creoles, blinded by resentment at the growing influence of their American neighbors, refused even to consider bilingual education and by this stance condemned their children to parochialism and isolation. As the years passed, the Creoles' attachment to their native language began to border on fanaticism. Some Creoles refused to allow any English to be spoken in their presence and ranted against the proliferation of the "barbarous" English language—yet these same linguistic purists showed utter unconcern when their children chattered away in the *gombo* dialect of their black mammies.

American administrators, like the Spanish before them, quickly realized that it would be extremely imprudent to proscribe the use of the French language in Louisiana. Until 1880, legislators were permitted to make their addresses in French as well as in English. Depositions given in French were acceptable in court, and the law provided for interpreters to be used when necessary. The victory of the English language was a gradual affair, effected without violence or trauma.

Yet one cannot help wondering whether the Creoles, so passionately attached to their language and culture, actually spoke good French. According to the French traveler Berquin-Duvallon, they did, except for certain idiosyncrasies of pronunciation: "They slur and drag out certain syllables, especially final ones, giving their speech a certain singing quality. Many of them pronounce the *j*s as *z*s and the *ch*s as *ce*." Audubon, on the other hand, refers with contempt to several "French Creoles" who visited him on his keelboat as he was descending the Mississippi to New Orleans: "This is a breed of animals that neither speak French, English nor Spanish correctly, but have a jargon composed of the impure parts of these three." It may be that Audubon had encountered Acadians or Chacalatas—a fact that might explain the severity of his judgment.

One might have expected the Creoles, as part of the effort to assert the validity of their culture, to have developed a strong native literature. Such, however, was not the case. Creole authors modeled themselves after contemporary French authors—the most popular rather than the best—and mimicked them so slavishly that their own work sometimes reads like parody.

Nothing was published in Louisiana during the years of French control. The first publication that we know of dates from 1777: two short anonymous poems, printed by Antoine Boudousquié, "printer for the King and the Cabildo." One of the poems was entitled, "The God and Naiads of the St. Louis River, to Don Bernardo de Gálvez"; the other, "Epistle to Don Bernardo de Gálvez." The second poem celebrated the virtues of the Spanish governor of Louisiana in such emphatic terms that it seems not improbable, as Edward Laroque Tinker has remarked, "that it was written to gain official favor."

Two years later, another poem was printed, also panegyric in nature: "The Conquest of Baton Rouge Bluff by Monsieur de Gálvez." This poetic effusion was signed by Julian Poydras—also, in all likelihood, the author of the other poems. The next work to appear, in 1798, was a pamphlet written by Doctor Masdeval, formerly physician to King Charles VI of Spain. The doctor claimed to have discovered an "infallible cure" for yellow fever. The remedy, in practice, must have seemed little better than the disease.

There also appeared during these years the printed text of the Code Noir; *Memoirs of the Merchants and Inhabitants of Louisiana Concerning the Events of October 29, 1768*, written by Chauvin de Lafrenière and Pierre Caresse, leaders of the uprising against the Spanish; several royal proclamations; and fifty-six public notices issued by the French prefect of the colony in 1803. These constitute the entire literary record of Louisiana prior to its acquisition by the United States.

Under American domination, and perhaps in reaction to it, there was a marked increase in literary production among the Creoles. The recent émigrés from France were particularly prolific, but the literary standards were not high. Two fine historians emerged from the Creole community: Charles Gayarré and François-Xavier Martin, whose *History of Louisiana* appeared in 1827. But on the whole the Creole style ran to high-flown rhetoric that was quickly and justly consigned to oblivion.

The climate of the region certainly seemed unhealthy for literature. The highest praise was reserved for the bombastic, the long-winded, the overblown. The following lines of verse, an attack by Doctor Charles Chauvin Boisclair-Deléry on the Yankee general Butler, offer an example of the style of the times:

> Tyrant of lowly birth, despicable wretch,
> Come to be measured for the gallow's last drop.
> What belly spewed you forth, what cave concealed the act?
> What name can I give to such a monstrous shape?
> Did not your reptile's scales tear your mother's womb?

It goes without saying that Creole authors did not live by their pens; literary activity was a mere avocation. Some were planters like Louis Allard, a distinguished Latinist but an abominable poet; journalists like Alexandre Barde; priests like Adrien Rouquette, an indefatigable versifier who has left us a large number of unreadable works on the life and customs of the Choctaws as well as several charming poems in *gombo* dialect; soldiers like LeBlanc de Villeneufve, author of a sentimental drama in five acts entitled "The Harvest Feast, or the Heroism of Poucha Houma"; or teachers and printers like the eccentric Tullius Saint-Ceran, originally from Jamaica, who wrote the following disconcerting verses upon the death of his young wife, Anna, in 1823:

> Without Anna my destiny falls in decay:
> While worms devour my wife in her tomb,
> Others my glorious future consume.

Saint-Ceran was much admired for his martial verse, and no farewell banquet for an officer of the Orleans Rifle Corps was complete without one of his odes to the departing hero. He dreamed of literary glory; when it was not forthcoming, he took to drink.

Presently a bookshop was opened on Chartres Street by the French émigré writer A. L. Boimare. He initiated a highly successful lending library: for $1.50 per month, or $15.00 per year, the subscriber could check out four or five volumes at a time and exchange his books every day of the week except Sunday. For $18.00 per year, out-of-town subscribers could check out fifteen or twenty volumes at a time. Boimare's bookshelves contained legal and medical texts, history, classics, and novels in French and Spanish.

However, the stock was not limited to books. On his return from a visit to France in 1828, Boimare advertised that he was offering for sale 140 hampers of champagne; 100 cases of kirsch; 25 cases of chambertin; 75 hampers of cherry brandy; truffles "from last year's crop"; a "very precious" miniature of Napoleon; a selection of "plaster figurines suitable for vestibules"; ladies' stockings in cotton, wool, and silk; hats; thermometers; and scientific instruments. In all probability, these items attracted far more customers than did the complete works of Jean-Jacques Rousseau or the latest novels from Paris.

At this period, the citizens of New Orleans could also draw on two large public libraries. The first, established in the early 1820s, was located in the governor's mansion; it contained over six thousand volumes and was intended primarily for French-speaking readers. The second was created at the instigation of an English-speaking group and endowed by a Jewish benefactor named Judah Touro. The avowed purpose of his bequest was "to enrich culture and to encourage a taste for the arts among the inhabitants of the city." The library was "open to all."

The people of New Orleans had little time for reading: the Americans were preoccupied with business, the Creoles with parties and balls. It was all the men could do to leaf through a newspaper—not the women, however, for newspapers were considered inappropriate, if not downright unhealthy, for the frailer sex.

THE NEWSPAPERS

"The newspapers of New Orleans are the most vapid and devoid of content I have ever seen," wrote the English author Harriet Martineau. Between the years 1820 and 1830, there were six newspapers published in the city, none of which, however, was likely to appeal to a cultivated or demanding reader. The Creoles could not be held responsible for this state of affairs, because the newspapers were almost entirely under the management of journalists from France. Most of these publications were bilingual. The best known were the *Louisiana Gazette*, the first American paper; *L'Ami des Lois*, which was replaced by *L'Argus* in 1824; *Le Courrier de la Louisiane*; and *L'Abeille*, founded in 1827. In an effort to fill the intellectual void, the bookseller Boimare launched *Le Passe-Temps*, "a medley of political and literary commentary," in 1827. It appeared six times a month but expired within a couple of years for want of readers.

This lack of readership was general and widespread and eventually prompted the publishers of the six local dailies, ordinarily bitter rivals, to agree on a staggered plan of publication for the summer months. From the first of July to the first of November, the period when many of the more solid citizens were out of town, the newspapers cut back their schedule so that only one appeared on any given day of the week.

The New Orleans dailies did not go in for bold headlines, eye-catching layouts, or tantalizing advertisements. Nor did they contain much in the way of local news. Several columns of the first page were devoted to want ads or public announcements—the sale of slaves, land, livestock, or merchandise; notices of theatrical performances and concerts; ads for cargo boats, doctors and dentists, hairdressers, and perfumers. Under a small logo of a running figure with a bundle on his back appeared the notices of runaway slaves. In *Le Courrier de la Louisiane* for June 7, 1828, we read: "Charles, small black male, letter-carrier for the southern district of the city, missing for several days; about fourteen years old, very slender, long arms and legs, stutter; has pleasant expression and small, widely spaced teeth." Under the heading "Stray Animals" appeared such items as the announcement of a black cow or bay horse found roaming in such or such street of the city.

The second section of the newspapers was devoted to foreign news. These items were often both fragmentary and out of date, having been collected by word of mouth down at the harbor. When reporters managed to get hold of a recent newspaper from Paris, London, or Washington, they had no scruples about lifting whole columns for the benefit of their readers. The news offered in the English-language section of the papers was not always identical to that printed in the French. For American readers, priority was given to bulletins from Washington and financial information; for the Creoles, political and cultural news from France received pride of place.

The Pen and the Rapier

During election periods, whether for mayor, governor, or president of the United States, political news usurped the newspaper columns. The French journalists, like their American counterparts, used their pens for bitter, slashing attacks on political opponents. Outspoken, vindictive, occasionally witty, they excelled at polemic but otherwise displayed little literary talent. An elegant prose style was of less use to a New Orleans journalist than speed, stamina, and a quick hand and eye; journalists were constantly challenging one another to duels, and it is probable that these well-publicized combats brought them more readers than did their editorial commentaries. "Only a steady diet of roast pelicans stuffed with firecrackers could explain their bellicose humor, their incredible sensitivity to insult, and their constant irritability," commented one Louisianian.

The tempestuous journalists dispensed with the elaborate dueling etiquette so dear to the Creoles. Insults were answered on the spot, both in public and private, and a self-respecting journalist never ventured out without sword-cane or pistol. Even badly wounded, they seldom conceded defeat. One day Jean Leclerc, founder of *L'Ami des Lois* and, according to Edward Tinker, "the wittiest, most stinging gadfly ever known in Louisiana," encountered at the exchange a fellow citizen who had recently felt the prick of his pen. After a few heated words, the two men drew their swords and proceeded to settle their dispute in the midst of the crowd. Leclerc, run through by his adversary's sword, crumpled to the ground. As the spectators gathered around him, he gasped out: "I call you all to witness that my adversary is, as I have always declared, a prize ass. In this hot weather I had need of a blood-letting, and the idiot has spared me the expense of going to a doctor."

No holds were barred in journalistic battles. Writers did not hesitate to libel a fellow journalist or a public personality, whether in article, public notice, or advertisement. The most vitriolic of the newspapermen was undoubtedly Charles de Saint-Romes, writer and publisher of *Le Courrier de la Louisiane*. His editorials lacked serious content, but his outrageous campaigns of slander and abuse and his numerous duels won him notoriety. His chief adversary was John Gibson, editor of *L'Argus* and leader of the anti-Creole constituency in New Orleans. Gibson had enraged the entire Creole population by asserting that the Creoles occupied a disproportionate number of public posts. When, in 1829, Gibson became a candidate for mayor, the following anonymous notice appeared in *Le Courrier de la Louisiane:*

Monsieur de Saint-Romes is requested to publish the following announcement of a candidate for the office of mayor. My name is well known to all of you, and no further description is required, but if someone wishes to be informed on the subject you may tell him: "Those who have never squandered the public funds of their precinct; who have never induced a young girl to leave her convent in order to lead her to ruin; who have never received a slap in the face from Mayor Clark without demanding retribution—all these are invited to cast their votes for Mr. John Gibson at the next election."

Gibson was furious and seized the first opportunity for a fight. Saint-Romes reported the encounter in the next day's edition of *Le Courrier*:

One would have thought that the editor of *L'Argus*, who claims to be a man of honor, would have inquired the name of the author of the notice before undertaking to punish him. Not at all! Instead he vented his wrath on me, though he is fully aware that an editor is responsible only for the content of those articles which he signs himself or to which he gives a byline. In yesterday's edition of *L'Argus* he spewed out a stream of venomous bile, and I dared to hope that his impotent ravings had run their course. But no! Still hoping to purge himself of the infamy clinging to his name, he sought to provoke me to commit an indiscretion. The perjured villain followed me to the café Hewlett, where I was peacefully watching a game of tric-trac. After prowling around me for some little while without daring to attack (I myself did not notice him, but numerous witnesses later informed me of the fact), he gathered about himself a group of like-minded villains, and then attacked without warning from behind, striking me a blow in the face that left me stunned in my chair. Scarcely had I recovered than I saw that same ignoble traitor, John Gibson, editor of *L'Argus*, reach into his coat as if for a weapon. I flung myself upon him and knocked him to the ground by a blow to the midriff delivered with my umbrella.

These were just the preliminaries. Saint-Romes continues:

I leapt upon him, seized him by the throat, and dragged him, or rather carried him, to the reading table, some ten steps from the spot where the scoundrel had first attacked me. I hurled him onto the table, face down, with all my strength, and endeavored to reenact the strangulation scene from *Virginius*, but the cowardly fellow refused to yield his last breath. Then, after searching in vain for my knife (in order to tear out his entrails), I was trying once more to finish him off with my bare hands, when I noticed a dagger and some pistols in his pockets. I was endeavoring to extract the dagger, with the intention of nailing him to the table on which he lay, when a contingent of friends and enemies intervened, and prevented me from accomplishing this noble purpose. The coward seized the opportunity to escape.

Not even Creoles were safe from Saint-Romes's malignant pen. In *Le Courrier* of June 28, 1824, the illustrious Marigny is accused of "not knowing a word of French," of posing falsely as a "purist," and of having a poor grasp of French grammar despite his frequent trips to France. On another occasion, the journalist made the claim that

"Marigny identifies his slaves by branding them on the back with the letters B. M."

Understandably enough, Saint-Romes and his colleagues made a point of working out regularly with a fencing master. But Marigny, at any rate, did not deign to duel with petty journalists. He simply turned the matter over to his lawyers, who took the newspapers to court.

FROGS, TOADS, AND OTHER FACTIONS

During election campaigns, the journalists worked themselves up to a fever pitch. Carried away by their own sonorous phrases, they wallowed in hyperbole. Their political commentaries were strong on sarcasm but often weak on logic and childishly silly. In *Le Courrier* of June 6, 1820, there appeared a lengthy editorial on the candidacy of Abner L. Duncan, a respectable American, for governor of Louisiana. The starting point of this elaborate whimsy is the pejorative nickname that each race had given the other: the Creoles referred to the Americans as "Méricains Coquins" (that is, American rascals), while the Americans, in reference to the French habit of eating frogs' legs, responded by calling the Creoles "Johnny-Crapauds."

The *Frogs* of lower Louisiana, meeting in assembly on the sixth of June, 1820, in broad daylight, in the Swamp district, passed by acclamation the following resolutions:

1. Resolved: that Mr. A. L. Duncan is an excellent fellow in private life, but there are good reasons to mistrust his demeanor in the public sphere.

2. Resolved: that Mr. Duncan has resided in this region for sixteen years, and for fifteen of those years has continually spoken ill of frogs.

3. Resolved: that under these circumstances, and with this record, it is very strange that he should seek their vote.

4. Resolved: that frogs are kindly souls, but don't like to be trod upon.

5. Resolved: that they also don't like to be made fun of.

6. Resolved: that the croakings of certain toads who have *personal motives* for singing the praises of Mr. Duncan, only offends our ears.

7. Resolved: that the above resolutions shall be croaked, sung, peeped, and chirruped in all the swamps, cypress groves, mudholes, backwaters, bayous, lakes, lagoons, and other such regions of the State to warn our fellow creatures not to let themselves be *swamped.*

During election periods, hostilities broke out not only between Americans and Creoles but also within the Creole community. Each

faction defended its candidate with equal vehemence and equal il-
logic. Political disputes sometimes served as occasions to settle old
scores. The presidential campaign of 1828 between the incumbent
John Quincy Adams and Andrew Jackson, hero of the Battle of New
Orleans, led to a violent polemic involving the illustrious Marigny
and Etienne Mazureau, a naturalized Frenchman who served as an
official for the State of Louisiana.

Marigny had published and distributed a pamphlet, signed simply
"by a Creole," in which he endeavored to establish the superior virtues of Andrew Jackson. Mazureau, who was supporting Adams, attacked the publication in an article in *L'Argus* signed "A Naturalized
Citizen." A few days later, Marigny retaliated with another pamphlet. Its opening pages were devoted to the presidential campaign;
then the author turned his attention to Mazureau, accusing him,
among other failings, of writing ungrammatical French and of having begun his career in Louisiana as a dancing master! Mazureau re-
futed both allegations in yet another pamphlet, signed this time in
his own name; but Marigny continued to press his attack. In his
next pamphlet, the issue of the presidential campaign was largely
forgotten; instead, Marigny reflected on his adversary's character
and private life in most unflattering terms. One of the anecdotes related by Marigny may cast light on the origin of their quarrel.

Some years earlier, Marigny and Mazureau had taken part in an
amateur theatrical sponsored by a number of prominent Creole families. The play was a tragedy entitled *Mahomet,* and Mazureau's role
called for him to collapse, mortally wounded, in the arms of Marigny. Unfortunately Marigny, in a spirit of buffoonery, had allowed
his fellow actor to drop to the floor with a thud. Leaping to his feet,
the enraged Mazureau hurled himself on Marigny, and the management was obliged hastily to lower the curtain on the unrehearsed
free-for-all. As Marigny recounted the incident in his pamphlet:
"When you were stabbed by the parricide Séide and fell back in my
feeble arms, 'you collapsed 'neath the weight of an overweening
pride.'"

On a different occasion, this same unfortunate Mazureau had provided another excuse for mirth. One spring, when the Mississippi
had overflowed in several areas of town, a passerby happened to

glance through the window of Mazureau's office. He saw the worthy gentleman seated solemnly at his desk, his feet ensconced in a bucket to protect them from the water that had flooded the floor. The spectacle caught the onlooker's fancy and inspired him to compose a ditty to the tune of "Michié Préval," a popular *gombo* tune of the time. Soon all New Orleans was singing:

> Michié Mazureau
> Dans son vié bureau
> Li semblait crapaud
> Dans ein la bail doleau.
> Dansé Calinda, bou-djoumb
> Boujoumb, boujoumb.

> Mister Mazureau
> In his ol' office
> Looked like a toad
> In a pail of water.
> Dance Calinda, boom-da-boom
> Boom-da-boom, da-boom!

GOMBO CULTURE

The French-language literature of Louisiana, although popular in its own time, is bound to seem tedious to a modern reader. Noble and high-flown, it is also curiously thin and empty—scarcely a literature for the ages. The black cultural heritage, in contrast—the *gombo* songs, folktales, proverbs passed on from generation to generation and preserved by such writers as George Washington Cable, Lafcadio Hearn, and Alcée Fortier—retains much of its original vitality.

For Alcée Fortier, *gombo* is not merely a corruption of French, but an idiom of its own:

It is the transformation by ignorant African slaves of the French language into a speech concise and simple, language at the same time soft and musical. The tendency is to abbreviate as much as possible, both in the form and in the construction of the sentence. All parts of speech not absolutely necessary to the meaning, are thrown out of the sentence. There is hardly any distinction of gender and the verb is simplified to a wonderful degree.

Thus "là-dedans" becomes "ladan," "monsieur" is transformed into "michié," "petit maître" becomes "timaite," and so on.

The *gombo* proverbs reveal a keen perception of animal life as well as a sense of the weaknesses of human beings: "Lapi pa capab gagnin piti sans gran zoreil" (Rabbits can't have baby rabbits without long ears); "Coupé zoreil milet, ça pas fé li choual" (You can't turn a mule into a horse by trimming his ears); and, on making a virtue of necessity, "Quand na pas choual, monte bourrique; quand na pas bourrique, monte cabri; quand na pas cabri, monte jambe" (When you don't have a horse, ride an ass; when you don't have an ass, ride a goat; when you don't have a goat, go on foot). In such maxims, humor and philosophy go hand and hand.

The folktales, almost all of African origin, have animals as heroes and are characterized by humorous tone, an element of surprise, and a touch of the supernatural. Some seem closely related to the *Märchen* of the Brothers Grimm—for example, the story of "The Singing Bones." Once there was a man and a wife, very poor, who had twenty-five children to feed. The man was good and kind, but his wife was very wicked. Every day, when the husband returned home from his labors, his wife set before him a dish of meat without any bones. Now, when you have twenty-five children around the house, you can't keep track of each and every one of them, but one evening the man summoned them all together, and he noticed that ten were missing. His wife explained that they had been sent to their grandma's for a visit; yet every day thereafter, another child was missing. Then one evening as the father stood in the doorway, thinking of his missing children, he heard distant voices singing:

> Nous moman tchué nous
> Nous papa manzé nous
> Nous pas dans la bière
> Nous pas dans cimetière.

> Our mama killed us
> Our papa ate us
> We have no grave
> We don't lie in the cemetery.

The voices were coming from a large stone in the man's field, and when he lifted the stone he discovered a large collection of bones, which promptly resumed singing. Then he understood that these were the bones of his murdered children. Full of rage, he killed his wife, buried the children's bones in the cemetery, and returned to his empty house. He could never eat meat after that, for it put him in mind of his children.

Other tales, like "Compair Lapin et Michié Dinde" (Br'er Rabbit and Mister Turkey), are typically African in flavor and obviously gained much from being told in the soft, lilting accents of a black mammy. An English translation by Alcée Fortier offers only the skeleton of the story:

> Every evening when Compair Lapin returned from his work he passed through a yard where there was a large turkey sleeping on a perch, and like all other turkeys that one also had its head under its wing to sleep. Every evening Compair Lapin stopped to look at the turkey, and he asked himself what it had done with its head. Finally, one evening, he was so curious that he stopped underneath the perch and said: "Good evening, Mr. Turkey."
>
> "Good evening," said the turkey without raising its head.
>
> "Do you have a head, Mr. Turkey?"
>
> "Yes, I have a head."
>
> "Where is it?"
>
> "My head is here."
>
> Compair Lapin looked in vain, but he could not see Mr. Turkey's head. As he saw that the turkey did not want to talk to him or show him where its head was, he went to his house and said to his sister: "Do you know that to go to sleep, turkeys take off their heads? Well, I believe I shall do the same thing, because it is less trouble to sleep without a head and one can speak without a head; the turkey spoke to me."
>
> Before his sister had time to tell him anything, he took an ax and cut off his head. His sister tried in every possible way to stick it on again, but could not do so, as her brother had killed himself.

BLACK MUSIC

It was in song that the creative spirit of the black slaves found its fullest expression. Unlike the American blacks, who from an early age were imbued with the Protestant religion or at least with the hymns and psalms characteristic of Protestantism, the blacks of New Orleans found their musical inspiration in the secular sphere. They had ample opportunity to absorb the sound of the rounds and minuets, waltzes and polkas played in the homes of their masters. They also attended operas and concerts and, as a matter of course, listened to the marching music that accompanied public ceremonies. In addition, some blacks received formal musical instruction. Their continual contact with music of every kind, including the instruments and rhythms of the whites, gave rise to their own lighthearted melodies, which often have the flavor of eighteenth-century France.

It must be admitted that the songs of the Creole slaves cannot match those of the American blacks for beauty or originality. Creole music lacks the emotional depth of the spirituals and blues, those outshoots of the Afro-American experience. But although Creole music occupies a different emotional plane, it also shares a bond with the music of the American blacks: the bond of all blacks transported to American shores. As Leroi Jones (Imamu Baraka) has remarked, the different forms of black music "show just how the African impulses were redistributed in its expression" and how the music itself was "Christianized and post-Christianized." Music and religion are intimately linked in black culture. "No matter what historical (or emotional) path we follow to trace the origins of black music," says Jones, "it leads us inevitably to religion."

However, this statement does not apply to the blacks raised in a Catholic environment. Afro-Christian music was virtually unknown among Creole slaves. No attempt was made to "Africanize" the Catholic liturgical music, and the voodoo chants retained their original African character. To be sure, a certain number of Catholic saints were introduced into the voodoo pantheon, and certain Catholic beliefs integrated into the voodoo rites, but the blacks never assimilated the music itself—Gregorian chants, for instance—into their culture.

The disassociation between sacred and profane music that we find among the Creole slaves is unique and surely attributable to their French Catholic heritage. In any case, the interest of their songs lies less in the music than in the words.

Music seems to have been the most natural form of expression for the black slaves, and their rounds, love songs, satirical ballads, and laments bring them vividly before us, allowing us a glimpse of the longings and frustrations that made up their lives. Improvisation was an important element in their music—which explains why so few songs have survived to modern times. Fortunately, however, Lafcadio Hearn and George Washington Cable collected and preserved some of the black songs of Louisiana.

The love songs are sentimental, occasionally sensual, with what Edward Laroque Tinker has called an "ingenuous" eroticism. In "Celeste, mo bel Bijou," for example, the central image retains its poetic integrity despite the double-entendres, and there is none of the deep, troubled sensuality characteristic of the blues. The song is touching in its simplicity and naïveté. And by one of those mysterious coincidences not uncommon in folklore, there are striking resemblances to certain ancient European ballads. In "Oh Sally, My Dear," an English folksong of the eighteenth century, the young man sings:

> If the women were hares and raced around the mountain,
> How soon the young men would take guns and go hunting!
> If the women were ducks and swam around the water,
> The men would turn drakes and soon follow after.

And in "Celeste, mo bel Bijou," the young man tells his love:

> Si to'tai zozo, zami
> Et mo'tai fisi, zami
> Mo tai tué toi, zami
> A fo'ce mo l'aimai toi
>
> Si to'tai bayou, zami
> Mo tai poisson, zami
> Mo tai nagé dans toi, zami
> A fo'ce mo l'aimai toi
>
> Si to'tai la boue, zami
> Mo tai cochon, zami
> Mo tai nagé dans toi, zami
> A fo'ce mo l'aimai toi
>
> If you were a bird, my friend,
> And I a gun, my friend,
> I would kill you, my friend,
> Because I love you so.
>
> If you were a bayou, my friend,
> I a fish, my friend,
> I would swim in you, my friend,
> Because I love you so.

> If you were mud, my friend,
> I a pig, my friend,
> I would wallow in you, my friend,
> Because I love you so.

Improvisation was part of the African musical tradition. Henry Edward Krehbiel, in his remarkable study of popular Afro-American songs, notes that each African king or chieftain had in his entourage a few men who served as "court jesters," and whose duties included improvising panegyrics, satirical songs, or songs of commemoration.

SONGS AND BALLADS

The blacks of Louisiana inherited from their ancestors a satirical bent and a gift for improvisation, and they utilized their inheritance for poking fun at whites and mulattoes. In their ballads, the black characters are invariably portrayed with sympathy and respect, the white or mixed-blood characters with derision, shading into cruelty when the subject is a man or woman of black ancestry who tries to pass for white.

Such is the case of Toucoutou, whose ungentlemanly lover has probably tired of her charms:

> Ah! Toucoutou, yé conin vous
> Vous cé tin morico
> Na pas savon qui tacé blanc
> Pou' blanchi vous lapo.

> Ah! Toucoutou, they're wise to you
> You're just a nigger wench:
> There is no soap so white, for true,
> Your sooty skin to blench.

Among the Louisiana blacks, songs often served as an accompaniment to dancing—another throwback to the African past. There were lively round-dances during which the slaves chanted an indecipherable mixture of African words and Creole *patois*. Sometimes anonymous minstrels composed formal ballads to be sung to a well-known dance tune.

"Michié Cayetano" is a song that tells of the wonders to be seen at the traveling circus that regularly visited New Orleans:

C'est Michié Cayetano
Qui sorti La Havane
Avec so chouals et so macacs
Li gagnein ein nomme qui dansé dans sac
Li gagnein qui dansé si yé la main
Li gagnein zaut, à choual, qui boit vin
Li gagnein oussi ein zein, zoli mom'zelle
Qui monté choual sans bride et sans selle
Po di' to' ça mo pas capabe
Mé mo souviens ein qui 'valé sab'
Yé en oussi tou' sort' bétail
Yé pas montré pou' la négrail'
Gniapas là dotchians do-brillé
Pou fé' tapaze et pou hirlé
Cé gros madame et gros miché
Qui ménein la tous pitis yé.

Dass Cap'm Cayetano
W'at comin' fum Havano
Wid 'is monkey an' 'is nag!
An' one man w'at dance in bag,
An mans dance on dey han'—cut shine
An' gallop hoss sem time drink wine!
An' b'u'ful young missey dah beside,
Ridin' 'dout' air sadd' aw bri'e;
To tell h-all dat—he cann' ne tole.
Man teck a sword an' swall'im whole!
Beas'es? ev'y sawt o' figgah!
Dat show ain't fo' no common niggah!
Dey don't got deh no po' white cuss!—
Sunbu'nt back!—to holla an' fuss.
Dass ladies fine, and gennymuns gran'
Fetchin' dey chilluns dah—all han'!
Fo' see Cayetano
W'at come fum Havano
Wid 'is monkey an' 'is nag!

(translation by George Washington Cable)

The song is revealing. Not only does it offer a glimpse of the circus and its clientele, it also casts light on the blacks' contemptuous attitude toward the "po' whites," the "sunbu'nt backs," and toward other blacks of different racial makeup. The author is probably a mulatto (that would account for the pejorative use of "niggah") and perhaps a free black. Or perhaps he is the domestic servant of some prominent New Orleans family and is merely asserting his privileged status at the expense of his less-fortunate black brothers. In any case, he is anxious to make it clear that he attends shows frequented by the better class of whites and thereby exemplifies a not-uncommon form of black snobbery.

The most famous song of our period was undoubtedly "Michié Preval," also called "Calinda" after the dance brought to New Orleans by refugees from Santo Domingo. The song tells of a Judge Preval who permits his black coachman Louis to hold a ball in his stables. All the blacks from "the best parts of town" arrive, many decked out in finery "borrowed" from their masters and mistresses. Again we encounter a mockery of white habits, mingled with desire to imitate them. According to the anthropologist Melville J. Herskovits, blacks often made an unconscious identification "with the life style and customs of those who had the power to procure the good things of life."

The "Calinda," which first gained popularity among the slaves of New Orleans, soon spread throughout the city and was sung and danced everywhere by blacks and whites alike. For many years, its captivating rhythms were heard throughout the city, giving Creole politicians and civil servants cause for reflection and sometimes troubling their dreams—for all the world like a naughty *loa* escaped from the voodoo pantheon of Santo Domingo.

6

Religion

Roman Catholicism came to Louisiana with the first white explorers. De Soto, Joliet, La Salle, and the le Moyne brothers were all accompanied by priests whose mission it was to convert the Indians as well as to minister to the spiritual needs of the members of the expeditions.

As we have noted, Louis XIV refused the Huguenots entry into the colony, and Louis XV's Code Noir made Catholicism the official religion of Louisiana, and mandated the expulsion of all Jews. Despite such harsh directives, the Catholic clergy in the colony exhibited a tolerance and open-mindedness that was all too rare at that moment of the Church's history. An effort to introduce the rigors of the Spanish Inquisition into the colony resulted in the newly appointed inquisitor, Antonio de Sedella, being summarily deported back to Spain.

Père Antoine

We must feel sorry for Père Antoine, as Father Antonio was called by his New Orleans congregation. His appointment as representative of the Holy Inquisition in Louisiana proved a sore trial for this gentle soul who had always conceived of Christianity in terms of charity and love. Directed by his superiors in Spain to stamp out heresy and castigate the Jews in the colony, Père Antoine was at a loss and simply kept his new assignment a secret. Months passed before Governor Miro learned of the good father's "promotion" in a communiqué from Madrid. Fearful that the presence of the Inquisition in Louisiana would act as a deterrent to American colonists, the governor ordered Père Antoine expelled. The year was 1790.

144

Five years later, Père Antoine returned to New Orleans as rector of the Church of Saint Louis. His appointment as Grand Inquisitor was tacitly forgotten. For more than forty years after his return, he ministered to his parishioners, baptizing and marrying virtually every Catholic in the city. His detractors muttered that he even extended his spiritual favors to the excommunicated, the unbaptized, and the divorced, for whom he performed marriage services out of the goodness of his heart.

Barefoot, dressed in the long brown robe of the Capuchin order, which he wore belted with a simple rope, Père Antoine was the very image of the man of God. He seemed to have a particular rapport with children, slaves, and the poor; and he never hesitated to ask his

Père Antoine.
The Historic New Orleans Collection

wealthy acquaintances for money, which he redistributed to the needy. The door of the parish house, situated behind the cathedral, was always open to all—as were the doors of the cathedral itself.

But Père Antoine was a controversial figure. The successive bishops of the diocese[1] accused him of being "disputatious," and his enemies condemned him for the "excessive" leniency he displayed toward his flock. Father Walsh, an Irish priest newly appointed to the parish, wrote to his superiors around the turn of the century: "With Father Antonio, a Spanish priest, we have a dangerous influence in our midst." Père Antoine was even spoken of in high quarters as a schismatic, and serious consideration was given to the idea of sending him into retirement in some Spanish monastery and replacing him with a strict disciplinarian who would bring the parish back into line. But it was all too clear that Père Antoine's parishioners were devoted to him and that, if any attempt were made to replace him, they would simply cease to attend church. And there would be no point in fulminating against laxness and corruption from the pulpit if there was nobody on hand to listen.

Father Dubourg, who was named bishop of New Orleans by the pope on September 24, 1815, quickly discovered that the people of his parish had a will of their own. Benjamin Latrobe reported that, while Father Dubourg was delivering his first sermon in the cathedral, the parishioners "sneezed, coughed, spat, and, as decency required, rubbed out their spittle on the floor with their feet." It is not hard to understand why Father Dubourg subsequently applied for papal authorization to transfer to St. Louis.

Roger Baudier, the author of a history of the Catholic church in Louisiana, explains: "The secret of Père Antoine's popularity is not difficult to find. For one thing, he was a charitable man. There is no denying this point. . . . However, there was another side to Père Antoine, which is far from flattering, but which also explains his popu-

1. While it was under French rule, the Louisiana Territory fell under the clerical jurisdiction of the bishop of Québec. Under the Spaniards, it belonged to the see of the bishop of Havana. In 1805, it was made part of the bishopric of Baltimore. In 1815, New Orleans became an episcopal seat, but the bishop appointed by the pope fell into a dispute with the local clergy and refused to assume his post. It was not until 1830 that the city at last acquired a resident bishop.

larity with the general public. . . . He took an attitude of 'laissez faire' and not meddling with people's morals."

We are told that the venerable Capuchin, who had been promoted to vicar-general of St. Louis Cathedral, never raised his voice against either freemasonry or dueling. He did not punish those who took mistresses, who failed to observe Lent or to take the Easter sacraments. He did not denounce those who divorced their spouses and remarried, and he seemed impervious to the presence of "usurers, apostates and prostitutes" in his parish. In fact, said Baudier, "he never condemned anything." Père Antoine baptized, married, and buried anyone who needed his services and asked no questions. When a Freemason died, his coffin was ushered into the cathedral regardless of the fact that it was bedecked with Masonic symbols and designs, and Père Antoine saw to it that the deceased was accompanied to the cemetery by priests and choir, candles and crucifixes, according to the proper Catholic rites.

When a memorial service was held for Napoleon in 1821, Père Antoine "authorized a layman named Canonge to preach a sermon from the dais." When a Jew wished to marry a Christian, he performed the ceremony without bothering to inquire whether the groom had undergone conversion. "Where were the laws of the Church, the decrees of the councils of the Church, the expressions of the Sovereign Pontiffs, canon law?" exclaims Roger Baudier. He concludes that "Père Antoine's days of 'glory' were a period of positive religious decadence, confusion and laxity. . . . Mass attendance fell to a low ebb, being confined mostly to women and Negroes."

It is interesting to compare these strictures with the comments of Protestant observers. Alexander Hamilton, for instance, had nothing but praise for the activities of the Church in New Orleans: "In a Catholic church the prince and peasant, the slave and master, kneel before the same altar in temporary oblivion of all worldly distinctions. They come there but in one character, that of sinners." Such a state of affairs came as a pleasant surprise for Hamilton, who remarks that Protestant churches, while not excluding blacks, generally confined them to "some remote corner, separated by barriers from the body of the church," whereas in New Orleans slaves were granted "all the consolations of religion . . . from the hands of the Catholic priests." Slaves were visited when sick, comforted in affliction, and their last breath was eased by "the sublime words: 'Depart Christian Soul.'" Hamilton continues: "Can it be wondered, therefore, that the slaves in Louisiana are all Catholics; that while the congregation of the Protestant church consists of a few ladies, arranged in well cushioned pews, the whole floor of the extensive Cathedral should be crowded with worshippers of all colours and classes?" He concludes with words of praise for the Catholic clergy: "For all that I can learn, the zeal of the Catholic priests is highly exemplary. They never forget that the most degraded of human forms is animated with a soul, as precious in the eye of religion as that of the Sovereign Pontiff."

Harriet Martineau, like Hamilton, seems to have been struck by admiration for the democratic spirit prevailing in the cathedral. St. Louis Cathedral, she declares, is

the only one in the United States where all men meet together as brethren. Within the edifice there is no separation. Some few persons may be in pews, but kneeling on the pavement may be seen a multitude of every shade of complexion from the fair Scotch woman or German to the jet black pure African. . . . During the preaching a multitude of anxious faces, thus various in tint and expression, turned toward the pulpit, afforded one of those few spectacles which are apt to haunt the whole future life of the observer like a dream.

Actually, this sense of fraternity was confined to the interior of the cathedral. Once the congregation had departed the sacred precincts, Martineau reports that they went their separate ways, "blacks and whites parting company as if they had not been worshipping side by side."

"The Most Tolerant Place in Christendom"

The Reverend Theodore Clapp, a Presbyterian minister from New England who spent thirty-five years in Louisiana, has left us an interesting account of the activities of the Church in New Orleans. "Catholic priests of New Orleans," he writes, "are models of clerical wisdom, decorum, and propriety. . . . Indeed, New Orleans is the most tolerant place in Christendom." His testimony is the more impressive when one realizes how prejudiced Reverend Clapp must have been at the outset. Before he departed for New Orleans, one of his colleagues had remarked that "he could hardly conceive of a greater calamity than for a pious and enlightened minister to be compelled to spend his days in Louisiana, where Christianity was encumbered by the corruption of the Roman Catholic Church."

Among the Puritans of New England, New Orleans was commonly known as "New Sodom," the "Godless City," or the "City of Sin." They fulminated against the Creoles for "profaning the Sabbath" and even condemned the Protestants of the city for lack of militancy—a weakness they attributed to the corrupting influence of the Papish environment.

Reverend Theodore Clapp. From a lithograph by Jules Lion.   The Historic New Orleans Collection

In his *Autobiographical Sketches*, Clapp admits that when he first came to New Orleans he was convinced that the most formidable enemy he had to encounter would be the Church of Rome. Several weeks later, at the home of a "liberal" gentleman of the city, he made the acquaintance of several Catholic priests who "had left their clerical robes at home" and who conducted themselves "with all the ease, elegance and affability characteristic of well-informed and polished laymen." In the best ecumenical spirit, the priests invited the minister to visit them at their private residences. And the instant liking that Reverend Clapp felt for his Catholic colleagues was soon reinforced by a profound admiration of their works. As he recorded in his journal: "The labor involved in the duties of the confessional is inconceivable to one who has not lived among the Catholics. I've known a priest engaged from daylight till noon, uninterruptedly, in receiving penitents, and that in the most inclement weather."

It is difficult to recognize in these descriptions the negligent and corrupt priests castigated by the Puritans and by such doctrinaire Catholics as Father Walsh. Undoubtedly the priests of New Orleans, with Père Antoine at their head, did occasionally interpret the teachings and instructions of the Church in a broadly libertarian spirit, but they did so in an effort to benefit their parishioners and the community at large. To be sure, they can be blamed for their failure publicly to denounce such Creole practices as gambling, dueling, and adultery, though we will never know whether they did not strongly admonish their parishioners in the secrecy of the confessional. Actually, it is unlikely that they did so: first of all, because there would be little point in scolding parishioners who were determined to persist in their ways; and secondly, because the Church had always displayed great tolerance for the carnal weaknesses of men, even while it insisted on virtuous conduct on the part of its women. We should not forget that the Fathers of the Church were for the most part misogynists and that the clergy in Louisiana traditionally adopted the role of healer of souls rather than arbiter of morals. In New Orleans, the clergy were less concerned with reproving the sinner and portraying the horrors of eternal damnation than with coming to terms with human frailty.

The priests of New Orleans extended a helping hand to their neighbors, cared for the sick, the poor, widows, orphans, slaves, and abandoned wives or mistresses. They welcomed back to the flock any sheep who had gone astray. St. Louis Cathedral was truly a house of God; although it may be true that during the week its attendance was limited to "women and Negroes," on Sundays and holidays every Creole family put in an appearance. *La Gazette* refers to the "huge crowd" that pressed its way into the cathedral on All Saints' Day in 1822. On that occasion, New Orleans took on a festive air and seemed "more like a Spanish or Italian city than an American one."

Latrobe reports that a large number of worshipers crowded the cathedral on Good Friday. He witnessed an unusual ceremony: a long procession of people winding past a crucifix set up on a table; they bent to kiss the crucifix, then placed a few coins in a platter beside it. "Each gave according to his disposition," he notes. The same ceremony was repeated at the front door of the cathedral. Latrobe notes also that Good Friday was officially observed: "Although the Catholic inhabitants of this city do business on Sunday as on any other day, yet on this day, Good Friday, even the notaries have, to my great injury, shut up their offices; and the police officer has summoned one of my carriers and threatened him with a fine of fifty dollars for hauling lime on this day."

In attempting to assess the religious habits of the population, we must make a distinction between the Creoles and the more recently arrived French. Most foreigners, whether they came from France or England, from the North or East of the United States, tended to apply the term Creole to the entire French-speaking population of Louisiana. But there were important differences. Among the political refugees newly arrived from France were revolutionaries and Bonapartists, many of them atheists or at least lapsed Catholics. Such was not the case among the Creoles, who, though seldom exhibiting the traits of piety and bigotry that are associated with many Catholic populations, were, according to historian Albert Fossier, "profoundly Catholic by inclination and belief." As Fossier explains: "They were baptized in their Church, married by their Church, and at the time of death fervently hoped to receive the last rites of their religion. They always insisted that their children be reared in the religion of their fathers and they encouraged the piety of their slaves."

There is much truth to this; but it should also be said that the Creoles took a disconcertingly offhand approach to conventional morality. One misses a certain idealism and moral rigor in their daily relationships. There were, of course, some straitlaced Creole families, but these were generally of Spanish origin and were so few as to be remarked on with interest and surprise.

Père Antoine's influence extended far beyond his own parish and made itself felt in the entire community. When he died in January, 1829, the city went into mourning: shops, offices, and even banks closed. His death was regarded as a "general catastrophe." The members of the municipal council voted to wear a mourning band for thirty days, and a group of Freemasons placed a notice in *Le Courrier* that described Père Antoine as a "venerable old man whose tolerance was matched by his goodness, his charity by his intelligence," and invited "masons of all rites and degrees" to attend the funeral: "Remember that Father Antonio never refused to accompany the mortal remains of our brothers to their final resting place, and that gratitude now requires us to bear him company with all the respect and veneration that he has so richly merited."

The lawyer Edward Livingston, grand master of the lodge, delivered a eulogy, singling out for praise the "holiness" and "virtues" of the beloved priest: "This holiness, his virtues, should have entitled him to canonization, and if his title to that distinction were to be tried, as it is said to be in Rome, the advocate of the Evil One would burn his brief and despair of showing one reason why he should not be received as a saint in heaven who led the life of one on earth."

Virtually the entire population of the city filed past his bier, and the Louisiana Legion, the Lafayette Rifle Corps, the members of the legislature, the magistrature, the legal profession, and the city council, as well as all the government officials, participated in the funeral procession to the cathedral. There Père Antoine was laid to rest under the altar consecrated to Saint Francis.

Such an outpouring of affection suggests both that Père Antoine was indeed a saintly man and also that tolerance promotes social accord. Certainly the Creoles of New Orleans were tolerant, but they were also obstinate. Neither the Capuchin priests nor the civil authorities ever succeeded in enforcing the directives issued by their superiors; and we have seen how Père Antoine expediently sidestepped his duties as Grand Inquisitor. The city's attitude toward its Jews is a further indication of its independent spirit.

THE JEWS

There were only a handful of Jews in New Orleans: merchants and tradesmen who had come from Portugal and Spain, Amsterdam and Bordeaux, to set up business in a promising new land. They constituted a quiet, law-abiding element that made solid contributions to the economic growth of the colony.

By order of Louis XV, and as stipulated in the Code Noir, the French West India Company had demanded the expulsion of all Jews from the Louisiana Territory. The royal proclamation was formally promulgated in New Orleans, but its enforcement was half-hearted at best. No one was molested, and the only Jews who left the colony, in effect, were those who chose to do so of their own accord. During Governor Kerlerec's administration (1743–53), there were six well-to-do Jewish families in New Orleans, each possessing houses and property of their own, who apparently found no difficulty in living there in violation of the Code Noir. The Jewish families were acclimatized to the country, its people, and its customs; and while professing to practice their religion, they seemed to do so more out of respect for tradition than from profound personal conviction.

In any case, when Louisiana came under Spanish rule and the energetic General O'Reilly set about enforcing the letter of the law, many Jews hastened to the Capuchin fathers to solemnize their marriages in the church, to baptize their children and slaves, and to receive baptism themselves. Some of them became exemplary Catholics. Others, as it seems, converted out of expediency. But the good fathers were sympathetic and never demanded exorbitant displays of fervor from their new charges. Although the parents might not take their religious duties very seriously, it was hoped that their children would in time become pious Catholics. That, according to tradition, is in fact what came to pass.

After this initial wave, there were some sporadic conversions over the next few years. Quite a number of them could be attributed to the charms of some Christian maiden who subsequently married the young convert. Père Antoine cheerfully presided over these "mixed" marriages, which were not at all to the liking of his superiors and scandalized his more straitlaced parishioners.

It was not until the territory was transferred to American rule that a Jewish community took shape in New Orleans. Even then it remained small. A prominent member during those early years was Judah Touro, a wealthy merchant from New England who settled in the city at the beginning of the nineteenth century. "Although an Israelite to the bottom of his soul," says Clapp, "it would give him the sincerest pleasure to see all the Churches flourishing in their respective ways." He was "heartily sorry that they did not more generally fraternize with love, and help each other."

In time, other Jews began to arrive from the East: merchants, businessmen, tradesmen, brokers. One of these, Levy Jacobs, was an important slave dealer of somewhat tarnished reputation. This disrepute was not attributable to his profession, for a prosperous slave trader enjoyed a social position comparable to, perhaps, a prosperous wine merchant. Like the wine merchant, however, the slave dealer was expected to label his merchandise with scrupulous care—and it was bruited about the marketplace that Jacobs had occasionally passed off slaves from Kentucky as Virginians. That was something like selling the product of a local vineyard as imported wine from Bordeaux.

Another Jacobs, a contemporary, found his marital problems the talk of the town when he placed a notice in the *Louisiana Gazette* stating that he would no longer be responsible for his wife's debts and then, a month later, felt constrained to inform the readers of the newspaper that he "had the pleasure" to announce that he was now living with his wife "in perfect harmony." (To complete the story, shortly thereafter he filed for both bankruptcy and divorce.) On the whole, however, the Jewish community was decorous and reserved. Most of its members were hardworking, and many were extremely wealthy; their standard of living equaled that of the wealthy Creoles. They did not, however, participate in the social whirl of New Orleans and never succumbed, as the Americans were to do, to the aristocratic Creole vices of dueling and gambling.

Under American rule, there was complete freedom of religion. However, the number of practising Jews seems to have been small, for we learn that the first public assembly of Jews in New Orleans, in 1824, numbered only some dozen people. In 1828 a civic document, drawn up in both French and English, authorized "Manis Jacobs and some others to form a congregation." That was the official beginning of the Jewish community in New Orleans.

In general, the Jews maintained cordial relations with the Christian community, especially with the Protestants. They often associated with them in business enterprises and on occasion offered them material aid. Through a generous donation, Judah Touro enabled a group of American Protestants to establish the public library that would bear his name, the Touro Free Library. This same Judah Touro came to the rescue of a debt-ridden Presbyterian congregation in 1824 by purchasing their church and land and then returning it to them for their continued use. When the church subsequently burned down, Touro had it rebuilt and contributed several thousand dollars toward its future upkeep. Reverend Clapp comments on this generous gesture: "He might have torn the building down at the beginning, and reared on the site a block of stores, whose revenues by this time would have amounted to half a million dollars at least." Such, however, were not Touro's intentions. When someone offered him a generous sum for the site, Touro replied that "there was not money enough in the world to buy it; there should be a church on this spot to the end of time."

THE REVEREND CLAPP

The Presbyterian Church, the second Protestant church in New Orleans, was situated in the Faubourg St. Mary, at the corner of St. Charles and Gravier streets. It was a fashionable neighborhood, and the church, accordingly, was both large and handsome. It had room for some five hundred worshipers. During the winter season, many of the town's most distinguished visitors attended services at the church, where certain pews were set aside for their particular use.

The Reverend Theodore Clapp was the second pastor of the Pres-

Reverend Clapp's Stranger's Church, *ca.* 1821. From a lithograph by Félix-Achille
Beaupoil de Saint-Aulaire.

The Historic New Orleans Collection

byterian Church. Its first pastor had been Reverend Larned, who died of yellow fever on August 31, 1820. Larned was a superior man who, according to historian Albert Fossier, "combined a dignified bearing with both grace and vigor," but at one moment in his career he had succumbed to panic and fled the city during an epidemic of yellow fever. On his return, he bravely confronted his indignant congregation, confessed his lapse from the pulpit, and pledged never again to flee in time of trouble, but rather to follow the example of the Catholic clergy who remained with their flocks "whatever perils assailed them." Reverend Larned declared: "The soldier of the Cross should always act on the motto: 'Victory or Death.' It is as ignominious for a clergyman to flee the approach of disease, as for an officer of an army to skulk on the field of battle."

In the following year, the yellow fever struck again, even more violently than before. For more than two months, the Reverend Larned gave himself unsparingly, visiting sick parishioners at their homes or in the hospital, burying the dead, and consoling the bereaved. On Sunday, August 27, he preached his last sermon:

I am ready to meet a final hour; to take a last look at the countenances of beloved relatives and friends, to see the fair and glorious scene of sublunary shadows no more. . . . O, let me die. . . . O, welcome, thrice welcome the hour when the portals of the tomb shall open to receive these mortal remains, and the light of a better world shall break in upon my forgiven, redeemed, and emancipated spirit!

That evening he took to his bed, and four days later he died of the fever.

The church soon found itself in grave financial difficulties. According to the Reverend Clapp, the congregation had borrowed some $45,000 from the municipality and now found itself "without a single dollar in its treasury." The church then obtained permission from the legislature to hold a lottery, but the money thus collected fell far short of its needs. At this moment Judah Touro appeared on the scene and became the benevolent proprietor of the church and its parcel of land.

Part of the church's difficulties could be traced to the transient nature of its congregation. The Americans seemed perpetually on the move and unable, as a consequence, to take much interest in the

problems of the parish. "The society is fluctuating and heterogeneous, almost beyond a precedent," lamented the Reverend Clapp.
"In a short time, the settled pastor sees his pews emptied, and filled
with new occupants. He has hardly time to form their acquaintance
before they vanish, to be succeeded by another set of strangers."

Under Clapp's ministry, the church on St. Charles Avenue became
the main Protestant center of New Orleans. In his *Autobiographical
Sketches*, Clapp commented that visitors to the city "never left . . .
without going to the American theater, the French Opera, and Parson Clapp's church." The "Parson" preached his first sermon before
a "noble looking audience," for the "ladies and gentlemen of New
Orleans dressed as finely to go to church as they did when they went
to the Opera, evening party or ball-room." The listeners found the
sermon and the new minister much to their taste—with the inevitable exception of those who disapproved of his broad-mindedness and
nicknamed him "the heretic parson."

Clapp had never been a stickler for doctrine, and in the course of
time he increasingly succumbed to the heterodox local influence.
He began to look with an indulgent eye on attitudes and practices
that formerly would have aroused his indignation.

With the steady growth of the American population in New Orleans, the influence of Protestantism also increased. Catholicism remained, of course, the "official" religion of the territory—with the
continued preponderance of Creoles and French émigrés, it could
scarcely be otherwise. But even among the French-speaking elements, there now existed a Protestant community.

The French Protestant congregation had no church of its own, but
the Episcopalian minister had placed his church at their disposal,
and every Sunday afternoon the Reverend Defernex conducted a service. It is difficult to estimate how many members of the congregation were descendants of those proud Huguenots to whom Louis
XIV had more than a century earlier forbidden entrance to his American domains. In time, however, the congregation grew large enough
to envision the construction of its own church. A general collection
was made among the French Protestant community, and the results
exceeded expectations. A year later, the cornerstone was laid for a
church on the corner of Bienville and Rampart streets.

In that same year, 1828, the Mariner's Church was erected at the foot of Canal Street. This church was intended to divert seamen from the pernicious appeal of the city's Swamp district, but the building was of such poor design and workmanship that the people of New Orleans soon came to consider it an eyesore and a disgrace and to call for its demolition.

In 1830, the Germans in the city opened a church of their own. Around this time New Orleans, like other American cities in the same period, witnessed an enormous proliferation of religious sects. The religious impulse seemed to be an integral element in the American character, as basic as the passion for freedom and thirst for equality. The Americans newly arrived in Louisiana seemed all to be associated with some sect; and even when they had neither church nor pastor, they sustained their devotion through Bible readings conducted at home by the father of the family or in public by some "elder" of their sect. Itinerant preachers flourished; though their sermons might be deficient in theological subtlety, they captured their listeners' imaginations through vivid descriptions of the delights of Heaven and the torments of Hell.

The New Gods

The Baptist and Methodist churches did not limit themselves to preaching their message to white people. Since the beginning of the century, their missionaries had endeavored to convert the Indians and to instruct the slaves. Like the Quakers, the Baptists and Methodists were beginning to feel that the sole justification for slavery rested in the hope that the slaves could be converted to Christianity. The Baptists were the first Protestants to train black pastors and deacons who could concern themselves with the religious life of the slaves on the plantations.

Long before the Protestant churches became possessed by missionary zeal, the slaves had already come to accept the God of their white masters. Such adaptability came naturally to the blacks of West Africa, the center of the slave trade. In their native land, they had already proved hospitable to new gods. In Dahomey, home of the Yoruba and Ashanti, it is common practice for both conqueror and conquered to adopt the divinities of the other tribe. If a tribe has been

defeated in war, it stands to reason that its gods must be less influential than those of the victorious tribe, and, according to anthropologist Melville J. Herskovits, "the gods of the conquerors are inevitably
added to the pantheon, joining company with the older, less powerful
deities." The conquerors, for their part, are anxious to appease the
indigenous gods, and therefore a mingling of deities is effected.

Clearly, this African tradition had a direct bearing on the religious
evolution of black Americans. The white man's God was of great importance to the enslaved blacks; they accepted Christianity with the
same spontaneous accord that they accepted the values and standards
of the white man's world. Some, indeed, converted even against the
wishes of their masters. There was no official policy among American Protestants to the effect that slaves should be baptized and instructed in the Christian faith, but many masters took these duties
upon themselves—at least as regards their household servants, with
whom they had daily contact. The situation of the field workers was
different and varied from one plantation to another. Some masters
felt it their duty not only to have all their slaves baptized and fully
instructed in the tenets of Christianity, but even to erect a church
for the use of the black community. John McDonogh, a rich planter
with vast domains on the outskirts of New Orleans, required his
overseers to assemble all his black laborers for prayers both morning
and evening, before and after their work in the fields—a practice
that the slaves found little difficulty in accepting, since in Africa
they had been accustomed to meet every evening to beg the gods for
protection against the evil spirits of the night. On small plantations
and farms, where religion assumed a familial character, the slaves
often formed part of the congregation that attended the prayer meetings or Bible readings conducted by the master. Until the beginning of
the nineteenth century, however, many masters showed no concern
at all for the religious well-being of their black field workers. On some
plantations, groups of slaves gathered to perform quasi-Christian
rites and to worship the white Christ. As Leroi Jones has remarked,
religion was of great importance to them, and because they were formally forbidden to worship their own African gods, they naturally
turned to the God of their conquerors. The slave who had been baptized enjoyed a certain prestige among his "heathen" brothers; he

was an initiate, the servant of a puissant and fearful deity. He could address himself to the "Holy Ghos'" of the white man—a spirit whom he somehow associated with the lost gods of his African past.

THE PROMISED LAND

Following the great evangelical campaigns of the Baptists and Methodists, missionaries were given a warm welcome by the slaves, and soon the worst epithet that one slave could bestow on another was "heathen." The preachers laid emphasis on the sufferings of Christ, on the equality of all men in Heaven, on the hardships and trials of the tribes of Israel. Inevitably, the blacks identified themselves with the Jews, and Israel became their Promised Land.

With the conversion of the slaves to Christianity, the cultural dislocation of the blacks became an established fact. Whereas the African slave had sung of his longing to return to his ancestral home, the black Christian now voiced his desire to "cross Jordan" and to "see the Lord." The yearning for Africa was replaced by a longing for death, which offered the only possible release from slavery. With death, the slave would journey "peacefully and majestically" "to the Promised Land." Evocative of this yearning is the following song, included by Leroi Jones in his book *Blues People*:

> Gonna shout trouble over
> When I get home
> Gonna shout trouble over
> When I get home.
>
> No mo' prayin', no mo' dayin'
> When I get home
> No mo' prayin' an' no mo' dayin'
> When I get home.
>
> Meet my father
> When I get home
> Meet my father
> When I get home.

The evangelical spirit of the Baptists and Methodists made a far greater appeal to the blacks than did the dogmas of the Episcopalians and Presbyterians. The slaves were especially attracted to the practice of baptism by total immersion, which was reminiscent of certain rituals practiced in West Africa, where the river spirits enjoyed particular status and power among the gods.

The Protestant slave in New Orleans attended his master's church every Sunday, and participated with his master in all religious observances. On the plantations, the master set aside a structure, designated as a church or "prayer house," exclusively for his slaves' use. This building became the social and religious center of the "clan," serving much the same role as the chief's hut in an African village. The slaves gathered there whenever they had the chance and conducted their own religious services without supervision or intervention. In the course of their prayer meetings, they gave their emotions free rein, and "gitten' the spirit" became the main goal of the assemblies, which were essentially charismatic in nature.

Music is an integral element of all African rites, and singing was soon incorporated into the Afro-Christian religious services. The tom-tom was forbidden, but the tempo of the music was conveyed through hand-clapping. The sermons, too, were delivered in a musical rise and fall modeled on African ritual chants. The preacher adjures the faithful, and the listeners respond—slowly and quietly at first, then with steadily increasing excitement, until the assembly reaches a peak of emotion. The worshipers pound the earth floor of the church with naked feet and sometimes exhibit signs of mass possession—a phenomenon associated with certain African rituals.

African tradition survived in the style and gestures of the black Protestants, as well as in the music. Over the course of several generations, however, the African gods themselves faded from memory. The Christian missionaries eventually succeeded in destroying the last traces of the slaves' ancestral beliefs. In the city of New Orleans, where the slaves lived in constant contact with whites, or in remote regions where there were only a few blacks in the midst of a white community, there was little opportunity for the slaves to perpetuate their African traditions, and all conscious memory of their past faith was quickly obliterated. Yet the same phenomenon occurred on the large plantations, where the slaves formed a close-knit society of their own: there too the assimilation of white culture was rapid and seemingly unopposed.

Nevertheless, the blacks retained certain aspects of their African past: their superstitions which, as Leroi Jones has pointed out, often hearken back to African religious practice, and their love of magic. Magic, by its very nature, flourishes in secrecy, and in all likelihood it continued to thrive sub rosa on the plantations and even in large towns, where forbidden practices could more easily escape notice. We shall see that New Orleans was to become the voodoo center of the United States.

Melville Herskovits has pointed out that the supernatural looms large in the life of the Afro-American. Because he has a passionate interest in the hidden forces that influence the universe and holds in fear and awe the magic powers that constantly threaten him, he has traditionally sought protection by means of a great variety of charms, which derive their power from all sorts of nonhuman spirits. The sorcerer, accordingly, is a personage of great influence; he knows how to bargain with occult forces and also distributes amulets and charms. He is admired, feared, and looked up to, and on some occasions makes use of his authority to foment an uprising.

It is therefore not surprising that the whites, from the early days of Louisiana's colonization, expressly forbade ritual ceremonies among the slaves. They recognized that the continued observance of African traditions could pose a grave threat—that the practice of the ancient rites, coupled with the influence of magic, could well end in insurrection. In Santo Domingo, the voodoo priests were a formidable element of the slave population, due to their authority and their close-knit organization. It was a voodoo priest, a runaway slave named Boukan, who instigated an uprising of the island's 100,000 blacks in 1791.

The slave owners were quick to realize that the tom-tom had other uses than to accompany songs and dances—that it could be used to transmit messages from one plantation to another and on occasion to sound the signal for revolt. As a consequence, all African drums made from hollowed logs were banned throughout the southern states. They were replaced by percussion instruments less suitable for transmitting messages and largely limited to providing a musical accompaniment for dancing.

THE MASSA'S RELIGION

We have noted the evangelical ferment among the black Americans, the obligation laid on Catholic slave owners to have their slaves baptized and instructed in the Catholic faith, and the fervor and sincerity with which blacks embraced Christianity. Nevertheless, vestiges of African belief could still be discerned in the slaves' religious practices and continued to inform their concept of the universe. At the beginning of the nineteenth century, with the arrival of black work gangs from Santo Domingo, voodoo made its appearance. For many years thereafter, this orgiastic cult, which invoked through magic the dualistic forces of Good and Evil, was to be a distinctive feature of the religious life of the Louisiana blacks. Just as Louisiana was the only place in the United States where one could still, in the mid-nineteenth century, witness authentic African dancing, so too it was the only place where African religious practices were still observed. The anthropologist Melville J. Herskovits finds no contradiction in the fact that many blacks were at once devout Catholics and participants in voodoo rites: "This apparently formidable contradiction was easily resolved by identifying the pagan spirit being invoked with some Christian saint; and as long as this spirit was not formally condemned by the missionaries and deprived of his prestige, the blacks saw nothing irregular in the practice."

Until 1803, Catholicism had been the official religion of Louisiana. In the Code Noir, Governor Bienville had decreed "in the name of the King" that all slaves should be instructed in the Roman Catholic faith and that all those who supervised them should be Catholic as well. The Code also stipulated that masters should make sure that their slaves observed Sundays and holidays (they were forbidden to work on those days) and that they were buried in consecrated ground. Any infractions of these regulations could result in the authorities' confiscation of the slaves. Article 7 of the Code stated that the regulations of the Declaration of Blois[2] and the Declaration of 1639 pertaining to marriage were to be observed "by both free people and

2. The Declaration of Blois, issued in 1579, made the Council of Trent's promulgations on marriage binding on all Catholics, as they still are today.

slaves, except that for slaves the owner's consent is required instead of the consent of the parents."

Despite these instructions, there is little reason to believe that the French and Spanish gave much more attention to the religious education of their slaves than did the Americans. They must have had them baptized, for the law demanded as much, and they saw to it that their household slaves acquired a veneer of piety. But it was only in New Orleans, where the priests took their duties to heart, that slaves and free blacks had the opportunity to receive proper instruction in the teachings of the Church.

The Catholic clergy consistently displayed a zeal for missionary work, but they were so few in number that it was impossible to assure compliance with the Code Noir except within the confines of the city itself. There were many parts of Louisiana where the blacks saw a priest no more than once a year, and where the whites had learned to make do without the ministrations of the Church. In the Mississippi Delta, marriages were conducted in a manner predating the Council of Trent, with the couple merely exchanging rings in the presence of witnesses. A French traveler, C. C. Robin, writing at the beginning of the nineteenth century, has left an account of the situation:

In the absence of clergy, baptism was a helter-skelter, devil-may-care procedure; and even under the Spanish government people can die without a priest and scarcely feel the difference. As for marriages, they are usually performed by the local military commander; otherwise, the charms of young love would wilt in the waiting. When a priest finally penetrates the region, he spends his time rejuvenating in the baptismal waters persons grown infirm with age, and instructing couples to "go forth and multiply" who are long past the age of childbearing.

On May 31, 1789, the pious king of Spain, mindful of the plight of his distant subjects, issued a decree that caused considerable stir in the colony. In effect, it ordered that every plantation have its own chaplain to oversee the religious instruction of the slaves and that the landowners take charge of the slaves' moral upbringing and put an end to all "irregular attachments." Henceforth, both blacks and whites were to be married only within the Church.

The planters protested that they could not possibly comply with this decree, for the colony was already critically short of priests. Given the increased cost of living, moreover, and the planters' diminished incomes, they could hardly afford to pay the salary of a chaplain, nor were their houses fine enough to maintain him in suitable style. On the subject of slave marriages, finally, the governor himself undertook to write to the king, explaining that slave couples often belonged to different masters and that it would be ruinously expensive for the owners to be compelled to buy that half of the couple who worked on another plantation. What is more, Charles Gayarré reports that the planters believed "Negroes have an almost insuperable aversion to marriage, and the efforts which have been made to encourage that institution among them have always proved fruitless." In summary, it appears that the French and Spanish were scarcely more conscientious than the Americans in providing blacks with proper religious instruction; if anything, they seem to have been more hypocritical.

Ritual songs and dances were transmitted from generation to generation of slaves, but until the arrival of immigrants from Haiti there appears no trace of organized African religion in Louisiana or even of a distinctive Afro-Catholic group. The Haitians' Saturday night or Sunday afternoon ceremonies involved not only the magical invocation of spirits, but also the phenomenon of mass possession. In Africa, there are no clearly defined frontiers between the sacred and the profane, and among many black Catholics there appears to have been a kind of mingling of the African gods with the saints of the Church.

It is in profoundly Catholic countries that the syncretism of Christian and African philosophy and religion achieves the most interesting results. Catholic dogma is too firmly fixed to permit the free interpretations that black Protestants could engage in. When they became Catholics, slaves were required to conform to set rules and beliefs, yet an important part of their emotional life remained unsatisfied. It was outside the Church, accordingly, that the encounter between Christian and African traditions took place. In Santo Domingo, this encounter gave birth to voodoo.

Voodoo

It is interesting to speculate why Santo Domingo, rather than Louisiana, was the first site of voodoo. Perhaps it was because in Santo Domingo large plantations were the rule and the proportion of whites to blacks was small. The slaves in Santo Domingo, unlike those in Louisiana, came into little contact with their owners and were therefore more inclined to maintain their African traditions. The shiploads of blacks newly arrived on the island managed to group themselves around religious or tribal leaders who encouraged them to preserve their heritage. According to a contemporary witness, M. L. E. Moreau de Saint-Méry, "the Arrabas Negroes [that is, the blacks from Dahomey] are the chief proponents of voodoo and the guardians of its aims and regulations." The word *vödum* is used by the peoples of Dahomey and the Guinea Coast to designate their gods: gods of the sea, thunder, iron, trees, mountains, fire, wind, rivers. Nothing could be accomplished without the consent of these gods, and the kings kept a tight control over the various religious cults.

Though baptized and instructed in at least the rudiments of Catholicism, the blacks of Santo Domingo still remained faithful to their ancestral beliefs. They made room in their traditional mythology for the Catholic saints, who seem to have coexisted on friendly terms with the African divinities.

A Haitian observer, Doctor Price-Mars, comments that the blacks "adopted a superficial allegiance to Christianity, and repressed their secret veneration of those primeval forces to whom they were bound by ancestral tradition." Under cover of darkness, they came together in the woods to perform sacred rites and to worship the snake god. On the eve of an uprising, the entire black population of the island had recourse to voodoo—not only the slaves, but the free blacks as well. The free blacks, who could travel at will throughout the island and were not affected by the harsh restrictions of the Code Noir, were generally the priests and priestesses of the cult.

As a resident of Santo Domingo in 1775, Moreau de Saint-Méry witnessed a voodoo ceremony. It began with the snake ritual, presided over by a voodoo "king" and "queen." The box containing the snake was placed on the ground, and the voodoo queen climbed upon it and began to "writhe about, possessed by the snake's spirit, and to give tongue to oracular pronouncements." The voodoo king then "traced a large circle with some black substance, and beckoned the candidates for initiation to enter the circle. A small bundle containing herbs, horsehairs, fragments of horn and other strange substances was placed in his hands." The king then tapped the initiate on the head with a wooden paddle, meanwhile intoning an African chant that was taken up by the crowd. Gradually the entire group of spectators fell into a trance. "Some fainted, some were overcome by frenzy. . . . They spun around, tearing their clothes and even biting their flesh in a sort of Bacchic fury, while others, fallen senseless to the ground, were carried by the dancers to an adjacent chamber where disgusting sexual practices took place in the dim light."

By 1820, voodoo had taken root in the region around New Orleans, due largely to the fact that many immigrants from Santo Domingo had settled there. In the city itself, the cult gained innumerable adepts among the black population, and a number of whites were attracted to it as well. Actually, the whites were less fascinated by the characteristically African elements of the rites and the cosmological vision that informed them, than mesmerized by the magical aspect, which was not, after all, wholly foreign to the European tradition. There were also those who insisted that it was the orgiastic aspect of voodoo that most appealed to the whites.

From the outset, voodoo in New Orleans was a matriarchal institution. Men were relegated to a minor role, though a certain "Doctor Jean" was prominent in voodoo circles at this time. An immigrant from Santo Domingo, Doctor Jean was a free black of enormous bulk who owned a number of slaves of his own and took pride in the fact that he had not one drop of white blood in his veins. Mulattoes, he declared, were "neither white nor black, but mules." For a fee, he would prepare amulets, read the future, devise charms, cast spells, and perform exorcisms. At no time, however, did he play a role in any of the ritual ceremonies.

The dominating female figure in the cult was a mulatto woman, also from Santo Domingo, named Sanité Dédé. Rumor had it that she had won her freedom through magic; the more prosaic truth, in all likelihood, is that she had purchased it with money earned through the sale of amulets and charms. She held an official license as an itinerant vendor and could be seen daily at the Place d'Armes, where she peddled ready-cooked foods. It was Sanité Dédé who converted Saint John's Eve into a great voodoo festival. Every year, hundreds of celebrants assembled on the banks of Lake Pontchartrain or along Bayou St. John to worship the snake god, known in Louisiana as the *gran Zombi*, and Saint John the Baptist, whom the voodoo adepts associated with an African deity or *loa* called Agomme Tonnerre, whose attributes included thunder and lightning. Sanité Dédé was accompanied at these ceremonies by a voodoo king, a secondary figure, generally her lover, whose reign terminated with the end of their liaison. Tafia was drunk, and chickens, cats, and goats sacrificed. Then, high with rum, dancing, and incantations, and in the grip of mass possession, the crowd followed the voodoo king and queen into the water to immerse themselves in a baptismal rite. Robert Tallant, a modern writer on voodoo, reports that a black adept recollected that in the rites of his youth "sometimes people was so drunk and excited they got drown. The water was just about up to their shoulders but they'd fall down and get stepped on."

In the City of the "Loas"

The traditional forms of voodoo depended on the personal interpretations of the high priestesses of the cult. The imagination of the blacks was constantly giving birth to new *loas* or divinities, while many older gods fell into oblivion. The adepts were not troubled by the contradiction between their proliferating polytheism and their faith in a supreme and all-powerful God. They cheerfully grouped their deities under three headings: the good spirits, among whom they counted Moses and a certain number of Catholic saints; the spirits of death and overlords of the cemeteries; and the evil gods, who were closely associated with magic. Because they looked on natural phenomena as supernatural forces, they made a place in their pantheon for Saint Sun, Saint Moon, Saint Earth, and the Sainted Stars.

Guinea, which had lost its geographical reality for them, became the dominion of the loas, an unspecified Valhalla from which the loas descended to Earth.

Just as Africans do not recognize a fixed boundary between the sacred and the profane, so too they do not specify a clear line of demarcation between good and evil. In Dahomey, a supernatural force can possess both benevolent and malevolent aspects; the same charm can cure illness or cause death. A loa often has a double nature. Erzulie, the Haitian Venus, and Legba, her Dahomian counterpart, are simultaneously the loas of friendship and of evil. In their latter role, they are known as Erzulie the Hang-Tooth and Legba the Slut.

In Louisiana, as in Haiti, Catholic saints were associated with African deities. Ogoun of Iron is related to Saint James; Erzulie reappears in tandem with the Virgin Mary or with Saint Barbara or the mythological Siren. Damballa is associated with Saint Patrick and Damballa's father with Moses, considered the greatest sorcerer of all time. Legba, who keeps watch at crossroads and temple doors, is sometimes equated to Saint Anthony, sometimes to Saint Peter. Legba is also the god of debauchery and lust, and he occasionally takes pity on mortals and helps them escape their destiny. Other popular gods are Agoussou, son of a panther and a mortal woman, and Saint Express, sometimes associated with the fearful Baron Saturday, god of the cemeteries. But voodoo adepts felt little impulse to codify their beliefs. They prayed to the gods for protection, in the full realization that such favors are never granted free of charge and that anyone who failed to repay the deities with offerings or sacrifices would draw down upon himself and his family the terrible anger of the gods.

Haiti was known for its man-eating loas, and gruesome accounts of human sacrifice were rife on the island. But the voodoo gods of Louisiana seem to have been satisfied with the blood of a cat, a dog, a cock, or a pig. Apparently the demonic spirits of Haiti had become somewhat domesticated when they reached American shores.

The loas made their presence known by dreams, signs, messages, and, most dramatically, by taking possession of an initiate in the course of a ritual ceremony. The phrase went: "the loa makes his servant dance"; and it was believed that the possessed individual assumed the role of the loa who had been invoked. Thus the servant of Damballa climbed trees, the servant of Bull Three-Balls threw himself on women, the servant of Legba rolled on the ground, the servant of Ogoun of Iron walked in blazing embers.

Many of the traditional rites and beliefs had been modified through time, but some—such as the snake ritual—survived intact. Every voodoo ceremony in New Orleans opened with this chant, intoned by the king or queen:

> Hear and come oh grand *zombi*
> Hear and come to work your magic.

An African ritual chant quoted by the Louisianian Henry Castellanos was also recorded in Santo Domingo by the French historian Moreau de Saint-Méry. It went this way:

> Eh Bomba! Hen! hen!
> Canga bafie te
> Danga moune de le
> Canga do ki la
> Canga li.

One is struck, finally, by the resemblances between the voodoo ceremony witnessed by Moreau de Saint-Méry in Santo Domingo and another ceremony that took place in New Orleans in 1825 and was described some years later by an eyewitness who had been fifteen years old at the time. Both ceremonies were structured on the ritual elements of dance, sacrifice, and orgiastic frenzy. In New Orleans, however, intoxicating beverages were served to facilitate "possession." Every account of voodoo ceremonies in Louisiana alludes to the drunkenness of the participants and the sexual orgies in which women were the most fervent participants.

Voodoo Rituals

Voodoo ceremonies were forbidden by law in New Orleans, as were all "public gatherings of Negroes." The rituals therefore took place at some sparsely populated spot along the banks of Lake Pontchartrain, where the celebrants could invoke their gods without simultaneously inviting police intervention. Sometimes voodoo gatherings were held in town, in spite of the prohibition—usually at the home of a free black. The newspapers of the time make great play with these "demonic" assemblies, at which slaves and free blacks indulged in "so-called voodoo orgies." On March 26, 1828, *L'Abeille* reported that "the police have on several occasions arrested a number of these cultists without, as it seems, deterring subsequent assemblies, and no sooner do the authorities strike down one of these temples of abomination, than another rises up in its place. . . . The incense still burns on the altars of the snake god."

When not officiating on the banks of Lake Pontchartrain, Sanité Dédé held her assemblies in a converted brick factory on the Rue de Maine. It was here that the young Orleanian, brought to the scene by a family servant, witnessed his first voodoo rite. He found himself in a large shed, lit at either end by a "fierce fire . . . casting a lurid light over the scene." Candles were placed "at equal distances," but their dim light "barely added to the darkling light of the two pyres." Some sixty people were assembled, each wearing a white bandanna carefully knotted around the head. "There were males and females, old and young, negroes and negresses—handsome mulatresses and quadroons. With them half a dozen white men and two white women." On a table stood two stuffed cats, one white, one black, flanking a small cypress tree set in a sort of wooden tub. Directly behind the tree and "towering above it," the boy saw "a black doll with a dress variegated by cabalistic signs and emblems, a necklace of the vertebrae of snakes around her neck, from which depended an alligator's fang encased in silver." Sitting by the table he recognized Zozo, an old sassafras-vendor "well known in New Orleans." Zozo was seated "astride of a cylinder made of thin cypress staves hooped with brass and headed by a sheepskin. With two sticks he droned away a monotonous ra-ta-ta, ra-ta-ta." At his feet sat a black man and woman who reinforced the rhythm by also drumming on the cylinder, one with "two sheep shank bones," the other with "the leg bones of a buzzard or turkey." Beside them a young black man methodically shook a gourd rattle.

At a given signal the four initiates formed a crescent before Dédé, who was evidently the high priestess or Voodoo Queen. She made cabalistic signs over them and sprinkled them vigorously with some liquid from a calabash in her hand, muttering under her breath. She raised her hand and Zozo dismounted from his cylinder, and from some hidden receptacle in or behind the large black doll drew an immense snake which he brandished wildly aloft.

He addressed himself to the snake and whispered something that it "seemed to understand," for the creature uncoiled itself and was thus passed over the heads of the initiates and wrapped around their necks, while Zozo intoned the name of the African sect: *"Voudou magnian."*

Now the climax of the ceremony approached, when the god seized possession of the crowd. The tom-tom beat grew , wilder, a banjo player joined the other musicians, and tensions mounted. Clay jugs of wine or tafia were passed around. Suddenly Zozo rose, once again removed the snake from its hiding place, wrapped it around his neck, and then "dexterously" hurled it into the fire. A great shout rose up; tom-tom, banjo, and rattle again began in good earnest, and to this "discordant" music were added the chants of the spectators.

The chorus of Dante's hell had entered into the mad shouts of Africa. . . . Up sprang a magnificent specimen of human flesh—Ajona, a lithe, tall, black woman, with a body waving and undulating like Zozo's snake—a perfect Semiramis from the jungles of Africa. . . . [She] began to sway on one and the other side. Gradually the undulating motion was imparted to her body from the ankles to the hips. Then she tore the white handkerchief from her forehead. This was a signal, for the whole assembly sprang forward and entered the dance. The beat of the drum, the thrum of the banjo, swelled louder and louder. Under the passion of the hour, the women tore off their garments, and, entirely nude, went on dancing. No, not dancing, but wriggling like snakes. Above all the noise rose the voice of Zozo:

> Now, dance Calinda
> Voodoo Magnian!
> Aie! Aie!
> Dance, Calinda!

The ceremony now turned to orgy. The candles were suddenly extinguished, leaving the entire room lit only by the dim glow of the dying fires. Sickened by the heat and overcome by an indefinable sense of terror, the boy dashed out of the shed and ran all the way home. Years later he wrote: "If I ever have realized a sense of the real visible presence of his majesty the devil, it was that night among his Voodoo worshippers."

MAGIC

Sanité Dédé was not the only grand priestess of voodoo, only the most famous. In the late 1820s, she was supplanted by a beautiful quadroon, Marie Laveau. Born in New Orleans in 1794, Marie Laveau was to dominate the voodoo scene there for forty years. A devout Catholic who made almost as free with holy water as she did with tafia, she was also a highly regarded clairvoyant, and her amulets were greatly prized by the recipients. She admitted to owing her divinatory powers to a snake, which, witnesses attested, was in the habit of "entering her bedchamber and conversing with her."

Laveau was also an astute businesswoman who managed to acquire a considerable fortune within a few years. The profession of voodoo priestess was lucrative, especially when the lady dealt in black magic. For casting spells, evoking the forces of evil, or making curses, a stiff fee was demanded.

Voodoo adepts believed in a supreme God, all the Catholic saints, African spirits, werewolves, ghosts; they believed in magic, fortune, and the efficacy of charms and curses. They endeavored to appease all the supernatural forces of the universe, and when misfortune struck they were as likely to have recourse to the Church, burning a candle by way of expiation, as to a voodoo "doctor" or priestess. For their own protection, they wore religious medallions or magic charms or both. They drew no sharp distinctions between their loyalty to the African tradition and their allegiance to accepted Catholic doctrine. And for the grand priestess, medallions and amulets, magic potions and holy water all shared the same supernatural potency.

As an intermediary between the loas and her clients, the voodoo priestess was by definition a maker of magic. Her amulets might serve many purposes, but they also carried with them certain restrictions that the user was supposed to respect in order for the charm to retain its power. If the magic failed to work, the client had only himself to blame. He could, of course, return to the priestess and purchase a new amulet.

Voodoo experts like Sanité Dédé and Doctor Jean were not applied to for protection alone, but as a sort of insurance against misfortune.

Their clients also sought them out as a means of gaining wishes or of inflicting harm on enemies. Some wished for money, others hoped to win the favor of an indifferent lover or gain back an unfaithful mistress. There were, inevitably, instances of an aging lady who wished to awaken the passion of an adolescent boy, or a young girl who longed for a Prince Charming. Others wished to rid themselves of a meddling neighbor, a professional rival, a superfluous spouse, or a jealous lover. And there were innumerable slaves who sought to get free of cruel or repressive masters.

Whites were not above applying to Sanité Dédé or her acolytes for their services. The Creoles as a group were extremely superstitious, especially the women, and their contact with the slaves reinforced this tendency. Many a Creole lady, her face thickly veiled, made her way through the back alleys to call upon a "seer." Her household slave, faithful and discreet, followed behind her. Albert Fossier cynically suggests that the clairvoyants used the knowledge gained from their extensive contacts to gain credibility: "Superstitious whites had great faith in them because in collusion with household slaves, they were able to reveal secrets and make prophecies that came true." Women who did not dare approach the voodoo practitioners in person sent their favorite slaves to request a potion or magic charm that would win back an errant husband or an amulet that would alienate him from his mistress. For in New Orleans, as elsewhere on the globe, the main business of the magic makers was to deal with the problems of unrequited love.

The recipes employed by these voodoo practitioners resembled those used by their European counterparts—witches, sorcerers, and the like—since time immemorial. A lady wishing to make a man fall in love with her was asked to supply the voodoo doctor with samples of her pubic hair and nail clippings, along with shreds of her flesh and pieces of her undergarments. These ingredients were shredded, crushed, and mixed together in a sachet that was then introduced into the house of the beloved, there to work its spell. For disposing of enemies, a popular recipe called for a dried toad, a dried lizard, the little finger of a person who had died by suicide, the wings of a bat, the eyes of a cat, the liver of an owl, and hair from a dead child, all of which were ground into a fine powder and made into an amulet. The cemetery became a much-frequented source of materials for the manufacture of evil charms.

If a man suffered from impotence, he could purchase an amulet made of the dried testicles of black cats, which he needed only to apply to his own testicles to be cured. If a woman wanted to assure her lover's fidelity, she could measure his erect organ with a piece of string, make nine knots in the string—and as long as she kept the string about her person, her lover would be faithful to her. There were also charms to assure success at cards or dice; to make one's enemies' teeth or hair drop out; to make them sick, impotent, or sterile; and to bring about their death.

The Voodoo Curse

The fatal curse has a history reaching far back into the shadows of time, and death by voodoo magic is a recorded fact. In most cases, however, the victim died of terror, not supernatural malice. The blacks believed implicitly in the magical power of the voodoo priests, and if one of them chose to issue a sentence of doom, the intended victim often succumbed to his own fatalistic certainty. Uncontrollable fear seized him when he discovered some voodoo object placed under his pillow or deposited on his doorstep. This fear might well produce a state of shock leading inevitably to death—unless he could procure the assistance of a rival voodoo expert, who could free him from the spell by means of an ingenious, and expensive, countercharm. It was rumored that Marie Laveau secretly planted charms in the houses of several of her best clients so that they would engage her to neutralize the malevolent influences. Many foresighted individuals invested in amulets to protect them from evil spells or to ward off sickness. Soon the majority of blacks, whether voodoo adepts or not, took to wearing amulets around their necks or legs.

Are such superstitions the sign of a naïve or credulous mentality? We need only think of the many rational intellectuals who daily consult their horoscopes or the vast number of Catholics who trust in the protective power of their medallions. It is hard to see much difference between the "primitive's" belief in a loa and the European's faith in a saint. Nor is it difficult to understand how the blacks came to confuse Catholic saints with African gods. In the voodoo rites, the saints came to have well-defined roles. Saint Michael was invoked to vanquish enemies; Saint Anthony of Padua brought good luck in games of chance; Saint Peter, without his key, guaranteed success, and with his key guaranteed even more rapid success; Mary cured the sick.

In St. Louis Cathedral, an altar dedicated to the Virgin Mary always attracted many black worshipers, particularly women. Whether their offertory candles were burning for the beautiful Erzulie or for the Mother of Jesus is hard to say, but their fervor was conspicuous and unquestionably sincere. Benjamin Latrobe remarked that the custom of burning candles had fallen into disuse among the Creoles in New Orleans but was continued among the blacks: "Considerable revenue must arise from this source. I once counted upwards of two hundred and ten candles burning or extinct upon the pavement before the three altars." One morning a choir boy reported to him that some four hundred candles were burning in the cathedral.

The candle industry was managed by the sacristan, who had a "kind of manufactory of them in a little court behind the church." He sold them "at twelve and a half cents each," and when they were three-quarters burned they were snuffed out by a choir boy, and the ends returned to the sacristan, who recycled them into new candles.

Another profitable source of church income came from burial fees and masses for the dead. Latrobe learned to his scandal that the funeral of Jean-Baptiste Thierry had cost $135.60. According to Latrobe, "tolling the big bells" cost ten dollars, "burning the six great candles" cost fifteen, and burning twenty-eight small ones cost seven dollars. The figures are so high that one suspects that Latrobe may have been misinformed.

THE RITES OF DEATH

The blacks of New Orleans seem to have been particularly attracted to the Catholic funeral services, and when one of them died, the attendance at the mass and burial was large and attentive. Until 1828, all funeral services were held at the cathedral, as were all other ceremonies. In that year, the municipal council, fearing that the lying-in-state of corpses might contribute to the spread of yellow fever, transferred all funeral services to a small brick chapel, Saint Anthony's, located on the corner of Rampart and Conti streets and consecrated by Père Antoine de Sedilla on December 27, 1827.

At the cathedral, as at the more modest Saint Anthony's, slaves and free blacks alike enjoyed the full splendor of a Catholic funeral. In his journal, Latrobe records two funerals that he witnessed:

First marched a man in a military uniform with a drawn sword. Then came three boys in surplices, with pointed caps, two carrying staves with candlesticks in the form of urns at the top, and the third, in the center, a large silver cross. At some distance behind came Father Anthony and another priest, who seemed very merry at the ceremony of yesterday, and were engaged in loud and cheerful conversation. At some distance farther came the coffin. It was carried by four well-dressed black men and to it were attached six white ribbons about two yards in length, the ends of which were held by six colored girls, very well dressed in white, with long veils. A crowd of colored people followed confusedly, many of whom carried candles, lighted.

The second funeral was of a slave "about one hundred years" old. Out of curiosity, Latrobe followed the procession. Over two hundred people accompanied the coffin. "Most of those who followed her to the grave were her children, grandchildren, great-grandchildren, their husbands, wives, and companions." Many of the women carried candles, and everyone was dressed in white. At the cemetery, Latrobe saw the grave, "three feet deep, of which eighteen inches were filled with water." Beside the grave was heaped a small pile of fresh earth mixed with bones—Latrobe, with his usual devotion to detail, identified them as "ten or twelve skulls" along with "ribs and thigh bones." The priests, five in number, entered the cemetery murmuring a hymn. The coffin was lowered into the grave, where "it swam like a boat in the water." The gravedigger, "a grey-headed negro, naked, excepting as to a pair of ragged, short breeches," tossed a shovelful of dirt onto the coffin. At this point, a woman, apparently overcome with grief, threw herself into the grave and found herself waist-deep in muddy water. The gravedigger "with very little ceremony thrust his shovel under her, and then seized her with both hands round the throat and pulled her up, while others took hold of her legs and arms, and she was presently removed." Meanwhile, a group of young men, climbing up "on the heap of bones, began to

amuse themselves by throwing in the skulls, which made a loud report on the hollow coffin, and the whole became a sort of farce after
the tragedy, the boys throwing about the legs and thighs and hunting
up the skulls for balls to pelt each other."

As the jazz musician Jelly Roll Morton has said, the people of New
Orleans took literally the scriptural command: "Rejoice at the death
and cry at the birth." In the words of the spiritual:

> Dere's a long white robe in the hebben for me
> I won't die no mo'
> Dere's golden slippers in the hebben for me
> I won't die no mo'.

7

Doctors, Medicine, and Yellow Fever

The Creoles were a long-lived race. There was an old slave saying: "A Creole dasn't die, he dry up." Louis Dubroca, a French traveler of the early nineteenth century, reported enthusiastically: "In Louisiana there are no devastating epidemics, and the happy inhabitants of this blessed land arrive at their final hour without having to endure the gradually increasing debilities of old age, which are more fearful than death itself."

It is hard to understand how this commentator could have overlooked the terrible epidemics of yellow fever that had decimated the population at regular intervals for almost a decade or the malaria that was endemic to the region. Yet another contemporary witness, Baudry des Lozières, also remarks on the "salubrious climate" of New Orleans—acknowledging, however, that "the Mississippi, like the Nile, overflows its banks every summer" and that the swamps around the city were "unhealthy," since they provided breeding grounds for thousands of insects, "known as mousquitoes, and far more bothersome than their French counterparts." But in his opinion the only truly mortal dangers confronting a citizen of New Orleans were boredom and the medical profession itself. His comments on the doctors are categorical and unsparing: "When a doctor tells a patient that he needs a change of air and recommends a trip to France, he is simply confessing his inability to treat him. It is not a healthier climate the patient is sent to seek, but more competent medical advice."

This judgment is supported by a document dating from 1804, written by a French physician, Paul Alliot, to President Jefferson. After accusing the Spaniards of responsibility for the many "consuming diseases and pestilences" in the city, he declares: "The ignorance of the local doctors is a further cause for the dwindling of the population; well-informed physicians who have visited Louisiana are unanimous in agreeing that the doctors there have little knowledge of that art which is so useful to the preservation of the human race." It is evident that Dr. Alliot ranks himself among those "well-informed physicians"; one wonders whether he is expressing his personal opinion, or a general one.

Licensing Regulations

Throughout the colonial period, and even under Spanish rule, virtually all the doctors and midwives practicing in Louisiana seem to have received their training in France. As Rudolph Matas explains: "Spain, which contributed little to the development of medicine in the eighteenth century, was in no position to supply medical men to her newly acquired colony of Louisiana." At an early date, General O'Reilly had laid down detailed regulations for the doctors, surgeons, and apothecaries of Louisiana. Apothecaries, for example, were forbidden to dispense medicines without receiving a medical prescription. Surgeons (who, we should remember, were at this period considered among the humbler members of the profession) were expected to meet a surprising number of qualifications. In the English colonies, anybody who so desired could set up in practice as a doctor. In Spanish Louisiana, the laws were more stringent; even surgeons had to possess a medical degree in order to practice.

The regulations were not proof against fraud, and in 1801 the Cabildo noted that several individuals were practicing medicine without possessing the requisite credentials. One was a free black; two others were apparently pharmacists who were illegally prescribing medicines.

If a doctor had a medical degree from Paris, he was assured of a flourishing practice among the Creole population. It was felt that French universities provided the most up-to-date training, and the doctors of Louisiana took pride in their "advanced" approach to medicine. They were among the first in the country to employ smallpox vaccinations, to treat venereal diseases with success, and to introduce improved childbirth procedures. For the Paris-trained doctor, as for his humbler locally trained counterpart, however, bleedings and purgings remained the principal stock-in-trade for most ailments.

When a doctor was summoned to the bedside of a fever patient, he invariably prescribed a bleeding or a purge—sometimes both—and made sure that the doors and windows of the sickroom were kept tightly shut. Even in summer, stringent measures were taken to guard against the nefarious effects of fresh air. Water too was looked on with suspicion. Patients were given as little to drink as possible; preferably a spoonful of orange-flower water or of champagne, administered at infrequent intervals. Most patients owed their recovery to a robust constitution.

The Frenchman Berquin-Duvallon observed that among both the black and the white citizens of Louisiana there were "few serious illnesses" and that in general the men were "still youthful and vigorous at sixty years of age." He also noted, however, that during the summer months the region was swept by "a sort of malignant fever of a particularly virulent nature, whose symptoms and effects vary so widely that doctors are at their wits' end in treating it," and that between October and July, "deaths are rare." Berquin-Duvallon lists the health problems of the population as "dysentery, bilious fevers, eye strain, coughs and congested chests, nervous disorders or spasmatic and vaporous attacks, epilepsy or 'falling sickness,' paralysis, childbirth complications (more often fatal here than is the case elsewhere), and intestinal worms, to which children are especially vulnerable and which occasionally result in death." In short, the typical ills of the period. Berquin-Duvallon adds: "People tend to lose their teeth at an early age—particularly the Creoles—due to the wetness of the climate and soil and the quality of the drinking water." He concludes that "the Creoles seem relatively free of birth defects; one sees few cripples, hunchbacks, etc." Cases of smallpox, he asserts, are rare and generally leave few traces, despite the fact that the civil government and clergy, "guided, as they believe, by reason and religion, or rather *misguided by* superstition, are opposed to vaccination." Although the Church did indeed object to smallpox vaccination on religious grounds, the government's opposition was at least partly based on medical experience. At this period, the English vaccine, in common use in New England, had not yet been introduced to Louisiana, and the local method of inoculation posed real dangers. On several occasions, the doctors had succeeded in spreading the disease rather than restricting it. In 1802, the city council decreed that inoculations could be authorized only when more than twelve cases of smallpox had been reported in the municipality; otherwise, patients should be confined in a small provisional hospital to be constructed for this purpose.

Immediately following the Louisiana Purchase, Governor Claiborne oversaw the introduction of the English smallpox vaccine. In 1817, the city council appointed one Doctor Smith the "official dispenser" of the "authorized vaccine," which was available to everyone for five dollars.

MEDICAL COSTS

The practice of medicine was a lucrative business in Louisiana. Writing at the beginning of the nineteenth century, Berquin-Duvallon noted: "With the possible exception of lawyers and bankers, medical practitioners have the surest means of rapidly acquiring riches." Few became millionaires, but many managed to accumulate a tidy personal fortune, and a few, endowed with prudence and sagacity as well as wealth, made their way to the highest rungs of the social ladder, becoming influential figures on the local political scene.

The fee schedule for the doctors affiliated with the New Orleans Medical Society in 1824 has been preserved:

For an initial visit (in town only)	$3
For each subsequent visit	$1
For a first visit at night	$4
For treating or dressing a blister	$1
For a consultation (in town only)	$5
For a written consultation	$10–$30
For treatment of a simple syphilitic condition	$20–$40
For treatment of syphilis complicated by bubos, caries, or condylomas	$50–$100

For a normal childbirth and follow-up care	$20–$50
For abnormal deliveries or prolonged labors, with follow-up care	$40–$100
For minor operations	$5–$30
For an amputation or major operation	$60–$200
For vaccinations and follow-up care	$4

Fixed by Agreement, April 18, 1824

Louisiana doctors fixed different rates for blacks and whites. In general, the fees charged blacks were about a third lower than those charged whites. Thus, a doctor in St. Francisville in 1825 charged a white man fifty dollars for surgical removal of an eye and a black man thirty dollars for the same procedure. The cost of treatment for gonorrhea was $15 to $20 for a white man, $10 to $20 for a black. On the other hand, the price for pulling a tooth was fixed at one dollar for whites and blacks alike, and black women paid about half the price charged whites for labor and delivery.

The French doctors in New Orleans were reputed to be excellent obstetricians, and highborn Creole ladies made a point of removing to the city as their delivery approached, even if they lived on distant plantations. One might have expected these ladies, raised by the Ursuline nuns and accustomed since childhood to taking their baths modestly clothed in a chemise, to have preferred a midwife to a male doctor. But that was not the case. As Berquin-Duvallon reported,

There are few women who are not convinced, or who do not pretend to be convinced, that their only hope for a safe delivery depends on their settling in the city one or two months before the appointed date, and submitting themselves to the hands of a surgeon rather than those of a person of their own sex, who could surely be expected to perform the operation with more dexterity and decency.

Of the fifty-three physicians registered in New Orleans in 1823, several specialized in obstetrics. About this time, Doctor Prévost, a refugee from Santo Domingo, successfully performed a cesarean section on a slave woman whose pelvis had been deformed by rickets. This was the first such operation in Louisiana and only the second cesarean in the United States. The procedure was successful, and when the woman became pregnant a second time Doctor Prévost triumphantly repeated the operation.

It was not always easy for a young doctor to establish a practice in New Orleans, for the city was already well supplied with physicians, both American and French. Many newcomers to the profession chose to become doctors-in-residence on a plantation, where, in return for the security of a fixed income, they looked after the medical needs of the planter and his family, as well as those of his slaves, for whom a building of some sort had sometimes been set aside on the estate to serve as a "hospital."

Slave owners took a strong interest in the health of their slaves. Good masters called in the doctor out of a sense of concern, bad masters out of avarice, for a sick slave was a financial liability, whereas a dead slave was a total loss. On the smaller estates, where the master could not afford to employ a doctor full time, a general practitioner would be summoned when emergencies arose. The masters' solicitude did not prevent them, however, from dealing out punishment to pregnant women who had fallen afoul of plantation rules. The women were made to lie on the ground with their stomachs suspended over a shallow ditch, so that the babies would come to no harm while the mothers were being whipped.

According to Berquin-Duvallon, the blacks were susceptible to "slight fevers in the spring, growing more violent in the summer," and to attacks of dysentery in the fall and of pneumonia in winter. The usual treatment for these illnesses was a combination of purges and astringents, along with the eternal bloodletting. The doctors were also called upon to reset dislocated bones, repair fractures, pull teeth, drain abscesses, perform amputations, and lend a hand in difficult childbirths. They were frequently required to treat cases of venereal disease.

In the nineteenth century, many Americans looked on venereal disease as a sort of divine punishment and were therefore inclined simply to let it run its course. The medical fraternity treated it with a certain offhanded disdain. The French doctors took the problem far more seriously than did their English colleagues, but the only treatment known at the time involved dosing the patient with mercury. Once the lesions had healed, the patient was considered cured. And if the patient was a slave, his owner sometimes refused to pay the medical fees if signs of the illness subsequently reappeared.

Louisiana had no medical school of its own at this period, though associated with the New Orleans hospital was a group of "apprentice surgeons." After the Spaniards' departure, Charity Hospital acquired an excellent phlebotomist, who happened to be a slave. According to tradition, he was so skilled that he was put in charge of surgery at the hospital. But on the whole, black physicians were a rarity.

Like the Spaniards, the Americans demanded that physicians possess medical degrees, and students were obliged to travel to France or the eastern seaboard of the United States to complete their studies. A degree from Harvard carried weight among the American settlers; among the Creoles, Paris and Montpellier commanded respect.

In medicine as in so much else, the French and Americans found themselves at loggerheads. Two separate medical societies formed in New Orleans, one French and one American. Among the French doctors were several colorful personalities who were as handy with a sword as with a clyster. Some of them were regularly found at dawn in the traditional dueling grounds of the garden of St. Antoine—not only in the role of medical attendants, a function prescribed by the Creole dueling code, but also as participants. Doctors generally fought other doctors—most often American doctors. On occasion, however, they also crossed swords with laymen who had dared to question their competence.

The feud between the two groups had less to do with styles of medical practice than with a rancorous conviction on the part of the French physicians that the Americans were usurping all the most lucrative medical posts. In 1824–25, the "Rogers Affair" brought these feelings to a head and filled the pages of *Le Courrier de la Louisiane* with a series of "open letters" whose vituperative tone alternately delighted and infuriated the reading public.

THE ROGERS AFFAIR

The affair began when *Le Courrier* announced that the position of chief medical officer at the Charity Hospital, which carried with it an annual salary of $1,200, had been awarded to an American, Dr. William Rogers. A strong contingent had favored the candidacy of Dr. Martin, a Frenchman who had served the hospital "with loyalty and zeal" for over seventeen years.

In a letter to the newspaper signed "Veritas," a local correspondent protested: "Why was Dr. Martin passed over? The answer was plain: 'I cannot say; but what I am well able to say, is that Dr. Martin is of *French Origin*, and that alone explains everything.'"

Let us keep an open mind on the matter and simply follow the train of events. Shortly thereafter, it was learned, to the great satisfaction of the French faction, that Dr. Rogers had fallen afoul of his superiors at the hospital due to a quarrel between himself and the chief surgeon, a Dr. Sanchez. In the course of the dispute, Rogers peremptorily demanded Sanchez's resignation, and the latter, in a rage, took his case to the administration, who, in turn, relieved Rogers of his functions. The French and Creole community of New Orleans greeted the news with jubilation.

Another correspondent, signing himself "Justice," claimed that Dr. Sanchez had been dismissed from the hospital staff after complaining about the American doctor's medical and administrative incompetence. It should be kept in mind that *Le Courrier* was a Creole organ and thus hardly objective in its treatment of the affair. Nevertheless, the pamphlets, letters, and editorials relating to the case, however biased their viewpoint, at least offer a vivid picture of the New Orleans medical community and of the conflicting attitudes, interests, and beliefs that separated the American from the Creole physicians. Among the most skilled of the practitioners, there was obviously little difference in medical knowledge or theory; nevertheless, one senses a deep-rooted antipathy.

According to "Justice," Dr. Sanchez had made the mistake of drawing the hospital administrators' attention to Dr. Rogers' "simple and expeditious" method of dealing with patients:

It consisted in passing through the different rooms, touching lightly the inferior jaw of the patients, in order to ascertain whether the salivary glands were sensible, and whether the mercury had produced the desired effect; after which the physician withdrew to the apothecary's room, and there, with the mere assistance of his memory, and without any notes, he prepared his prescriptions for eighty or ninety patients, more or less.

Sanchez had also criticized Dr. Rogers for putting a ward supervisor in charge of the pharmacy "after he had had only six lessons in pharmaceutical work." "Justice" recounted, finally, how one day, while

Rogers was making one of his whirlwind tours of the hospital, he noticed that one of the patient's arms felt "quite cool" and ordered that the patient be placed on a convalescent diet and allowed to walk in the garden. "But," replied the assistant, "he is dead." "Dead!" answered the doctor. "Well, have him buried."

Dr. Rogers was subsequently replaced by Dr. David C. Ker, whose appointment provoked a fresh outcry in the Creole press. Two correspondents, probably members of the medical fraternity, vehemently challenged the administration's claim that the appointment was justified by Dr. Ker's "financial need." One of the writers, signing himself, appropriately enough, "Indignatissimus," protested that the new doctor had a "large list of patients," had "just won a lottery prize of twenty thousand dollars," and was the annual recipient of "the sum of one thousand dollars as a depository of the smallpox vaccine." However justified the fury of "Indignatissimus," one cannot but suspect that it was to some degree inspired by envy.

THE CHARITY HOSPITAL

In the end, the choice of Dr. Ker seems to have been a good one. The editor-in-chief of the *Louisiana Gazette* wrote favorably of the appointment, extolling the doctor's "civic and professional" virtues. The editorial continued: "Since he has already distinguished himself in private practice, it is to be expected that Dr. Ker will take firm charge of a hospital which has, alas, long suffered from a lamentably poor reputation." Dr. J. N. Picornell, a Spanish physician, wrote in 1819 that the hospital was "badly situated, badly organized, and badly operated." The following year, the *Louisiana Gazette* reported: "Sick people are left to die in their own filth. . . . We wonder how the physician finds the courage to set foot on the premises." And in 1823 another medical observer, Dr. P. F. Thomas, commented: "To date the hospital administrators have effected no change for the better." Yet in 1826 a visitor from New England, Timothy Flint, could write: "The charity hospital . . . is probably one of the most efficient and useful charities in the country. . . . Here misery and disease find a home, clean apartments, faithful nursing, and excellent medical attendance." This transformation was the work of Dr. Ker.

The poor were admitted to the hospital free of charge; for those who could afford it, the fee was seventy-five cents a day. Don Andrés de Almonester, the founder of the hospital, had stipulated that a certain number of beds be reserved for slaves. An outbuilding not far from the central structure served as an asylum for the mentally ill and as quarters for those suffering from contagious diseases. This building contained twenty-four beds.

Deaths were frequent, not so much because of the quality of the medical care at the hospital, but because the hospital had such a bad name that patients delayed entering it until they were beyond help. It was for this reason that the city council, in August, 1820, made the decision to employ three doctors and three apothecaries to visit poor patients in their homes—a service that found favor with the public while also reducing the pressure on the hospital staff.

The Charity Hospital was not the only facility for treating the sick and infirm in New Orleans. There were two or three private clinics in the city, the best known of which was run by Dr. Davidson. Here the patients were free "to choose their own physicians"; the clinics offered "private rooms, comfortable beds, and efficient nurses." The rates ranged from seventy-five cents to two dollars a day; the lower price was the one charged to slaves, who were lodged in a separate building. Dr. Davidson succeeded in obtaining a government contract to establish a hospital specifically for sailors and merchant seamen. He subsequently added a wing to his clinic, which was now called the Orleans Infirmary and Marine Hospital. For the Charity Hospital, which had long suffered from overcrowding, the transfer of the seamen to Dr. Davidson's new establishment was a great boon. For the seamen themselves, the opening of the Marine Hospital meant that they need not fear being turned away from the Charity Hospital to risk death in a wretched boardinghouse or in the streets.

Bleeding, Calomel, and Advertisements

The American doctors considered their French colleagues old-fashioned, unenterprising, and generally ineffectual. But if the French practitioners seldom cured their patients, the Americans often killed them. American doctors seemed temperamentally inclined to "battle nature." They believed that if a small dose of medication was helping the patient, a stronger dose would be sure to cure him. The

patients themselves encouraged this attitude, for they tended to regard a prudent physician as indecisive, a reckless one as bold and
courageous. This was the age of calomel ("sweet mercury") and
phlebotomy. According to Rudolph Matas, the doctors, with the encouragement of their intrepid invalids, prescribed mercury in doses
that "they would hardly dare administer to a mule" and then bled
the patients white.

Yellow fever claimed many victims every year. So also did calomel, which the American doctors frequently mixed with rum "to
sustain the patient." Under the circumstances, we can understand
why some of them died laughing.

The French physicians had little faith in calomel as a cure for
yellow fever. But, like the Americans, they had a tendency to pre-
scribe medication in very strong doses. In his *Essay on the Yellow
Fever in America*, the eminent Dr. P. F. Thomas, Secretary General
of the Medical Society of New Orleans, addressed his colleagues as
follows: "European physicians will generally find the recommended
doses excessively large . . . but they must take into consideration the
fact that medication here requires double the dosage used in Europe
to attain the same degree of efficacy, because of the relaxation of the
fibrous tissues conditioned by the warm and humid climate."

In addition to calomel, doctors employed herb teas, laxatives, and
emetics. Quinine, castor oil, and morphine formed part of their
medical arsenal; and in treating venereal diseases, each had his own
favorite mercury compound. Syphilis and gonorrhea were widespread
in Louisiana, especially among the blacks, and the newspapers of the
period are filled with advertisements for sure-fire remedies. Some of
these announcements refer euphemistically to a "liquid" or "lotion"
for relief of "personal complaints"; others frankly proclaim the merits of their product in curing venereal disease. One physician, with
rarified tact, offered his services to "foreigners (and others) who had
in a moment of inattention contracted a certain illness."

Many doctors, especially those recently arrived in the city, used
the public notice columns of the newspapers to make themselves
known to potential clients and to advertise their specialties. A
French physician, for example, announced in 1825 that he practised
"the latest methods developed in France to cure hunchbacks"; an-

other undertook to cure hemorrhoids, while assuring his female clients of the greatest "discretion." Still another, who managed "a large hospital for blacks," informed his public of a change of address and announced that the new premises would contain "a fumigation chamber for whites," located in his own apartment and wholly separate from the quarters for the blacks.

Throughout the 1820s, a Dr. Raynard de Laferrière extolled the virtues of sulphur baths in the *Louisiana Gazette* and *Le Courrier*. The baths promised a cure for "fungus, ringworm, scabies, ulcers, leprosis (in its early stages), recent attacks of paralysis, long-established rheumatism, low fevers, gout, and all inflammations due to atmospheric conditions, humors, clogged pores, or weak membranes"—a list that would have delighted Molière. Dr. Laferrière's baths, "taken in conjunction with the proper medications," would also bring prompt relief to sufferers from "aching bones, yaws, and all skin ailments resulting from venereal diseases." In short, the baths seem to have been a veritable panacea.

Druggists and dentists also had recourse to the newspapers, the former to cry their wares ("The freshest and purest medications!"), the latter to proclaim their professional qualifications and announce their rates. R. Cowell, we learn, is a dentist from London who "sets artificial dentures with inimitable artistry" and whose "botanical powder" sweetens the breath. Another dentist offers "subscription rates" of ten dollars a year or five dollars a head for families. His price for an artificial front tooth is nine dollars; for a back tooth, five dollars. Another dentist offers "artificial teeth and complete dentures of pure enamel" and announces that he will pull teeth and tooth stubs and also manufactures his "own excellent tooth cleansers."

The practice of medicine was far from being limited to physicians and pharmacists. The countryside was crisscrossed with medicine-men, carrying their patent medicines and "miracle elixirs" to the most remote farm communities. In the streets of New Orleans, black and Indian peddlers proclaimed the virtues of their medicinal roots and herbs. The local newspapers frequently offered their readers home remedies for tumors, boils, and other minor disorders. The *Louisiana Gazette* of July 28, 1820, proposes the following treatment for a wen:

Indian method: first take a pound of new butter, without salt, and lay it in a coal oven; get a bull-frog without hurting it, says the Indian; the frog must be alive; lay the frog with the back down in the butter; bake the frog until it is well done; take it out; pour off the butter in a vessel, and anoint the wen as often as you please in the course of a day. This cure has been tried on a wen that had been growing for thirty years, and had become quite painful with an itching. Ceased the first day this was tried. . . . The application produced a curious sensation as if it was scorching the roots. . . . In eight or nine months the body of the wen was squeezed out without pain.

For yellow fever, it was recommended that a plate of raw onion rings be placed beside the patient's bed to absorb the infection. The onions were to be removed and burned after two or three hours and replaced by fresh rings. The healthy members of the household were encouraged to purge themselves twice a day, wash from head to toe with alkaline soap, and carry about their person a bit of camphor or a clove of garlic. Señor Pontalba, a wealthy and dignified Spaniard resident in New Orleans, had another method for fighting the disease: he sprinkled his home, his servants, and himself with liberal doses of vinegar. He also had some rather original theories on yellow fever, claiming that it was particularly fatal to Englishmen and unmarried women, and that the Americans, who were its first victims, were responsible for introducing the disease into the region.

Berquin-Duvallon saw the matter somewhat differently. He believed that the Americans were particularly susceptible because they came from a cooler climate; their veins, in consequence, were "full of a thicker, more abundant flow of blood," which rendered them more vulnerable to the weakening effects of the local climate than were those who were acclimatized to the heat. Moreover, he explained, the Americans "thoughtlessly indulge themselves with rich, highly spiced foods and strong drink." By way of contrast, he cited the Spaniards, who were accustomed to a simple diet flavored only with garlic, "which they regard as beneficial for the health." He concluded that, on account of their eating habits, "yellow fever, while deadly for the Americans, is of little concern to the Spaniards, and a continual menace to the French."

Dr. P. F. Thomas, a "specialist" in the treatment of yellow fever, had his own theories about the disease. "Young men," he wrote, "are more likely to contract the disease than children or old men, precisely because they are more vigorous" and therefore more prone to "excesses." Newcomers to the region were also susceptible, he explained, because "the rapid and very dramatic change from a cool to a warm climate is accompanied by an increase in the caloric content of the blood, which is generally more free-flowing and more aerated than is that of the local inhabitants." In view of these theories, it is easy to understand why so many doctors resorted to repeated "debilitating" bleedings in their treatment of yellow fever.

THE "VOMITO NEGRO"

Generally speaking, the blacks and the Creoles seem to have been immune to yellow fever. However, the sickness regularly depleted the American and European populations in the city. It was particularly dangerous for newcomers to the region, and recent arrivals were well advised to follow the example of the well-to-do natives and quit the city during the summer months.

Business slowed down during the summer. The cotton and tobacco crops that formed the bulk of the commercial traffic had already been dispatched to Europe or the eastern states; the new harvest would not be in until late October or early November. During this period of respite, Latrobe reports that the merchants took long holidays:

A very large proportion of the commercial community, from October to July, consists of strangers, who purchase or sell as agents or principals, and leave the city when their business is concluded. . . . Those permanent inhabitants of New Orleans who can afford it, and dread the fever, the solitude, and the *ennui* of the city during July, August, and September, go to the Bay St. Louis, or to other places of public resort at that period, and do not return until the middle of October or the beginning of November.

If business kept the menfolk in the city, they dispatched their families to the country during the dangerous period. Only the poor and the imprudent stayed on. In the summer of 1822, when the city was gripped by a virulent epidemic of yellow fever, Mayor Louis Philippe de Roffignac made a commendable effort to aid those citizens most threatened by the disease. He announced that "newcomers and those with limited funds who desire to leave the city will be provided with the means to withdraw to the shores of Lake Pontchartrain until the epidemic comes to an end." Yet few chose to accept the offer, and Dr. Thomas recorded several days after the announcement that "the mayor told me that there were currently three thousand newcomers in town who were likely to contract yellow fever."

Epidemics swept the city in 1817, 1819, 1820, 1822, 1824, 1827, 1829, and 1830. According to the Reverend Clapp, more than nine hundred people died during the summer of 1829. Rudolph Matas notes that the Charity Hospital admitted 1,135 patients in 1821 and 1,689 patients in 1822. The record shows that in 1822 1,082 of the entering patients were cured, 34 "escaped" (whatever that may mean), and 573 died, almost all of them victims of yellow fever. In the same year, the fever attacked the town late but with particular vehemence, claiming the lives of some 1,400 people—"a terrifyingly high number," commented Dr. Thomas, "if one considers that there were few strangers in town, and that the epidemic did not strike until September." Among the victims of the epidemic of 1820 were the architect Latrobe and Pastor Larned. Latrobe, whose vivid descriptions of the New Orleans cemeteries constitute some of the most memorable portions of his memoirs, was himself buried in the Protestant section of the St. Louis cemetery at the side of his son, who had died of yellow fever in 1817.

The doctors could do nothing to control the spread of the disease, and their treatments—washing, bleeding, and calomel—failed to relieve the sufferings of the victims. The causes of the *vomito negro* or "black vomit," as the Spaniards termed yellow fever, eluded the medical profession.

Many doctors believed that the source of the disease was "internal body heat, combined with the humidity of the climate." Dr. Thomas offered a dissenting opinion, contending that "the decay of animal and vegetable matters in the waters, which give off noxious vapors," brought on yellow fever. The eminent émigré French physician, Dr. Nicolas Chervin, conducted a long and painstaking investigation of the disease. His conclusion—that yellow fever was not contagious and that it owed its origins to "the unhealthy air emanating from the swamps and drainage ditches that surround the city"—came close to uncovering the truth. But even if he had succeeded in identifying mosquitoes as bearers of the disease, contemporary medicine would have been powerless either to check its spread or discover a cure.

Any doctor who claimed to have discovered a cure for yellow fever was invariably besieged by patients. The treatment generally consisted of some new technique for purging or a novel method of bloodletting. Some doctors offered bleeding accompanied by pain-killing drugs, gentle laxatives, and tonics; others recommended "the use of moxas over the abdominal region and along the spine," which could be varied with cupping glasses applied to the stomach. Leeches also had their advocates, and the French were partial to a laxative regimen consisting of a potion of potassium nitrate and sodium sulfate, followed by enemas. Naturally, all yellow fever patients were placed on a rigid diet.

In treating yellow fever, the American doctors tended to rely on calomel and massive bloodlettings. A certain Dr. Marshall, "member and Secretary General of the Medical Association," would open a vein in the patient's arm at the onset of the disease, immerse the arm in hot water, and draw off blood until "the head pains disappeared." He then administered diluents and laxatives. If the headaches recurred, he recommenced the bleedings. During the epidemic of 1822, Dr. Marshall employed this method with, we are told, "astonishing success."

Rudolph Matas records that the medical profession also had its share of eccentrics. In place of bleedings, a certain Dr. Dow recommended a good beefsteak and a half-bottle of port, "opportunely administered." Dr. Flood plunged his patients, as a last resort, into an ice-cold bath. One lived to tell the tale: "They (Dr. Flood and the black nurse) poured it, unsparingly, bucket after bucket. It seemed as if the very Mississippi were pouring over me. The shock was terrible." The patient was then vigorously rubbed with towels and wrapped in blankets to make him perspire. This cold water treatment was held in the same scorn by the Creole doctors as were the immoderate use of calomel or the lancet. They prescribed only *warm* baths.

The fear that accompanied an outbreak of yellow fever was due partly to the disease's unpredictable character. The Reverend Clapp has left a graphic account of its symptoms. Some victims, he writes, "are able to work until the last moment, feel quite fine till they fall down and die." Others, after appearing "very sick, then seem to recover." He tells of a man who wrote to inform his family of his recovery and died before his servant had returned from posting the letter. He himself had visited a sick friend one morning, to find him seated at the table reading a newspaper. The invalid seemed in fine fettle. He spoke in such humorous terms of a visitor who had left minutes before "that we both burst into a peal of laughter"—and a moment later he "breathed not again."

The symptoms of yellow fever were frightening and repulsive:

Perhaps there is no acute disease actually less painful than yellow fever, although there is none more shocking . . . to the beholder. Often I have met and shook hands with some blooming, handsome young man to-day, and a few hours afterwards, I have been called to see him in the black vomit, with profuse hemorrhages from the mouth, nose, ears, eyes, and even toes; the eyes prominent, glistening, yellow, and staring; the face discolored with orange color and dusky red.

The appearance of the dead was equally horrible:

The physiognomy of the yellow fever corpses is usually sad, sullen, perturbed; the countenance dark, mottled, livid, swollen, and stained with blood and black vomit; the veins of the face and whole body become distended . . . and though the heart has ceased to beat, the circulation of the blood sometimes continues for hours, quite active as in life.

It was not until the end of the eighteenth century that yellow fever assumed epidemic proportions—"coincidental with the expansion of American commerce into the city," as Berquin-Duvallon remarked pointedly. Many Creoles were not above blaming the Americans for the introduction of the disease.

A City Besieged by Sickness

The epidemic of 1820 was responsible for two hundred deaths. In 1821, yellow fever bypassed New Orleans entirely. The following year, not a single case had been reported in the city by the end of August, and the inhabitants rejoiced that they had been spared once more. At the beginning of September, however, the fever struck with unparalleled violence. "In a short time the number of deaths reached thirty a day, and continued at this terrible rate through the end of October," recorded Dr. Thomas.

The actual figures were undoubtedly higher. Even in ordinary times, some deaths and burials went unrecorded, and during an epidemic, when the doctors, priests, pastors, and gravediggers were overburdened with work, it is understandable that they could not report every victim who passed through their hands. There were also those who died without ever having been seen by a doctor or were hastily buried by self-appointed gravediggers, and those who had been struck down in a backwater bordello and whose bodies were unceremoniously dumped into the adjacent river or swamps.

On September 2, the mayor proclaimed via *Le Courrier*: "Death is within our gates; the whole town is in mourning; most families are in deep bereavement, and everyone is touched by grief." A makeshift hospital was hastily established, and nurses and attendants hired. Chain-gang slaves were commandeered to help the gravediggers, and additional help was recruited from outside the city among indigent laborers. The clergy were instructed to abbreviate their funeral services, and the singing that customarily accompanied funeral processions was curtailed. All the theaters were closed down.

A warm, humid breeze drifted lethargically in from the river. In their patios and gardens, the citizens burned small piles of animal skins, horns, and hooves to ward off infection. Wavering columns of smoke ascended to a leaden sky. The streets were quiet, almost deserted; despite the heat, windows and doors were hermetically sealed against the sickness and death that had taken possession of the town. Occasionally a public official, a minister, a sister of mercy, a doctor, or a slave came into sight, furtively going about his business. At sunset, a few families ventured outdoors to seek some fresh air along the riverbanks; a horseman galloped up the Esplanade, and a pair of lovers could be seen gazing up at the stars.

The levee itself was strangely altered. The river was still crowded with boats, all rocking gently at anchor, but a sinister stillness had descended on the port. The usual jostling mob of people at the market was drastically thinned out; everyone seemed in a hurry to finish his business and get home, with none of the customary lingering at the cafés. Yet although a note of fear pervaded the scene, there was neither panic nor despair. Yellow fever was a presence with which the inhabitants had learned to reckon; its departure, they knew, would be as sudden, as unpredictable—and as certain—as its arrival had been. Shops and places of business remained open, and the newspapers continued to appear. Work continued on the construction sites, though it was slowed down by an inevitable depletion in the size of the crews. In the gaming houses, a faithful band of gamblers still bent absorbedly over their games, and in the sordid dives of the Basin region, where the fever claimed many victims because of the unhealthy condition of both inhabitants and habitations, the whiskey and rum continued to flow. Everyone believed that alcohol prevented infectious illnesses. Drunkards, however, died like everyone else.

It was a trying time for doctors and clergymen. According to the Reverend Clapp, the epidemics never lasted less than six weeks and more usually eight; during that time, he never enjoyed a full night's rest. The only sleep he got was snatched at odd moments in the midst of tending the dead and dying.

One Dr. Cabarrus, writing on September 8, 1824, to a friend, reported: "The fever continues to rage without abatement, except probably a little more manageable than at first; still we bury from 12 to 15 per day. Two of the faculty have gone the way of all flesh, and two others hovering over eternity." The next day he added: "They are both dead this morning. Thank God I still injoy [sic] good health and spirits, tho every day exposed to the fumes of the dying and the dead."

All the hospital beds were taken up, but new patients were continually being brought in. Some lucky ones, aided by a strong constitution, survived both the fever and the overcrowded hospital conditions. The steaming wards and corridors of the hospitals were pervaded by the odor of blood and decay. Black attendants quietly wove their way through the maze of beds and stretchers; a priest passed by bearing the Sacrament; a doctor, his features contorted by fatigue and nausea, leaned over the livid, transfigured countenance of a dying patient. Dr. Thomas noted that many victims died "as though of suffocation, their faces a deep blue."

Behind drawn curtains and closed shutters, families nursed their sick, mourned their dead, or rejoiced in the recovery of a stricken relative. Often they rejoiced too soon. After four or five days, the disease typically went into remission and the patient thought himself cured. Then the fever abruptly returned with renewed strength, striking its victim down just as he had found new hope. Because the doctors seemed helpless to combat the disease, people often had recourse to miracle-workers or healers. Creole slaves and free black women were reputed to possess secret remedies for yellow fever. Karl Pöstl claims: "In 1822, hundreds of patients died in the hands of expert physicians while these old women commonly succeeded in restoring their own patients."

Meanwhile, in households that had remained untouched by the sickness, the family members anxiously awaited the end of the epidemic, which would come in several days or several weeks. Consciously or unconsciously, many of them nourished the belief that if Death had claimed a victim elsewhere, their own chances of being stricken were reduced.

BRING OUT YO' DEAD!

Early in the morning, when the town began to stir and birdsong lifted over rooftops and gardens, a different cry reverberated through the streets. "Bring out yo' dead!" it went; and from the Faubourg St. Mary to the Faubourg Marigny, the municipal hearses made their lugubrious rounds, collecting the previous day's victims among the city poor. The bodies, many of them already in an advanced state of decay, were wrapped in plain linen and piled unceremoniously onto the mule-driven vehicles. The process was often accompanied by heartrending scenes as parents said farewell to their children, husbands and wives to their spouses. But in many instances the bodies were those of friendless transients, newcomers to New Orleans who had taken up residence in small boardinghouses or hotels, while launching themselves on the conquest of the "big town."

The bodies were hastily trundled off to the cemetery to avoid contagion. At the gates of the cemetery, an incongruously festive atmosphere reigned. Street vendors had collected there to cry their savory wares. Inside the gates, the stench was overwhelming, the spectacle horrific. Open graves filled with muddy water were everywhere, as were mounds of bones and disorderly heaps of coffins. The funeral processions were often compelled to make wide detours, axle-deep in mud, to reach their designated gravesite. The coffins, exposed to the noonday sun, attracted clouds of flies whose incessant buzzing and voracious swarming added to the horror of the scene.

The gravediggers, generally black or Irish, hustled the coffins into the hastily dug graves, while the priests or pastors murmured brief prayers at the graveside. Despite the devastating force of the epidemic, the conventions were observed: Catholics, Protestants, and blacks were each relegated to their proper burying grounds. The municipal officials and the population in general took the notion of separation seriously; it was not until the terrible cholera and yellow fever epidemic of 1832 that these regulations were for a few weeks entirely suspended. To keep up their spirits, the Irish gravediggers sang bawdy songs and refreshed themselves at frequent intervals with generous lashings of rum and whiskey. The bones disinterred in the course of the digging were rudely thrust aside with the spade or a kick of a boot, along with the curse: "Room for yo' betters, God damn ye!" It sometimes happened that the number of fever victims exceeded the supply of coffins; then some of the bodies were lowered into their graves wrapped only in a sheet and subsequently covered over with a thin layer of lime.

The gentry, of course, were buried with more dignity and decorum, though with the same haste. Their bodies were accompanied to the cemetery by those members of the family, if any, who had not fled the city at the outbreak of the epidemic. If a vault or tomb was not available, the grave was dug by the family slaves. Edward Tinker writes that it frequently happened that the grave was filled with water and the coffin floated on the surface. "They would not sink until the slaves, holding hands to balance themselves, stood on each end and see-sawed." If the coffin still refused to sink, a gravedigger punctured a hole in the lid with his pickax to release the captive gases.

There was a steady flow of traffic between the hospital and the burial grounds, and funeral convoys crossed and recrossed frequently on route. However, there came a time when the traffic began to diminish as the weather grew less stifling and the outbreaks of fever less frequent. One by one, the shuttered houses began to open, and people could be seen taking the evening air on their balconies. Gradually the streets regained their animation, the cafés their clientele, the city its atmosphere of frivolity. The doctors and clergymen were finally able to get some rest. In the midst of the burgeoning joy and good humor, people again turned their conversations to marriage, parties, balls, the theater. As Reverend Clapp reports,

The epidemy is over. Then in New Orleans, health reigns again; absentees and strangers are rushing back home. The weather is as charming as that of paradise. All is stir, bustle, cheerfulness, gaiety and hope. Doctors are at leisure; posts of employment, made vacant by the recent mortality, are soon filled by strangers, as young, ardent, hopeful and sanguine as were their predecessors, and destined, most of them, to share the same fate.

New Orleans had resumed its cheerful aspect.

8

Pleasures and Pastimes

Life in New Orleans seemed an endless round of entertainments. On the slightest excuse, plans for a party, ball, parade, or public celebration were set afoot. During the "season," the whole city put on its dancing shoes. One American visitor, Joseph H. Ingraham, remarked that "during a single winter" the citizens managed "to execute about as much dancing, music, laughing and dissipation as would serve any reasonably disposed, staid and sober citizens for three or four years." Saxe-Weimar noted: "No day passed over this winter which did not produce something pleasant or interesting; each day, however, was nearly the same as its predecessors. . . . Dinners, evening parties, plays, masquerades, and other amusements followed close on each other, and were interrupted only by little circumstances which accompany life in this hemisphere, as well as in the other." Until 1830, every concert was customarily followed by a ball; sometimes a theatrical performance or an opera also served as the occasion for a ball. During carnival season, all levels of society had the opportunity to indulge their passion for dancing. There were balls for everybody, even for children as young as four years old. A contemporary newspaper account reveals that the popular balls at the Orleans and Saint-Philippe ballrooms were often preceded by "children's balls"; apparently the children behaved with a suavity and grace that did credit to their dancing instructors. Saxe-Weimar reports that the little girls, from the age of ten on, were "dressed and coiffured like grown up young ladies."

On the night of Mardi Gras, all the places of amusement were thrown open to the public, and the Théâtre d'Orléans was the site of a grand ball attended by the city's social elite. A platform was extended from the parterre to the stage, and a passageway was created between the theater and the adjacent Orleans Hall, where a second orchestra held forth. This passageway permitted the gentlemen to move back and forth between the society ladies in the theater and the quadroons in Orleans Hall without attracting attention. The duke of Saxe-Weimar observes that there were many wallflowers at the society balls, for the men tended to drift off to the ladies of mixed blood, with whom "the white women could not hope to compete for attractiveness."

Nevertheless, the society balls were splendid occasions. Commenting on the carnival of 1824, the *Louisiana Gazette* editorialized:

The six balls held on successive Fridays at the Orleans Hall presented a gracious blend of beauty, good taste and decorum. The allure of our ladies owes little to the glitter of gold, sapphires, emeralds or diamonds. It is due rather to the diaphanous stuff of their gowns, the clinging tulle that sets off their slender figures, while the very flowers that adorn their lustrous hair blush for envy. In our spacious, richly ornamented ballrooms, where the glitter of a thousand candles is multiplied a thousandfold by mirrors, two hundred young beauties rival each other for grace, elegance, vivacity and youthful ardor. Paris himself would have tried, without a doubt, to divide the apple among each and every one of them.

In contrast to such effusions, Saxe-Weimar soberly reports that at the balls given every Tuesday and Friday at the French Theater, to which only the best families were invited, the ladies were "pretty, well-dressed and danced well." The quadroon balls were clearly more alluring for men in search of amorous adventure.

BALLS

During his stay in New Orleans, the duke of Saxe-Weimar explored all the strata of local society. He was a frequent and sought-after guest in the homes of both the Creole and the American aristocracy. He visited the cafés "where the common people pass their time" and attended both the society balls and the public dance halls. He also dropped in on the quadroon balls, attended the American and the French theaters, visited John Davis' gambling casino, and took part in almost all the dinner parties and evening entertainments that occurred during his sojourn in the city. Because of the broad range of his activities, his accounts are of exceptional interest to us, and their value is enhanced by his level-headed tone. Thanks to Saxe-Weimar's memoirs, it is possible to evoke with some accuracy the daily life of the New Orleans man-about-town at the period with which we are concerned.

The "society balls," which enjoyed high favor around this time, were a compromise between public balls and strictly private affairs. They were sponsored by a group of bachelors and young married men, who elected committees to oversee various aspects of the ball's organization: the selection of an appropriate hall, procedures for maintaining order and for keeping out undesirable elements, the sale of tickets. Tickets were generally offered by subscription: for a price between nine and twenty dollars, one could subscribe to a series of six to ten balls. The subscribers could invite up to three ladies of their choice to each dance; heads of families were authorized to bring their wives and daughters. Occasionally, an extra dance was added to the schedule and announced to the subscribers through the newspapers. *L'Argus* for April 20, 1824, announces:

In compliance with the request of a number of distinguished subscribers to the Easter Sunday Ball, we are pleased to announce that a ball will be held this coming Saturday, the 24th. Subscribers may obtain tickets from M. Gicquel, goldsmith, at the corner of Toulouse and Royale Streets; or from M. Duval, 319 Dauphine Street, between St. Philippe and Ursuline Streets.

Society balls were sometimes organized to mark a holiday or honor a visiting celebrity. The ball held for Lafayette in 1825 was such an occasion—though, unlike the usual society ball, that one was thrown open to all who could afford the price of admission. Some eight hundred revelers attended.

The Kings' Ball, a Creole institution dating to colonial times, served as kick-off to the carnival season. It was one of the most elegant and exclusive of the balls. Admission was limited; the organizers took pains to assure that only the very best families received invitations. But all those who had been left out organized their own rival balls, and every January 6th all New Orleans gave itself over to dancing and gaiety. Special pastries were baked for the occasion; toasts were drunk to the newly installed "King and Queen of the Twelfth Cakes," who ruled benevolently over the festivities. Twelfth Night inaugurated a series of parties, both public and private, that continued without pause until Mardi Gras.

Despite its exclusivity, the Kings' Ball was a traditional favorite. A piece of doggerel that appeared in *L'Abeille* in 1828, evidently composed by a writer of republican sentiments, suggests the spirit of the public response:

> If the kings who rule on earth, I say,
> Were kings such as we chose this day,
> Then to those kings I'd lift my glass
> And vow undying love.
> But the world's great monarchs are a sorry lot,
> When compared to the kings our joy has begot,
> So to our kings alone I'll lift my glass
> And vow undying love.

The public balls were far more numerous. The entrance fee was generally a dollar, though there were always some who managed to wangle free tickets. The masquerade ball at Mardi Gras cost two dollars for men and one for women.

The clientele of the public balls was a mixed lot. A French traveler, the baron de Montlezun, who attended a function for "white ladies" at the ballroom in the Rue Condé, recorded with evident bemusement: "A young woman, on finishing a waltz, took up her infant son and offered him the breast, which from the extreme candor of her attire had long been in evidence." Clearly the mores were not those of the highest New Orleans society; Saxe-Weimar reported that, although the ladies' toilettes were often elegant, "most of the dancers did not belong to the highest social stratum." Excitement ran high, and at some point in the evening a fight was certain to break out—which explains why the authorities requested the dancers to check swords, canes, and pistols at the door.

The brawls began in the ballroom with kicks or punches and sometimes continued all the way to the checkroom, where more lethal weapons were called into play. Although gentlemen of good family were not above putting in an appearance at these affairs, a respectable woman would never risk attending a public ball, even under cover of a mask or domino.

MASKED BALLS

Public masked balls were forbidden by the civic authorities until 1827, as were all street masquerades. However, the tradition of the annual Mardi Gras masquerade dated back almost to the founding of the city. Masked balls were a form of entertainment much enjoyed by the wealthy and the common folk alike. Kaintucks, military deserters, thieves, outlaws, desperadoes, and ruffians of all sorts swelled the ranks of Mardi Gras revelers, adding a note of menace to the festivities. The blacks added to the confusion: under cover of masquerade, they mingled with whites in places normally denied to them, in public ballrooms and even private homes. After a number of disturbing incidents, the Spaniards made it illegal to wear a mask in public. The ban was lifted when the city passed into American hands but was reinstated in 1806, when it was thought that Aaron Burr and his fellow-conspirators were intending to take refuge in New Orleans.

Of course, the members of high society continued to hold their own masked balls, and because they produced no public scandal, the authorities did not interfere. *L'Argus* spoke in 1824 of the "many magnificent" masked balls held in the city during Mardi Gras and emphasized that these events were attended by "order and decorum." During the next few years, there were numerous attempts to persuade the town fathers to rescind the ban, but a few leading citizens always intervened to block these efforts. Finally, in 1827, a group of merrymakers decided to go ahead with plans to organize a series of "masked balls and masquerades" to conclude the carnival season, despite the fact that the motion to restore masquerades was still pending before the city council. On December 15, Mayor de Roffignac made a formal appeal to the council to amend the existing regulations. A special committee was appointed by the civic authorities to gather information on this delicate matter. Meanwhile, on December 19, two hundred "respectable citizens" addressed a petition to the mayor; they too requested the restoration of masquerades. After a long and acrimonious debate in the council, the "yeas" won the day. On January 5, 1828, a delighted populace learned that henceforth masked balls would be permitted in the city from January 1 until Mardi Gras. *L'Abeille* jubilantly proclaimed: "At long last the wearing of disguises has come back to public usage! Rejoice all ye rakes and boulevardiers who are somewhat past your prime, and ye fair ladies whose charms have been tarnished by time! Rejoice, for masks are no longer forbidden!"

Masked balls and costume balls became the rage. Often the dancers were requested not only to disguise themselves, but to act out a role appropriate to their attire. Such was the case at the "grand costume ball and charade" given on Saint Joseph's Day, 1828. Although addicted to this entertainment, the people of New Orleans do not seem to have displayed either originality or finesse in acting out their assumed roles. Ann Farrar, the young daughter of a Natchez plantation owner, who regularly wintered in New Orleans along with her mother, reported that at one such ball she saw a masked reveler playing the part of "an intoxicated Indian," another "disguised as an old woman"; as she wrote to her father, she could not understand how anyone could take pleasure in such carryings-on. Karl Pöstl, for his part, noticed several young businessmen and planters attired as poor Irish laborers and conducting themselves in what they imagined was an appropriately rowdy manner—a spectacle that he found devoid of charm or edification.

In general, the Americans failed to appreciate the Creoles' buoyant good humor and joie de vivre, nor did they share their devotion to dancing and other forms of revelry. In addition, they strongly disapproved of participating in such pastimes on Sunday, the Lord's Day. As Henry Kmen reports, the concept that "religion ought to inspire cheerfulness and that cheerfulness is associated with religion" was completely alien to the Puritan mentality. The Americans hoped that their upright example would lead the Creoles to mend their ways. Actually, the influence seems to have gone the other way. Although the Protestants continued to hold the Sabbath in respect, they relaxed their standards for the rest of the week and joyfully succumbed to the pleasures of the dance. It was the Americans, in fact, who eventually converted New Orleans' Mardi Gras into a celebrated tourist event that attracted visitors from all over the world.

The first Mardi Gras parade—a simple, spontaneous affair—took place in 1827. A group of young men, "newly returned from Paris" and dressed in "outlandish" garb, marched through the streets of the Vieux Carré, swinging cowbells, banging on pots, blowing toy horns and whistles, and singing at the top of their lungs, to the half-irritated, half-admiring glances of the local populace. Each year after that, the celebration grew in size and ambitiousness, with assembled crowds of Creole and American youth parading noisily through the town on their way to various Mardi Gras costume balls. They shouted, sang, hurled ribald compliments at the young ladies who gazed down on them from their balconies—and, in short, behaved with total abandon. Yet these early processions were still informal and spontaneous. The first organized Mardi Gras parade, planned and sponsored by the civic authorities, did not take place until 1838. According to witnesses, "the spectacle surpassed anything seen before."

The return of the masquerades prompted an outburst of popular enthusiasm and popular raucousness. An article in the *Louisiana Gazette* for February 17, 1829, refers to the brawls following "every dance" at the public ball held in the Union Hall and to the "many occasions for disorder because of the disguises." It appears that the honest burghers who had opposed legalizing masquerades may have had some justification. However, according to the *Gazette*, "the police was so active and the surveillance and vigilance" so good that the brawls did not degenerate into riots. That there were some very close calls we learn from the same *Gazette* journalist. Returning to his rooms in Ursuline Street at the small hours of the morning, he found his path strewn with prostrate forms. Even when he was safely indoors, "it was impossible to sleep, for at every instant the noise from the blows by the fist, the cane, and the daggers mingled together with the cries of those assaulted and the furious shouts of those who were attacking." The journalist concludes his article: "For once, what a pleasant Mardi Gras!" Evidently there is no accounting for tastes.

Sumptuous Repasts

Of the three main ballrooms of New Orleans, the Orleans was unquestionably the most splendid. Situated on the second floor of an elegant building adjacent to the Théâtre d'Orléans, the ballroom was a long rectangle with a high ceiling and three rows of benches arranged as in an amphitheater. The room was illuminated by seventeen crystal chandeliers, suspended from the ceiling by wrought-iron garlands of roses. In every corner, colored glass reflected the light. A row of windows opened onto a long balcony overlooking Orleans Street; at one end of the room, a broad stairway led down to the garden, where the dancers could repair to catch their breath and quench their thirst. When the hall was rented for a society ball, a supper was laid in the adjoining room. The food was undoubtedly sumptuously prepared in the best Creole tradition, but the service seems occasionally to have been less than elegant.

The architect Latrobe reports on a "magnificent ball" that he attended on the occasion of Washington's Birthday:

There were about three hundred gentlemen present, and probably four hundred ladies. When supper was ready, old Mr. Fortier, an old creole of about seventy . . . stopped the dancing, and wailed out: "Il y a cinquante couverts, cinquante dames au souper, au souper, au souper!" About one hundred, however, sat down, and the gentlemen stood behind their chairs; another and another set succeeded. The third set did not fill the table, and the gentlemen scrambled for seats.

Several local dignitaries, including the governor of Louisiana and the mayor of New Orleans, were, however, left standing; but the fortunate young men who had secured places showed no inclination to relinquish them. Latrobe qualifies this incident as "a remarkable instance of the democratic character of the citizens"—a generous description of what to most eyes would have appeared simply a remarkable instance of bad manners.

Caught up in the rhythm of the orchestra, the Creoles danced on for hours, and the balls were invariably prolonged far into the night. Saxe-Weimar reported that "two cotillions and a waltz are danced in succession, and there is hardly an interval of two or three minutes between the dances. The music was performed by negroes and gens de color and was pretty good." Most of the musicians were blacks, slaves, or freemen; occasionally, however, ensembles were made up of musicians newly arrived from Europe. Henry A. Kmen notes: "In 1829, even in a ballroom of the second rank, one found orchestras with fifteen musicians." The owners of the cafés, cabarets, and saloons often hired musicians to satisfy their customers' craving for dancing; and in 1826 the first "dime-a-dance" halls appeared in the city—though the actual price was then six and a quarter cents.

BLACK AND WHITE BALLS

We possess little information on the dance hall girls, their identities, or conditions of work. In all probability, they plied their trade in the dance halls and dives of the Basin, where the humblest elements of New Orleans society—laborers, artisans, free blacks, and slaves—mingled with sailors on shore leave, Kaintucks on a spree, and a mixed lot of drifters, ruffians, and thieves. The sordid establishments of the Swamp had no monopoly on vice, however, and it is likely that the dance hall girls did not limit their business to the dance floor. They were probably free black women, too dark of skin and curly of hair to pass themselves off as anything but what they were, and obliged to sell their bodies for a few coppers to any customer who came along. They could not aspire to the neat little cottages on Rampart Street.

Those desirable habitations were reserved for the prettiest, most fair-skinned, and accomplished of the courtesans, whose outward poise and polish concealed the poverty of their backgrounds. The landscape architect Frederick Law Olmsted summed up their situation, which was well understood by all:

Their beauty and attractiveness being their fortune, they cultivate and cherish with diligence every charm or accomplishment they are possessed of. Of course, men are attracted by them, and, not being able to marry them legally and with the usual forms and securities for constancy, make such arrangements "as can be agreed upon." When a man makes a declaration of love to a girl of this class, she will admit or deny, as the case may be, her happiness in receiving it; but supposing she is favorably disposed, she will usually refer the applicant to her mother. The mother inquires into the circumstances of the suitor; ascertains whether he is able to maintain a family; and if satisfied with him in these and other respects, requires from him security that he will support her daughter in a style suitable to the habits she has been bred to, and that if he should ever leave her, he will give her a certain sum for her future support, and a certain additional sum for each of the children she shall then have.

The negotiations were usually initiated at the quadroons' ball. Their elaboration and outcome depended on the attractiveness of the subject, the fairness of her complexion, and her mother's ability to play her off against the competition.

The origin of the quadroons' ball—or the Blue Ribbon Ball, as it was sometimes called—is unknown, as is the name of the founder. What is known is that in 1799 a Monsieur Coquet, along with his associate Monsieur Boniquet, obtained permission from the municipal authorities to organize a public ball for the city's free blacks. We also know that, during the carnival season, the officers of the free black militia units had been accustomed to organize their own balls. In November, 1805, this same Coquet began to organize twice-weekly balls for free black women; with the exception of the musicians, black males were excluded. Yet similar balls had apparently been held in New Orleans for some time, to judge from the 1805 account of Judge Thomas C. Nichols: "Drums beat occasionally at the corners of the streets . . . to inform the public that on such and such night there would be a grand ball at the salle de Condé, or to make announcement of a ball of another sort, for coloured ladies and white gentlemen."

From 1809 on, Blue Ribbon balls were held in all the city's public ballrooms; by 1815, they had become as much an institution as had Mardi Gras itself. At the beginning, these balls attracted an unsavory element of the white population; Henry Kmen reports that they were prone to "smelling bad, starting fights or chewing tobacco and spitting vanilla." In order to remedy the situation, the price of admission was raised. "A ticket to the Quadroons' Ball," wrote Saxe-Weimar, "is now two dollars, so that only people of a certain social rank can afford to attend." During his stay in New Orleans, Saxe-Weimar saw a number of these balls, and he was favorably impressed by the grace, modesty, and good manners of the quadroons: "Several of these females have enjoyed the benefits of as careful an education as most of the whites; they conduct themselves ordinarily with more propriety and decorum and confer more happiness on their 'friends' than many white ladies to their married lords."

The gentlemen attended the quadroon balls singly or in groups, arriving after a party or a formal dinner or dropping in for a few minutes in the midst of a society ball. Fathers brought their sons, uncles their nephews, godfathers their godchildren. Gentlemen passing through New Orleans made a point of stopping by, and visiting dignitaries were ceremoniously conducted to a Blue Ribbon ball by their hosts.

The white women maintained a discreet silence when their menfolk excused themselves in the middle of a social function to "take a bit of fresh air," or "drop in at the gaming rooms." Even the most naïve of them knew the true disposition of things, but their strict upbringing forbade all protest, and feigned ignorance seemed the best means of saving face. As Saxe-Weimar confesses, "We returned to the white ball without disclosing where we had been." One can imagine the ironic smiles and piercing looks with which the women greeted their errant escorts.

The quadroons' ball was a subject that no gentleman ever mentioned in mixed company. When the ladies were by themselves, however, they must have discussed the topic at great length, with great curiosity and little charity to spare for their rivals the quadroons.

A PASSION FOR DANCING

Though black men were banned from the Blue Ribbon balls, they had ample opportunity to dance elsewhere. In the exuberant city of New Orleans, every social group had its balls and celebrations—especially at carnival time. The owners of the public ballrooms sponsored dances for whites, for quadroon women and white men, and for blacks. The whole town danced, but not together.

The Creoles seemed never to get enough of dancing. When they were not going out to balls, they danced at home, with friends, or simply with family. The *soirée dansante* or dinner-dance was a common form of entertainment dating back to the time of Governor Vaudreuil. The marquis de Vaudreuil had set the tone for Creole society; according to contemporary accounts, his balls and receptions were not unworthy of Versailles. Among the upper-class Creoles, evening at-homes were sumptuous affairs, even when the guests were limited to relatives and close friends.

The at-homes usually took place on Sunday evenings. They began with an elaborate dinner, after which young and old alike danced to the music of a piano or an orchestra. Around eleven o'clock, more refreshments were served. The guests took their leave shortly after midnight.

During Lent, everyone piously refrained from dancing, except when the occasion absolutely demanded it. Fortunately, that was quite often: there was always a birthday or anniversary to commemorate, a distinguished visitor to honor, or a fund-raising ball for some deserving charity—a widow with five children, a destitute family, abandoned infants. Washington's Birthday on February 22 provided the occasion for a series of splendid balls that involved almost the entire city. Without calling the patriotism of the citizens into question, one suspects that Washington's Birthday was the more fervently celebrated because it came as a break from the sobriety of the Lenten season.

To tell the truth, the people of New Orleans danced all year round, except for Holy Week itself. Baudry des Lozières notes that their passion for dancing "reached its height during the winter," but this should not lead us to believe that they lost interest during the long months of summer. Neither the dreadful heat, nor the long distances they were obliged to travel, nor the torment of the mosquitoes could turn them from their favorite pastime. Gentlemen were known to ride twenty miles on horseback in the dark of night through forests and swamps in order to attend a ball. At the height of the season, entire families boarded a steamboat or crowded into a coach to attend a dance at a friend's plantation.

The hospitality at the plantations matched the generosity of their proportions, and an evening ball often served as an opportunity for guests to spend several days in the country. In the course of the spring and summer, a plantation owner made sure to host at least one ball and often several. Some planters had the foresight to train their slaves as musicians; thus, the estate was never without a resident orchestra. In addition, the planter's family generally included some musical members: an aunt who played the piano, an uncle whose lively fiddling set the pace for the quadrilles. Some of the more prosperous landowners, whose estates were not too distant from New Orleans, made it a practice to import dance orchestras from the city.

The annual exodus of the city's first families at the outset of summer failed to dampen the ordinary folk's enthusiasm for balls and dances. During the hottest months, they could seek out the popular dance halls along Bayou St. John or on the shores of Lake Pontchartrain. There they could dance all night long and gamble as well. For gambling was another New Orleans obsession, perhaps an even stronger one than dancing.

A Craze for Gambling

Throughout the eighteenth century, visitors to New Orleans were wont to remark on the citizens' predilection for gambling. During the nineteenth century, this predilection developed into an all-consuming passion. In New Orleans, people bet on a hand of cards, a throw of the dice, races, lottery tickets. They gambled day and night, at home and in gaming houses. And they played for large stakes: at this period, there were no limits placed on bets, and it sometimes happened that a player lost $25,000 in a single sitting.

Fortunes changed hands with a roll of the dice; men were known to play away their homes, land, furniture, and slaves. Gambling became the chief vice of the Creole community. It was by no means limited to the aristocracy: virtually the entire male population, from Bernard de Marigny to the most down-and-out Chaca, haunted the gambling tables. "Most after-work social gatherings are convened for the purpose of gambling, and access to the tables is only too easily granted," remarks Claude Robin in the account of the region that he published in 1807. He continues:

The most solidly founded fortunes totter and fall, while those just being established collapse even more quickly. A sea captain loses at a sitting the profits of a long voyage, and even enjoins in his loss the cargo entrusted to his care. The boatman relinquishes the fruits of his far-flung journeying. The frontiersman is stripped of the money earned by much toil and peril, and now lacks the wherewithal to resume his labors. The farmer, who has come to town to dispose of the year's harvest and supply his family with provisions for the coming year and his poor blacks with clothing, is compelled to return home empty-handed, unless he resorts to the ruinous ministrations of the towns' many moneylenders.

If this account appears exaggerated, we need only recall that Bernard de Marigny, whose fortune appeared limitless, ended his days in penury.

The same reckless spirit that prevailed in the city's gaming houses could be found in the homes of the rich. The Louisianian W. Adolphe Roberts has an anecdote whose subject, Antoine-Julien Meffre-Rouzan, was a respected Creole social leader and an inveterate gambler who regularly assembled his friends at his home for a game of cards. Before his guests arrived, Meffre-Rouzan would fill a large Sèvres vase that stood in the hallway with banknotes. If, in the course of the game, any player lost all his money, he could discreetly withdraw from the room, replenish his supply from the Sèvres vase, and leave a promissory note in the vase for the amount he had borrowed. If he proved unable to recoup his losses in the course of the evening, he would send around a slave first thing next morning with the money he owed his host. Meffre-Rouzan "never counted or checked" the money in the vase or the sums remitted him in the morning. When a guest once commented on this seeming indifference to gain, Rouzan disdainfully replied that he had no reason to suppose that any of his acquaintances would ever take advantage of his trust.

Until the 1820s, the city's gaming halls had few pretensions to elegance. Even the establishment run by John Davis, the ambitious and enterprising proprietor of the Théâtre d'Orléans, was described by Saxe-Weimar as "obscure chambers, resembling caverns." But in 1827 Davis built a gambling casino on the corner of Orleans and Bourbon streets that was designed to give full expression to his grandiose imagination and to flatter the tastes of the wealthiest and most discriminating citizens in the city. The rooms were large and elegantly appointed, with soft velvet and damask complementing the glittering chandeliers and the giltwork. To encourage trade, Davis kept the casino open day and night, seven days a week. He staffed the rooms with croupiers and dealers imported from Europe, who relieved one another on four-hour shifts. On Sunday nights, the proprietor treated his clientele to a sumptuous dinner, complete with fine wines. Not surprisingly, the fame of the Davis casino quickly spread beyond the confines of the city and state to every part of the country. A few years later, Davis opened a casino on Bayou St. John that rivaled the earlier one for luxury but was open only from Saturday noon to Monday morning.

The other gaming houses in the city were drearily functional compared to Davis'. Nevertheless, they were seldom short of clients, who flocked there to play roulette, faro, or twenty-one. Poker was introduced around 1825. It came via the steamboats and soon spread throughout the city. At first, it was the game of sailors, Kaintucks, and quick-witted adventurers who had perceived that handsome profits could be derived from the game. In the smoky back rooms of taverns and dance halls, poker soon became the game of choice. At this period, there were already a good many professional cardsharps in New Orleans, but they restricted their activities to the brothels and saloons of Girod Street or Tchoupitoulas Street. Their physical appearance—shifty, shopworn, prone to violence—entirely suited their setting. The dandified gambler in his immaculate white suit, with courtly manners and a fine Havana cigar between smiling lips—the figure so beloved of Hollywood—was a product of Mississippi steamboat travel and was seldom seen ashore.

In polite society, there were innumerable ways for a gentleman to part with his money. The general public, as we have seen, was partial to faro, roulette, and twenty-one; the aristocracy favored écarte and braque. The Americans, except for those of Puritan stock, were equally addicted to gambling. One of the city's most celebrated gamblers was the brilliant Virginia lawyer, John R. Grimes, who was said to have lost about fifty thousand dollars a year over the course of ten years. Grimes was known locally for his huge gambling losses, his eloquent courtroom appeals, his extravagant tips, and his elaborate dinners, which were attended by the cream of New Orleans society. Saxe-Weimar has left an account of one such occasion:

After the second course large folding doors opened, and we beheld another dining room in which stood a table with the dessert. We withdrew from the first table and seated ourselves at the second, in the same order in which we had partaken of the first. As the variety of wines began to act upon the tongues of the guests at liberty, the ladies rose, retired to another apartment and resorted to music for amusement. Some of the gentlemen remained with the bottle, while others, among whom I was one, followed the ladies. . . . We waltzed until ten o'clock.

The Americans were evidently quick to adapt to Creole habits, abandoning themselves without shame or apology to a passion for gambling. The craze was not confined to the men. At teatime in the best Creole houses, one might see the ladies assembled around a gaming table, playing among themselves for very tidy sums.

GAMES AND ENTERTAINMENTS

Billiards, backgammon, checkers, and dominoes were the most popular games of the period. In 1828, there existed no less than thirty-nine billiard parlors in New Orleans. The other games were played not only at home, but also in the cafés, where many idlers spent entire days. These games were not altogether harmless: they too were played for money. One could stake the contents of purse or wallet on a game of dominoes or backgammon. The higher the wager, the greater the excitement of the players—and of the onlookers, who crowded around the table, commenting on every move and even laying down bets of their own on the outcome, for all the world as if they were attending a cockfight.

Saxe-Weimar had the impression that the cafés were the meeting place of the common folk of New Orleans. In point of fact, many of the cafés of the Vieux Carré also counted among their clientele both American businessmen and Creole aristocrats. The most fashionable cafés were situated on Royale and Chartres streets, with the exception of the Café des Améliorations, which stood at the corner of Rampart and Toulouse streets.

Every day for many years, a small group of elderly Creole revolutionaries gathered at the Café des Améliorations to vilify the American regime and elaborate schemes for liberating the city from the "barbarian oppressors" and returning it to the just and beneficent dominion of France. One of the group, a gentleman named Chevalier, remained loyal to the fashions of his youth and affected a powdered wig, knee breeches, silk stockings, and buckled shoes.

Among the best known establishments was the Café des Refugiés. In former days it had been a tavern, frequented by brigands, with the colorful name of the *Veau qui tête* ("The Suckling Calf"). Its present clientele consisted mainly of refugees from Santo Domingo, who indulged in interminable discussions over innumerable glasses of *petit Goyave* (a concoction whose recipe has, alas, been lost to history) concerning a subject dear to their hearts: the French government's failure to compensate them as promised for their losses.

The café most popular with the ordinary folk was the Maspero, located on the second floor of the Maspero Exchange, a long wooden structure erected during the early years of the nineteenth century. This unpretentious building, with its exposed beams and simple decor, served as the site for almost all the commercial transactions between the merchants, brokers, and exporters. When the English threatened to attack the city in 1814, it was here that General Andrew Jackson and his staff met to draw up the battle plans that would ultimately result in the defeat of General Pakenham's redcoats.

One section of the café was reserved for members of the press. For many years, there was only one mail delivery a day, around eleven o'clock in the morning, and all the newspapermen in town congregated at the Maspero at lunchtime, both to discuss the latest news and to match wits over backgammon and dominoes.

Horse races were another popular form of entertainment. The Jockey Club, whose membership included most of the gentlemen of good family in the city, held regular meets on a track made available by General Hampton, a well-to-do planter and raiser of livestock. In 1826, the meets were transferred to the municipal racetrack at Jackson, a few miles downstream from New Orleans. The meets were patronized by a large and elegantly dressed public whose fervor was assured by the extravagance of their bets.

New Orleans offered both inhabitants and visitors a wide range of entertainments, some of which, it must be admitted, catered to their baser tastes. Cockfights, dogfights, and bullfights were held on a regular basis. Newspapers carried advertisements for these bloodthirsty contests. On a single Sunday, for example, the public could choose between four such events. In the first, an Attakapas bull would be pitted against "six of the largest dogs of the region"; in the second, six bulldogs would fight a Canadian bear; the third would pit a "tiger" against a brown bear, while the fourth would feature twelve dogs and an Opelousas bull. "If the tiger is not vanquished by the bear," the announcement continues, "he will engage in single combat with the last-named bull; and if the latter vanquishes all his adversaries, fireworks will be set off on his back, which is sure to supply an amusing spectacle."

The fact that these entertainments were held on Sunday made them all the more shocking to visitors from New England or Britain. It is easy to see why New Orleans came to be regarded by outsiders as a notoriously wicked city.

In 1830, an English traveler, James Stuart, came to the city's defense: "British writings about looseness of manners among the people (of New Orleans) is false. Excepting only the appearance of lottery offices and billiard rooms, vice is much more prominent in London, and even in Edinburgh, and, I suspect, in most of the European cities, than in New Orleans." On the subject of prostitution, Stuart comments:

Females of light character are nowhere seen on the streets, or public resorts, or at the doors or in the lobbies of theaters; and there seems to me to be more perfect propriety of conduct at the theaters here than at any public place of any description in Britain, and more general attention to dress here than there. In fact, everybody who goes to the French Theater here must dress in the same way as if going to the opera house in London.

THEATER AND OPERA

The Creoles were devoted to both theater and opera and for many years cherished the hope that they would be able to establish a resident company of first-class performers. In 1791, the dream came partly true. A small acting troupe from Santo Domingo arrived in the city. Because no theater was available, they staged their performances out of doors, in a tent, or on the patio of some hospitable café or hotel. Soon the company took up residence in a hall on St. Peter Street. There it remained for some years, performing Molière and Boieldieu with rudimentary sets and a great deal of verve. In 1810, the company moved to the newly built Saint-Philippe Theater. This structure is said to have cost some $100,000; it boasted a spacious parterre and two tiers of boxes and could accommodate up to seven hundred people. Plays were presented alternately in English and French, to please both constituencies. It was at this theater that New Orleans' first ballet performance was staged—an event that made a lasting impression on the theater-going public. But the Saint-Philippe Theater could not withstand the competition of the Théâtre d'Orléans and the American theater, and by 1832 the building was being used only for dances.

Théâtre St. Philippe, 1810. From an engraving by Jacques Tanesse.

It was, in fact, no easy matter to enter into competition with two such dynamic and indefatigable promoters as the Santo Domingan John Davis and the American James Caldwell. Both men were fervently committed to making their theater the best in the region, not only from the point of view of profits, but of artistic prestige as well. The honor of their constituencies—one Creole, the other American—was at stake. Their rivalry worked to the advantage of the people of New Orleans, for it meant that the city had two theaters

Théâtre d'Orléans, 1813. From an engraving by Jacques Tanesse.
Louisiana Collection, LSU Library

whose renown extended beyond the city and even the state. However, the quality of the productions was uneven and did not always live up to the ambitions of the producers.

Karl Pöstl and Saxe-Weimar have both left valuable accounts of the theatrical life of New Orleans. The French theater remained open eight months of the year at this period, the American theater for five months. Pöstl writes that the latter "is gaining rapidly in popularity, although its audience is presently drawn largely from the humbler elements: boatmen, Kentuckians, Mississippi merchants, hunters and trappers." Pöstl, who was something of a connoisseur of music, attended a performance of Weber's *Der Freischütz*, "here transformed into *The Black Huntsman of Bohemia*"—an alteration which, he feared, boded ill for the production. Pöstl's premonition was unhappily justified:

Six violins, which played anything but music, and some voices far from being human, performed the opera, which was applauded. The Kentuckians expressed their satisfaction in a hurrah, which made the very walls tremble. The interior of the theater had still a mean appearance. The curtain consists of sail cloths, and the horrible smell of whiskey and tobacco is a sufficient drawback for any person who would attempt to frequent this place of amusement.

By coincidence, Saxe-Weimar attended the same production. He echoes some of his compatriot's strictures on the quality of both performers and audience:

The orchestra was very weak and badly filled; hardly any of the performers could sing. The decorations, nevertheless, were tolerably good. I found the boxes and galleries thronged; in the pit were but a few spectators, and those consisted of sailors and countrymen from Kentucky who made themselves quite at ease on the benches and cracked nuts during the finest piece of music—a custom I have noted in all English theaters.

Saxe-Weimar is much kinder, however, about the ambiance. The theater, he remarks, was decorated "not untastefully," and the gas-lit auditorium possessed "a very handsome chandelier."

The French theater attracted a more refined and less heterodox audience, and Saxe-Weimar naturally felt more at ease there. The elegant hall contained a parterre, two tiers of boxes (some of them screened off, permitting families in mourning to view the spectacle without being seen), a first balcony for free blacks, and a second balcony for slaves. The duke found the actors "just tolerable" and compared the level of performance to that of a French provincial theater—hardly a compliment. The resident companies seem to have been mediocre, although from time to time visiting actors enlivened the scene. In the winter of 1827–28, the great tragic actor Edwin Booth, father of Lincoln's assassin, played the roles of King Lear and Richard III before rapt audiences in the Camp Street Theater, as well as offering two performances of *Orestes* to overflow crowds at the Théâtre d'Orléans.

There was only a limited number of professional musicians in the area, and the two rival theater directors were hard pressed to assemble the personnel for their ambitious projects. In order to put an opera on the boards, it was often necessary to trim the score, rearrange the orchestration, and modify the arias. Quintets became quartets and quartets trios; where fifty musicians were called for, the production made do with twenty-five. Good singers were particularly hard to come by, and the producer had to learn to make the most of his one or two truly dependable soloists. When one of the singers in a duet was clearly not up to his task, the other was instructed to sing all the more loudly. The score was often adapted to suit the limitations of some aging tenor or tremulous soprano.

None of these handicaps dampened the enthusiasm of the citizens for theater and opera. Davis and Caldwell deserve credit for having striven to improve the artistic quality of their productions. Both frequently traveled to Europe to engage recognized talent. In 1822, John Davis brought an excellent ballet troupe to New Orleans; it quickly won the hearts of the local audience. "Terpsichore is within our walls!" proclaimed one of the newspapers. Unfortunately, the corps de ballet proved a costly experiment, and the public had henceforth to content itself with home-grown dancers. But the next year, on March 4, 1823, John Davis brought to his French theater an uncut performance of Rossini's *Barber of Seville*—three years before the opera was seen in New York.

The Creoles and the Americans had decidedly different tastes in theater. The Creoles loved opera, but they also loved vaudeville. At this time, every opera performance was preceded by a vaudeville act or other "special attraction": a Spanish dance with castanets, a tight-rope walker, an acrobat, a Chinese dance with tambourine, a lecture on natural philosophy. Tragedies or "heroic comedies" (a popular form of melodrama) were invariably preceded or concluded by one or two vaudeville skits. These were generally rather bawdy slapstick performances that provoked hilarity among the Creole spectators and scornful smiles among the Americans.

In 1829, an American journalist, speaking for his compatriots, castigated "the indecencies and inanities of French vaudeville." French newspaper readers hotly replied that the plays of Shakespeare were infinitely more "indecent." They cited chapter and verse from *King Lear* and *Othello*: "Let copulation thrive!" "An old black ram / is tupping your white ewe." Their indignation becomes more comprehensible if we remember that Voltaire himself referred to Shakespeare as "a genius full of force and richness, but totally devoid of taste, and lacking the faintest knowledge of literary form."

In New Orleans, cultural enthusiasm cooled as the weather grew hotter. From May on, attendance at the theater tapered off. The well-to-do departed for the country, and those who remained preferred to seek amusement out of doors, taking long walks along the levee. To entice people into his theater during the summer months, Davis tried leaving the doors and windows open during the performances and replaced the oil lamps, which smoked badly, with gas light. But nothing worked. Eventually Davis decided to follow the example of his American rival. He closed his theater during the summer and took his company on tour, traveling as far as St. Louis, Nashville, and even New York.

Financially, theater production was anything but a sure thing. Many tickets were purchased on credit and never paid for. The price for a season ticket at the French theater in 1821 was $80 for a reserved box seat, $60 for an unreserved seat. The ticket allowed the holder admission to two performances a week, on Tuesday and Sunday. A season ticket for blacks, in the first balcony, cost $50. In 1824, Davis lowered his rate for the best reserved seats to $60 in an effort to boost attendance but simultaneously ended his policy of selling tickets on credit. Henceforth, they were sold on a cash basis only.

The burgeoning success of Caldwell's theater was a constant source of irritation and anxiety for Davis. He could, of course, console himself with the thought that the quality of his productions attracted a better class of audience than did Caldwell's—but high-quality productions were expensive to mount, and he required full houses to make ends meet. At one point, he decided to appeal to the patriotism of his French-speaking audience. In announcing a play entitled *The Friend of the Laws,* Davis addressed a plea "to all those who realize how vital a society such as ours is to the maintenance of civilization." At that very moment, he declared, "this island of culture" was threatened by the tidal wave of American immigration; the time had come for the French population of New Orleans to manifest its "patriotism." This kind of argument never failed to elicit an emotional response from the Creoles.

CONCERTS

Because the Creoles were fond of music, local musicians could always count on an audience at their concerts. Indeed, some French composers who had never succeeded in getting their work performed in France had the pleasure of hearing it played in New Orleans. A few of these neglected talents enjoyed a measure of success in the New World. Operas were even composed especially for the New Orleans audience by musicians who, had they remained in France, would never have succeeded in hearing their work performed.

Concerts were often organized as charity benefits, most frequently for widows and orphans, sometimes for some destitute immigrant or family in distress. In 1827, a concert was arranged to benefit one Captain Romati, a former soldier in Napoleon's army who had "lost everything except his liberty." Occasionally, an impoverished musician put on a concert for his own benefit, as did the violinist Desforges, "who had lost all his possessions in a fire."

The usual price for a concert ticket was one dollar for adult whites, fifty cents for children and blacks. At many concerts, special sections were reserved for slaves. Generally speaking, however, the blacks preferred gay marches to the music of Haydn and Mozart, and they swelled the crowds in the Place d'Armes on Sunday mornings, when the municipal militia regiments paraded to music in full uniform. Clusters of spectators clung to the iron grillwork surrounding the square; their rapt expressions were clearly due less to the glittering weaponry and splendid uniforms than to the music of the marching band.

In fact, the entire population, blacks and whites alike, loved parades and military music. This passion seemed to increase with the passing years. Almost any public occasion—the laying of a cornerstone, the unveiling of a statue, the anniversary of some famous military victory, whether French or American, a distinguished visitor's arrival, an election, a wedding—served as an excuse for a parade. The blacks integrated music into their burial rites. And the day was not far off when the first funeral procession would wind its way through the streets, accompanying the deceased on his last journey with a blare of trumpets.

The "Bamboula"

In New Orleans, Sunday was a day of relaxation, even for the slaves. Dressed in their finest, they gathered by the hundreds under the sycamores in Congo Place, and from early afternoon until nightfall they danced to the rhythm of tom-toms and crude stringed instruments. The dances were lively and fast paced, with quick steps and many pirouettes. There were sensual, even blatantly erotic dances, in which the dancers mimicked the motions of lovemaking. There were bright, joyful dances that reflected the influence of European music; dances that were little more than a stamping of feet; dances with sacred undertones, such as the calinda; dances like the carabine, in which the man spun his partner like a top; frenetic dances like the bamboula and the counjaille; and mysterious dances like the pilé chactas, in which the man first circles his partner, then sinks to his knees before her and writhes at her feet like a serpent.

The slaves danced barefoot on the grass, as the civic guard looked on from a discreet distance and a horde of white spectators pressed around the gates of the square, their faces registering a mixture of amusement, astonishment, shock, scorn, and indulgence. The African rhythms and dances were obviously not to everyone's taste, and some of the Americans in the crowd must have looked on the scene as a display of savagery that no one but a black—or a Creole—could either savor or condone.

Latrobe has left a graphic description of these occasions. One Sunday he heard from the road "a most extraordinary noise" that resembled many horses "trampling on a wooden floor." He soon perceived "a crowd of five or six hundred persons, assembled in an open space or public square," and he drew nearer to see what was happening. Groups of very dark-skinned blacks formed circles of varying sizes around the groups of dancers. Latrobe's attention was caught by two women who were dancing together, each holding "a coarse handkerchief, extended by the corners in their hands." They danced with great deliberation, scarcely moving their feet or bodies, and executing steps that Latrobe considered "dull."

The women were accompanied by two tom-toms and a stringed instrument: "an old man sat astride of a cylindrical drum, about a foot in diameter, and beat it with incredible quickness with the edge of his hand and fingers." The other drum was "an open-staved thing" that the drummer held between his legs and played on both with his fingers and the palm of his hand. The stringed instrument was a "most curious" affair, resembling a long-necked banjo, at the end of which was carved a seated male figure whose body was formed from a calabash. The musician was a little man, "apparently eighty or ninety years old." Latrobe thought that all the dancers were executing the same dance steps but that the accompaniment differed for each group. He took particular notice of another stringed instrument that had "something of the form of a cricket bat with a long and deep mortise down the center." The instrument was rapped with a small stick, producing a "terrible" racket. Other musical instruments included "a square drum, looking like a stool, which made an abominable, loud noise," and a "calabash, with a round hole in it, the hole studded with brass nails, which was beaten by a woman with two short sticks."

The emphatic beat of the tom-toms and calabashes underscored the singing of many voices and the clapping of many hands. "A man sang an uncouth song to the dancing, which was, I suppose, in some African language, for it was not in French, and the women screamed a detestable burden on one single note." Clearly, Latrobe was no devotee of African music.

"The allowed amusements of Sunday," Latrobe noted, "have, it

seems, perpetuated here those of Africa among its former inhabitants." He concluded: "I have never seen anything more brutally
savage and at the same time dull and stupid." John Paxton, writing
about the same spectacle, concurred: "It is a foolish custom that
elicits the ridicule of most respectable persons who visit the city."

Members of the Anglo-Saxon population made repeated attempts
to outlaw these dances. But they ran into stubborn opposition from
the Creoles, who fully appreciated the role that music played in the
life of their slaves, and who, in any case, considered these dances a
perfectly innocent form of amusement. As long as the festivities in
Congo Square did not get out of control, they saw no reason to ban
them. The only restriction they placed on their slaves was that they
return to their quarters by sundown, as on any other night. The curfew was signaled by a cannon fired from the Calaboso. The dancers
dispersed quickly, chanting, "Good-night dance, the sun has gone to
bed," and exchanging promises to meet again the following Sunday.

By means of these gatherings, ancestral songs and dances were
faithfully transmitted from generation to generation. Creole patois
sometimes supplanted African dialects, but the basic structure of
the songs remained intact: the theme, announced by a soloist, was
taken up in the refrain by a chorus, or a short musical phrase sung by
the chorus was appended to the longer melodic line of the soloist.
Melville Herskowits maintains that it is safe to say that Louisiana
was the only state in North America where one could witness performances of authentic African dances: the calinda, the congo, and
the bamboula.

According to contemporary accounts, the great majority of the
dancers in Congo Square were of pure African extraction. Latrobe
saw "hardly a dozen cafe-au-lait faces in the crowd." Quadroons,
mulattoes, and most of the Creole blacks regarded these Sunday rev-
els as beneath them, and American blacks were rarely in evidence—
partially out of deference to the opinion of the Creole blacks, partially out of fear of their Protestant masters' disapproval. From the
Protestant point of view, it was a sin to dance on the Lord's Day or to
sing anything other than hymns.

The festivities in Congo Square met with the disapproval of the
more respectable elements of the population, not only because they

disturbed the peace of the Sabbath, but because they served as an occasion for performing ritual voodoo chants and for some dances which, admittedly, were obscene. The erotic gestures of the dancers and the frank simulation of sexual acts shocked even the most broad-minded whites. Yet the large numbers of white onlookers who flocked to the square every Sunday were not coming merely to be shocked. Perhaps their sense of outrage was mingled with an irresistible surge of pleasure.

An Illustrious Visitor

The arrival of a distinguished visitor offered the people of New Orleans the chance to indulge their taste for ceremony to the limit, while also displaying their fine sense of etiquette and decorum. The visit of the marquis de Lafayette was the great social event of the year 1825. As soon as the fact of his visit was confirmed, a planning committee was established under the chairmanship of the then governor of Louisiana, Henry Johnson. The committee's first task was to find suitable lodgings for Lafayette. Every leading citizen offered the hospitality of his own home, but after long discussion it was decided that since the marquis was the whole city's guest, the most appropriate place to lodge him would be city hall.

A sum of $15,000 was allocated to transform the old Cabildo into a residential palace worthy of the Revolutionary hero. The offices of the mayor and the other officials were transferred to new quarters, rented from the baron de Pontalba, and the city's foremost artisans were recruited to transform the vacated space into gracious private apartments. The armaments room became an elegant dining room, while the council chamber, the *sala capitular* of the Spanish governors, was transformed into an ornate sitting room. The ceilings were all decorated with cornices and rosettes; the old wooden mantles on the fireplaces were replaced with marble; and the walls were covered with luxurious fabrics. The furniture, mirrors, chandeliers, rugs, and paintings were the best the city could offer. Henceforth the old Cabildo would be known as "the Lafayette home."

The city also commissioned a triumphal arch for the Place d'Armes. According to Colonel A. Levasseur, Lafayette's secretary, the arch was "sixty-eight feet high, rising twenty-eight feet above the keystone, and fifty-eight feet wide, with an opening of twenty-feet; and twenty-five feet thick." The arch "rested on a pedestal faced with Sera Veza marble; the base of the pedestal, in green Italian marble, was decorated with large statues depicting Liberty and Justice." The front, faced with yellow Veronese marble, featured two statues personifying Fame, both holding in one hand a trumpet, in the other a laurel wreath. One wreath was entwined with a banner bearing Lafayette's name, the other with a banner bearing George Washington's. A relief of an eagle crowned the whole edifice. The pedestal bore the inscription, in both French and English, "A grateful Republic has erected this monument to Lafayette." At the very summit of the arch stood a statue of Wisdom, her hand resting on a bust of the "immortal Franklin."

This "splendid edifice" was fashioned of wood and covered with canvas painted to resemble marble. The effect was electrifying: Levasseur declared solemnly that the triumphal arch was "monumental in conception, and displayed exquisite taste."

Early in April, the city dispatched a comfortably appointed steamboat, the *Natchez*, to meet Lafayette at Mobile. On board was a welcoming delegation of citizens headed by Joseph Armand Duplantier, a local planter and former comrade-in-arms of the marquis. There was also a small military band on board.

Having taken on Lafayette and his entourage, the *Natchez* crossed the Gulf to the mouth of the Mississippi, passing the Balize, where, according to Levasseur, "enormous alligators with shifty eyes and lethargic movements could be seen reclining on tree trunks in the middle of the river, and seeming to challenge the other river traffic."

On April 10, the shore batteries at New Orleans fired a hundred-gun salute to announce the imminent arrival of the "guest of the nation." At daybreak on the tenth, the *Natchez* drew up at the site of the Battle of Chalmette, where in 1815 the motley forces of Andrew Jackson had routed the British army under General Packenham. Lafayette and his companions were moved to see that the riverbank was lined with troops in French uniform. He stepped ashore "to the boom of cannons and the cheers of a large crowd which, in spite of the inclement weather and the distance from town, had turned out to greet him." The visitor was welcomed by a contingent of cavalry;

twelve dignitaries served to lead the escort. Lafayette was conducted to the Macarty plantation, which had served as headquarters for General Jackson during the late war, where he was greeted by the governor in the name of the people of Louisiana. This welcome was the first in a long series. In the course of his five-day visit to New Orleans, the marquis was subjected to no less than sixteen such discourses, to each of which he was of course expected to reply. As the historian Edward Laroque Tinker remarked, "it seems that every municipal official, with the sole exception of the dog catcher, had the right to deliver an address."

Everybody who had managed to gain entrance to the house was introduced to Lafayette. Levasseur records that "a great number of ladies had come to meet the general, and through the medium of Monsieur de Marigny, they congratulated him on his arrival in Louisiana and informed him of their respectful regards." It is reported that Marigny's high-flown rhetoric touched the old soldier deeply.

The procession soon regrouped and, "in spite of a driving rain," set off for New Orleans. The general was seated with the governor and Duplantier in a large landau pulled by six greys; they were closely followed by a calèche carrying Colonel Levasseur and the general's son, George Washington de Lafayette. Under the unremitting rain, the roads turned to mud and the vehicles crept forward with great difficulty. As the procession reached the outskirts of the city, the crowds along the route grew steadily larger. Levasseur reported that, on entering the city limits, "we passed through lines of troops bordering the streets, to the accompaniment of martial music." In spite of the mud and the driving rain, Lafayette insisted on reviewing this honor guard on foot. At last the group reached the Place d'Armes. There, writes Lavasseur, "the gaily bedecked buildings bordering the river, the boon of cannon both on land and on water, the chiming of bells and the acclamation of the multitude—all this made an impression that defies description."

The general was conducted through the triumphal arch and then met by Mayor de Roffignac, who "addressed him on behalf of the people of New Orleans." He proceeded to the courthouse, where he "was addressed by Mr. Prieur on behalf of the city council." The next stop was his residence in the refurbished Cabildo, where he was able to snatch a few minutes of rest. But only a very few minutes, for soon a military band could be heard in the distance with the entire roster of Louisiana's armed forces marching behind, determined to honor the general with a full-scale military review. Lafayette took the salute from the balcony of the city hall. "All the troops that passed in parade," noted Levasseur, "were remarkable for the elegance of their turn-out and the dignity of their bearing." First came the grenadiers, then the artillerymen, the dragoons, the infantry, various honor guards, and the Louisiana Riflemen, "whose name conjures up many heroic deeds."

Lafayette was particularly delighted by a contingent of one hundred Choctaw Indians in headdresses and full war-paint, marching in single file behind the Riflemen. He was moved to learn that "these Indian braves, who had fought alongside the American troops in the Seminole War," had been camping on the outskirts of New Orleans for over a month in order to see "the great warrior, the brother of Grandfather Washington."

"LONG LIVE LAFAYETTE!"

The general must have been pleased but exhausted by his welcome. In the days to follow, he appeared at a continual round of receptions, banquets, dances, public entertainments, and parades. He paid calls, received delegations, and entertained thirty people at dinner every night in his apartments. Despite his age and his ordeal at Olmutz, Lafayette clearly possessed a hardy constitution in order to endure the schedule imposed on him by the "Lafayette Planning Committee."

On Monday, April 11, for example, he received a visit from members of the legislature and the Bar Association and paid calls on the mayor, the governor, and "several ladies." In the evening, he went to the theater. Both Davis and Caldwell had made a bid for his presence on the same night, so "the general was obliged to choose by lot which theater he would attend. Chance favored the English theater." Here, where a specially improvised production was to be performed, Lafayette was greeted by "an indescribable outburst of enthusiasm." When, a short time later, he put in an appearance at the French theater, "the play was interrupted by a burst of applause, and cries of

'*Vive* Lafayette!' The entire audience rose to its feet: the scene resembled Themistocles' entrance at the Olympic Games."

On Tuesday, the general received "a delegation of Spanish residents and émigrés," a deputation of Temple Knights, and a "delegation of state militia and legionnaires." In the evening, he attended a ball, followed by a supper held at the Théâtre d'Orléans and attended by the cream of New Orleans society.

On Wednesday, Lafayette paid a number of calls "on ladies and distinguished personages" and received, among other visitors, the venerable Père Antoine. The aged Capuchin friar embraced him warmly, exclaiming, "O my son, the good Lord has shown me great favor in allowing me to see and speak with the worthy apostle of Liberty." The tears ran down the friar's "long beard, bleached by time," as he spoke of the condition of his unhappy fatherland, Spain. That afternoon, Lafayette viewed a parade and some artillery maneuvers. In the evening, the Place d'Armes was illuminated in his honor. Hundreds of small colored lanterns were suspended from the trees, the triumphal arch, and the grillwork surrounding the square. The cathedral and parish house were decked out with bright banners, and all the houses around the square were lit up. Twice the general made the tour of the square, while the crowd cheered, fireworks went off from the top of the triumphal arch, and cannons fired a hundred-gun salute. Lafayette then put in a brief appearance first at the American theater, then at the Théâtre d'Orléans. He ended the evening at a ball in Saint-Philippe Hall.

On Thursday, there were even more visitors than on the previous days. Lafayette received a delegation of free blacks, members of the medical society, and "a great many ladies and citizens of all social ranks." In the evening, he attended a meeting of the Grand Lodge of Louisiana, where he dined with three hundred Freemasons. Returning to the Théâtre d'Orléans, he saw a performance of the opera *Aline* and of a play written especially for the occasion, *Lafayette in New Orleans*.

On Friday the fifteenth, the day of Lafayette's departure, his apartments were crowded with well-wishers anxious to pay their parting respects to the venerable "Champion of Liberty" and "Friend of Washington." Many fathers had brought their children, so they could "behold the noble features of our country's benefactor." Marigny was in attendance, as was the wealthy German merchant Vincent Nolte. Nolte was a long-time friend of Lafayette and had visited the general every morning of his visit, immediately after breakfast. In the course of their conversations, the general had confided to his friend that he was hard pressed for money. The American Congress had voted him the generous sum of $200,000, but he had yet to receive a penny of this gift. Nolte obligingly responded with the immediate loan of $1,200. He was to be one of the party accompanying Lafayette to Natchez.

The moment had come for Lafayette to say farewell to the city. As he left his quarters, he found the streets packed with people, all shouting, "Vive Lafayette!" He crossed the Place d'Armes, "where several companies of legionnaires and other troups stood to attention as he passed," and entered the carriage that was to take him to the pier. There the steamboat *Natchez* was waiting to carry him to Baton Rouge and Natchez.

Another enormous crowd lined the levee. "All the balconies and rooftops, all the sailboats and steamboats were overflowing with spectators." Lafayette went on board amid the cheers of the crowd. A final round of cannon signaled the ship's departure.

Accompanying Lafayette on the first leg of his journey were the governor and his staff, the mayor and other municipal officials, and the Lafayette Planning Committee. As Levasseur reports: "Two miles upstream most of the passengers were obliged to disembark. It was with a pang of real emotion that we parted from these worthy magistrates. We had known them briefly, it is true, yet long enough to come to recognize their sterling qualities."

On board ship, Lafayette was able to catch his breath before embarking on a new round of festivities at Natchez and Philadelphia. Back in New Orleans, his visit dominated drawing room conversations for a long time to come. In business circles, however, talk reverted almost immediately to cotton. April was the season for cotton speculation: attention turned to the latest market reports from Liverpool, and the price of cotton was the talk of the town. Only a visitor of Lafayette's stature could briefly distract the merchants, middlemen, and speculators of New Orleans from their principal preoccupation. And the fact that the venerable marquis had been able for a few days to usurp the place of King Cotton in the minds of the American businessmen is perhaps the truest testimony to the respect and affection in which he was held.

9

The World of the Mississippi

On board the *Natchez*, great pains had been taken to make General Lafayette's voyage as comfortable as possible. The cabin usually reserved for gentlemen travelers had been entirely set aside for his use, and the forward bridge had been transformed into a sitting room complete with sofas and card tables, playing cards and books. From the bridge, the passengers could enjoy a splendid view of the great river, confined by the levee that ran all the way from New Orleans to Baton Rouge. On either side of the river, a series of panoramas opened to view: fields of sugarcane; wild forests interspersed with sawmills; colonnaded mansions surrounded by orange trees whose delicate aroma wafted over to the steamboat. From somewhere on board, a black deckhand could be heard singing a wistful lament:

> De night is dark, de day is long
> And we are far from home.
> Weep, my brodders, weep.

The river teemed with activity. In addition to the cumbersome steamboats, it was crowded with flatboats resembling large floating arks, keelboats propelled by long oars, and dugouts carved from tree trunks, in which farmers, fishermen, and Indians carried fruits, vegetables, fish, crab, and wild game to market in New Orleans.

THE STEAMBOATS

At this period, the steamboats held dominion among the numerous vessels that traveled the great American waterways. Little by little, the Mississippi, like the Ohio and the Hudson, had been invaded by flotillas of large ships, flanked by paddle wheels, bristling with smokestacks, and laden with elaborate superstructures that gave them the look of gigantic wedding cakes. These vessels transported passengers, grain, cotton, tobacco, agricultural implements, furniture, housewares, molasses, rum, sugar, firewood, coal, slaves.

The plantation owners whose estates bordered the river often entrusted passing steamboat captains with lists of purchases to be made in town. These purchases ranged from the trivial to the momentous: from a few yards of muslin to a grand piano, from eau de cologne to bonnets that tied under the chin and were all the rage that season. To deliver his commission, the planter dispatched a slave down to the levee, who hailed the vessel by waving a torch or a bright piece of cloth. The captain seldom failed to heed the summons, unless his boat happened to be involved in a race with another steamboat. Up to 1840 or so, the steamboats made little effort to adhere to a rigid timetable. The captain would delay his departure until he had taken on a full complement of passengers and freight, and there were numerous unscheduled stops en route to procure fresh supplies of firewood to stoke the ravenous furnaces, to pick up new passengers and cargo, or to deliver messages and drop off parcels.

River travel on the Mississippi was perilous, even when accomplished by steamboat. The captains were a daredevil breed, the river shoals were treacherous, and the boilers had an unpleasant habit of exploding on the slightest provocation. Accidents were common and often grave. Sometimes a steamboat ran aground, and there were numerous cases of ships blowing up or catching fire. Few captains could resist the challenge of a boat race. Urged on by the excited shouts of their passengers, they tended to throw caution to the winds and prime their boilers to the bursting point.

In the earliest days of steamboat travel, the crews were almost entirely white, but soon slaves were brought aboard to serve as stokers, deckhands, and stewards. Many of the steamboat captains were former sailing men, and they retained the habits and traditions of their seagoing days. They continued to bark their orders through a megaphone, despite the fact that they no longer had ocean waves and gales to contend with; and their conversation, especially their oaths and curses, had a distinctly salty flavor. Like the sea captains of old, they liked to be in complete command of their vessels and crews—though they had, in fact, no authority whatsoever over the pilot.

The pilot was often a former keelboat captain and as such was long familiar with the ways of the Mississippi. His quarters were on the topmost deck of the steamboat. From there he surveyed the changing course of the river, paying particular attention to the strength of the current and to any abnormalities in the watery terrain. After all, the drop of a single foot in the water level could spell disaster. The pilot's skill and knowledge were crucial to the safe operation of the boat, and the pilot was by no means unconscious of the importance of his role. Many pilots addressed their captains with a certain condescension, even arrogance, and they barely deigned to cast a glance at their former associates, the keelboat men.

Yet the keelboats had once ruled the Mississippi, and at first their boatmen had ridiculed the ungainly steam-driven vessels with their "fire-pump" engines, which were continually breaking down or blowing up. The first steamboats to venture on the river had been so slow that they were easily passed by rowers, who had the current to help them. By now, however, the keelboatmen had come to realize that these "floating volcanoes" were dangerous competitors; by 1825, most of the agricultural produce of the lower Mississippi Valley was being transported to New Orleans by steamboat, and river passengers were finding the commodious and colorful vessels much to their liking. Only the most impecunious traveler now elected to travel by keelboat.

LIFE ON BOARD A STEAMBOAT

During the 1820s, the steamboats still had only two cabins: one for the men, the other for the women. Mrs. Trollope reported that the gentlemen's cabin was more luxuriously appointed than the ladies'—a situation that deeply disturbed her. "The breakfast, dinner, and supper are laid in this apartment," she reported, "and the lady passengers are permitted to take their meals there." The rest of the time they were strictly excluded. On the better boats, the cabins were elaborately decorated. A German traveler, J. G. Frugel, has left in his journals a detailed description of the second *New Orleans*, a steamboat designed by Robert Fulton in 1815 and built in Pittsburgh at a cost of $65,000.

The boat had a crew of thirty-four, with four officers, and could carry two hundred tons of cargo and about fifty passengers. Frugel informs us that the captain received $2,500 per annum, that the passengers on the voyage upstream paid twelve and a half cents per mile, and that those on the voyage downstream paid only six and a quarter cents per mile. He describes the passengers' quarters as follows:

The ladies' cabin is below deck, it being the most retired place. It is elegantly fitted up. The windows are ornamented with white curtains and the beds, twenty in number, with red bombazette curtains and fringes and mosquito bars, besides sofas, chairs, looking glasses etc. . . . and an elegant carpet ornaments the floor. . . . Above deck is an elegant round-house of 42 feet in length and 28 in breadth for gentlemen. This room for the convenience of the passengers is provided with 26 berths in 13 state rooms . . . each berth has a window. Sofas, or settees and chairs, two large tables, a large gilt framed looking glass, several elegantly finished recommendation cards and the regulations of the boat in gilt frames —all these adorn the room, and finally an elegant carpet covers the floor.

The shipboard regulations pertained only to the gentlemen, for it was assumed that the ladies would need no guidance on matters of conduct. The regulations included:

No gentleman passenger shall descend the stairs leading to, or enter the lady's cabin unless with the permission of all the ladies, to be obtained through the Captain, under the penalty of two dollars for each offense. . . .

No gentleman shall lie down in a berth with his shoes or boots on under penalty of one dollar for each offense. . . .

Cards and games of every description are prohibited in the cabin after ten o'clock at night. . . .

At noon, every day, three persons to be chosen by a majority of the passengers shall form a court to determine on all penalties incurred and the amount collected shall be expended in wine for the whole company after dinner. . . .

It is particularly requested that gentlemen will not spit on the cabin floors as boxes are provided for that purpose.

Mrs. Trollope, who traveled on the *Belvedere* with her daughter in 1828, reports that the carpet in the otherwise "handsomely fitted up" gentlemen's cabin was so soiled that she would have preferred "sharing the apartment of a party of well-conditioned pigs to being confined to that cabin." She was repelled by the American habit of incessant spitting. The shipowners soon introduced spittoons into the gentlemen's cabin—one for each passenger. These humble implements were subsequently transformed into decorative objects adorned with gilt.

The speed of the second *New Orleans* was four miles an hour against the current and ten miles an hour downstream. In 1817, steamboats made the trip from Louisville, Kentucky, to New Orleans in twenty-five days and two hours. By 1828, the voyage had been cut to eighteen days and ten hours; by 1834, to eight days and four hours.

On the first steamboats, a cabin passenger paid $140 to travel from New Orleans to Louisville. Ten years later, he paid $100 for a passage from New Orleans all the way to Pittsburgh. By 1833, the price of the New Orleans-Pittsburgh run had dropped to $40, and the rate for noncabin passengers was only $10 or $12. These passengers got precisely what they paid for; they traveled with the cargo and were expected to supply their own food. Sometimes impecunious travelers could earn their passage by helping take on firewood along the route.

The river was bordered for most of its length by vast forests, so the captains had little difficulty in obtaining fuel for the voracious furnaces. In the early days of steamboat travel, the crews were expected to cut their own firewood, but as the traffic grew, the settlers along the riverbanks set up makeshift fueling stations and sold cordwood to the passing steamboats. These woodcutters were a desperate and dispirited lot, living as they did in the midst of alligator-infested swampland and prey to malaria, malnutrition, and the sheer brutality of wilderness life. Their principal link with civilization was the whiskey sold them by the passing boatmen. Whiskey cast a hazy glow over the stark misery of their existence, enabling them to continue in the face of sickness, loneliness, and poverty.

Few on shipboard paid any heed to the plight of these miserable wretches. For the steamboat passengers—at least those who had paid for a cabin—the days passed in a series of agreeable pastimes: taking the air on deck and admiring the scenery, striking up interesting conversations with travelers of the opposite sex, or taking pot-shots at the alligators—a sport much favored by the gentlemen. The steamboat was a world unto itself, populated by a strange medley of characters: long-haired evangelists, merchants and planters, brokers, doctors, wealthy foreigners, fugitives from justice, backwoodsmen, marriageable daughters chaperoned by mothers, aunts, or black mammies, professional cardsharps, immigrant adventurers, slaves. Each boat bore an identifying emblem, usually placed between the two smokestacks, and the outer cases of its paddle wheels were distinctively decorated in vivid colors.

THE KAINTUCKS

The keelboats could not compete with the steamboats, whose speed increased, as we have seen, even as their cost went down, and whose attractions and comforts far surpassed the humbler vessels'. For more than a century, the river traffic had relied entirely on the keel-boats and flatboats. Keelboats were long, slender boats, navigating the river both upstream and down, occasionally propelled by sail, but more often by oars or by means of poles along the riverbank. The keelboats employed from eight to twenty rowers and sometimes more, depending on the size of the vessels. As a group, the rowers were hardy, rowdy, and quarrelsome; they feared neither God nor the devil and struck terror into the hearts of the citizens of New Orleans. C. C. Robin describes them as "drunken gamblers and whoremongers . . . who are often pennyless within a few days of being paid."

A Mississippi boatman doffed his hat to nobody. The story is told by Harnett Kane that when the keelboat transporting the duke of Or-léans—the future King Louis-Philippe—and his brothers ran aground on a sandbar, the captain shouted out, "You kings down there! Show yourselves and do a man's work, and help us three-spots pull off this bar!" And the royal party hopped to it!

Although the keelboats did not displace much water, they were capable of carrying heavy cargoes, and some of the boats were not lacking in amenities. John James Audubon, the naturalist, traveled from Natchez to New Orleans by keelboat in January, 1821, and described the accommodations: "Our situation in this boat is quite comfortable. We have a good servant to wait on us, are served with regular meals, clean and in plates." Audubon was the more appreciative of these niceties from having made the trip from Cincinnati to Natchez on "Mr. Jacob Aumack's flatboat," during which he almost perished from the cold, while also losing all his drawings. He lost them "amongst 150 to 160 flat boats and houses filled with the lowest characters. No doubt my drawings will serve to ornament their parlour or will be nailed on some of the steering oars."

Until the end of the 1850s, flatboats were a common sight on the Mississippi, and they seem to have undergone few modifications over the years, for Berquin-Duvallon's description of the vessels in 1803 is virtually identical to Harriet Martineau's in 1838:

These are large boats, of rude construction, made just strong enough to hold together, and keep their cargo of flour, or other articles, dry, from some high point on the great rivers, to New Orleans. They are furnished with two enormous oars, fixed on what is, I suppose, called their deck; to be used where the current is sluggish, or when it is desirable to change the direction of the boat. The cumbrous machine is propelled by the stream; her proprieters only occasionally helping her progress, now by pulling at the branches of overhanging trees, now by turning her into the more rapid of two currents. She is seen sometimes floating down the very middle of the river; sometimes gliding under the banks. At noon, a bower of green leaves is waving on her deck, for shade to her masters; at night, a pine brand is waved, flaming, to give warning to the steam-boats not to run her down.

A certain William Richardson has left an account of a trip he made by flatboat in 1816. He purchased the boat in Louisville for $60, loaded it with $1,800 worth of cargo, hired a captain for $60 and two oarsmen for $30 each, and started out for Natchez. Richardson and his crew camped at night on little islands in the river; they procured food by shooting ducks and bartering whiskey for eggs or chickens. Richardson sold the boat in Natchez for $25 and proceeded on to New Orleans in another vessel, which reached the city in seventy-six hours. "No river in the world is more beautiful," he reported, "the navigation easy and not dangerous."

RIVER PIRATES

Contrary to Richardson's opinion, the Mississippi was reputed to be a particularly dangerous waterway, and not only because of its irregular contours, capricious currents, and numerous shoals. During the first half of the nineteenth century, the river was much frequented by brigands—especially at the confluences of the Red River and of the Ohio. The favored prey of these fresh-water pirates were not the professional boatmen, who were excellent riflemen, always ready for a brawl, but the sober farmers of the Ohio Valley, who regularly brought their produce downstream to market, or the pioneers setting off in search of new homes with all their worldly goods in tow.

"Colonel Plug," one of the most notorious of the river pirates, developed a standard *modus operandi*. He slipped aboard a moored vessel, concealed himself amidst the cargo, and drilled holes in the boat's hull. Timing and precision were essential, for the boat must not begin to flounder until it had come within hailing distance of Plug's lair. At that point, Plug gave the signal, and his gang hastily rowed out to the "rescue." Of course, nothing was actually rescued from the sinking boat except the cargo and the Colonel. The boat's passengers and crew were left to fend for themselves in midstream; if they offered any resistance to the pirates, they were cut down without mercy.

One day Plug drilled one hole too many, or he drilled it too large or drilled it too soon. At any rate, the boat sank to the bottom before his piratical colleagues could arrive to save their leader and the merchandise.

Other pirate bands, like that led by the celebrated Bully Wilson, had no hesitation in boarding vessels in broad daylight, armed to the teeth—although they took care to make sure that the odds were in their favor before venturing an attack. Every year a sizable number of boat crews and passengers mysteriously disappeared "somewhere between Louisville and Memphis," or "somewhere between Natchez and Baton Rouge." In 1824, the combined crews of a dozen flatboats resolved to lay an ambush for a large band of pirates encamped on an island at the confluence of the Mississippi and the Red River. On July 1st, some eighty resolute and well-armed boatmen concealed themselves amidst the cargo of a flatboat and descended the Red River toward the pirate stronghold. Only a handful of men were visible on deck. As the boat passed the island, a flotilla of canoes containing about thirty armed men in all set off to overtake it. The moment the pirates, brandishing knives, rifles, and hatchets, set foot on the flatboat, the full force of boatmen burst from cover and flung themselves upon the attackers. In a few minutes, ten bandits were killed and the remainder taken prisoner. The captives were blind-folded and pushed overboard. As they bobbed about helplessly in the water, a group of boatmen armed with rifles held a shooting match: a bottle of whiskey was awarded to the sharpshooter who dispatched the greatest number of pirates.

Yet life on the Mississippi had its compensations. At dusk, when the flatboats and keelboats were moored for the night, the crews gathered around campfires to drink and sing or swap tales of past adventures. They told of battles against the English or the Indians; of epic bear hunts in the wilderness; of other pursuits in the bars and brothels of New Orleans and Natchez—Natchez, where to refuse grog before breakfast would degrade you below the brute creation.

On the subject of New Orleans women, the conversation never ran dry. Walter Blair and Franklin J. Meine, in their biography of Mike Fink, recall a typical description of these alluring ladies: "They have clothes like—like angels, by God, and hearts like devils. They spray the fringes of their petticoat with gold and they wear gold slippers and their stockings are decorated likewise with the same precious metal, all sewed around in pretty little god damned flowers on the prettiest legs in the world.

Mike Fink the Boatman

The hard-bitten, swaggering rivermen were inveterate storytellers, and one of the heroes who figured in their tales was Mike Fink, once a hunter of Indians, now a keelboatman. Mike hailed from Pitts-burgh and described himself as "half-horse, half-alligator." His boast was: "I can out-run, out-jump, out-shoot, out-brag, out-drink and out-fight, rough and tumble, no holds barred, any man on both sides of the river from Pittsburgh to New Orleans and back to St. Louis."

Mike Fink, the bearded giant with huge muscles and bright blue eyes, who always dressed in a red shirt and a leather frontiersman's jacket, soon became a figure of mythology, and today it is impossible to separate the facts concerning him from the legend. In the Ohio Valley, he was known as the Snapping Turtle; on the Mississippi, he was called the Snag. He was said to have a passion for women, whis-

key, and brawling, and to detest Indians and blacks. The story goes
that while tracking a deer in the forest, he noticed an Indian also
moving in on his prey. Fink said to himself: "If I shoot the Indian,
the deer will run away; if I shoot the deer, the Indian will shoot me."
He therefore waited until the Indian had shot the deer, and then shot
the Indian.

This brand of brutal cunning made Mike Fink a hero among the
Mississippi boatmen and the prostitutes of Natchez, Memphis, St.
Louis, Vicksburg, and New Orleans. He boasted a woman in every
port, and no man dared challenge him. He thrived on violence: he
once murdered a man who attempted to rival him for a prostitute's
favors and was reputed to have killed for far less. Fink disappeared
abruptly from the Mississippi in 1822. Some said he could not put up
with the steamboat's victory over the keelboat; one source claimed
that his boat had been sliced in two by a steamboat to which he
refused to yield the right-of-way and that Fink himself had been
drowned. Still others reported that he had quit the river and become
a trapper after the bordellos and taverns of New Orleans, deciding
they had had enough of him, banned him from their doors.

Along the lower reaches of the Mississippi, Bill Smedley's was a
name to be reckoned with. The towering Kentuckian first came to
public attention one night in July, 1817, when he led a band of fifty
boatmen on a rampage through the streets of New Orleans. After
they had put several members of the police force out of commission,
the rioters burst into the tent where the Cayetano Circus was entertaining a crowd composed largely of women and children. Panic en-
sued; the women and children fled screaming, while the men tried
to subdue the rampaging boatmen, only to be trampled in the melee.
Meanwhile, the boatmen had opened the animal cages, and Bill
Smedley personally clubbed to death a buffalo and a tiger. By this
feat he won lasting glory among the roughnecks of New Orleans,
while confirming the Creoles in their belief that the Americans
were basically little more than savages.

Smedley presently set himself up as the king of the city's red-light
district. He abandoned his keelboat to live with Annie Christmas,
who ran a floating bordello on the Mississippi. Annie was almost six
feet tall and weighed close to two hundred and fifty pounds; she al-

ways carried a whip, and many a pimp, pander, or boatman could testify to her skill in using it. She saw to it that her establishment was run in a businesslike manner; using the principle of incentive rewards, she offered a free shot of whisky to the girl who could satisfy the greatest number of customers during a given period of time. The girls on board were dressed in red and received their clients in small alcoves constructed in the hold. When business was especially brisk, tents were set up on deck to handle the overflow.

The bordello was moored at the foot of Tchoupitoulas Street, where the majority of the flatboats were tied up, and accordingly attracted a good many customers. Annie Christmas ran a tight ship. Once Mike Fink got out of hand, and she let him know that he was no longer welcome: not on her boat, not in New Orleans. If he valued his life, he would make himself scarce. Annie Christmas herself came to a violent end, killed one night in a New Orleans gaming house. The identity of her murderer was never determined.

THE SWAMP

After spending three or four months on the river, the boatmen's thoughts were fixed obsessively on women and drink. New Orleans was well prepared to supply both. On arriving in the city, the boatman with money to spend often headed for Annie Christmas' or some similar establishment. But for real action, the place to go was the Swamp, haven of seamen and stokers, pimps and prostitutes, drunks, gamblers, military deserters, cut-throats.

Crime pays, and a number of enterprising individuals had set out to reap the profits. The Swamp was infested with sordid dives, dingy one-night hotels, and makeshift gambling dens. The visitor could purchase bad rum and worse whiskey, lose his money at cards or dice, and spend his last few cents on a young girl of any race he desired. The visitor entered the region at his own risk; a moment's distraction or indiscretion could cost him his money and sometimes his life. Yet, despite its dangers, the Swamp exercised an irresistable attraction for many boatmen and sailors.

The flatboatman's first task was to dispose both of his cargo and his boat. To return upstream in a keelboat was no mean feat, even for the likes of Mike Fink and his hearty companions, but to do so in a flatboat was almost impossible. Accordingly, the boats were dismantled after they reached New Orleans and sold as lumber, much of which was used to construct sidewalks in the city.

Although the keelboatmen were professional rivermen, many of the men who descended the Mississippi in flatboats were farmers. With true pioneer initiative, they had knocked together a boat in order to sell the produce of the family farm in the New Orleans markets. The big city dazzled them. The more prudent and upright among them scrupulously avoided the disreputable parts of town. They limited themselves to the Vieux Carré, the levee, and the public market, perhaps going so far as to buy a drink in one of the popular cafés, take in a play at the American theater, or shop for souvenirs to bring back to their mothers, sisters, sweethearts, or wives. After a brief tour of the city's attractions, they boarded a steamboat or keelboat to return home. Their enterprise had netted them a pile of "dixies"—the ten-dollar bills indigenous to New Orleans, whose name derived from the French word for ten, *dix*, prominently displayed on their face.

The less prudent young men, however, headed straight for the Swamp. There they were promptly relieved of their earnings. They could, indeed, consider themselves fortunate if they escaped with their lives. Country bumpkins were no match for the desperadoes of the big town.

Along the Natchez Trace

Those unfortunates who could not afford to pay their passage home on a riverboat were condemned to travel by land. The route leading from Natchez to Nashville was an old Indian path, known as the Natchez Trace, which led through the territory of the Choctaws and the Chickasaws. The route was notoriously dangerous, not because of the Indians, with whom the Americans had concluded a treaty in 1801, when the path was converted to a post road, but because of the white outlaws who preyed on the wayfarers. Travelers along the Natchez Trace tended to band together in groups. Even so, many failed to reach their destination.

A common means of travel along the Natchez Trace was known as "whipsawing." Three men would pool their meager resources to buy a horse; then lots were drawn to determine the order of riding. The first rider would set off at a good clip and continue on for a couple of hours. Then he would dismount, tie the horse to a tree along the route, and proceed on foot. When his two companions came on foot to the place where the horse was waiting, the second rider would mount and gallop ahead for the next two hours, then leave the horse for the third traveler. In this way, all three had a chance to alternate walking with riding, while the horse was allowed to rest every two hours. In this fashion, many made their way through the dense forests of the Natchez Trace. Some reached their homes; in other cases, the horse was stolen or expired from fatigue, or the travelers themselves were killed by highwaymen.

One of the most notorious of the Natchez Trace bandits was John A. Murrel. He specialized in the kidnapping of blacks, whom he subsequently sold on the slave market. Murrel did not hesitate to murder those whom he held up to eliminate the risk of his being recognized at some future time by one of his victims. He was a familiar figure in the cafés, cabarets, and bordellos of New Orleans, which he frequented not only for his own amusement, but also to gather information on future traffic along the Natchez Trace and the economic status of the travelers.

Nobody in New Orleans seemed to associate this handsome, well-dressed stranger with the "butcher" of the Natchez Trace; even in the Swamp, where the inhabitants keep their eyes well peeled, he passed unrecognized. Most took him for a well-to-do planter from Tennessee in search of a little out-of-the-way entertainment.

The entertainments of the Swamp were indeed out of the way. The women suffered from venereal diseases, the drinks were doctored, and the card games fixed. Stabbings and shootings were routine, and the slightest dispute ended in a bloody brawl. The only law was that of brute force. In the gambling dens, it was the proprietor, not Lady Luck, who controlled the winnings. If by chance a player succeeded in pocketing some money at the gaming tables, he was jumped by thugs the moment he left the establishment. Sometimes he was simply accused of having cheated at play and forced to give back his winnings. But if a murder took place—and this was often—the victim was either left to lie in the streets or stretched out on the bar of the gambling den by way of cautionary example. When the odor of the decaying corpse began to be offensive, it was unceremoniously dumped in the river. Such, at any rate, was standard operating procedure at one notorious establishment quaintly named the "House of Rest for Weary Boatmen"!

Another celebrated nightspot was the Sure Enuf Hotel. Its proprietor, Mother Colby, was an old harpy as broad as she was tall. The hotel itself was a dilapidated two-story stucture with a broken-backed roof. The ground floor held a bar, which overlooked the street; in the back was a small room for faro and roulette. In a corner of this chamber, separated by a thin partition, was Mother Colby's apartment: a tiny area that served at once as kitchen, dining room, and bedchamber. In another corner of the back chamber, makeshift rooms had been curtained off. There, for payment of a picayune (six cents), clients could rent a little privacy for entertaining the women they had picked up on the streets.

On the second floor, in a large attic under the eaves, rows of mattresses were laid out. The man who occupied a mattress in the center of the room, the only spot where one could stand upright, was charged twelve and a half cents; the others, who had to crawl to reach their sleeping spaces, paid only a picayune. This sort of arrangement prevailed in most of the hotels of the Swamp. The plutocrat who occupied the center mattress was often murdered in the course of the night, in order to obtain his supposed riches.

One day Mother Colby decided to sublet the ground floor to two Mexicans—brothers by the name of Contreras—and devote herself to the management of the hotel portion, as well as to a new bordello that she had just opened on the other side of the Swamp. The Contreras brothers had scarcely installed themselves in the Sure Enuf when they received a memorable visit from Bill Smedley. He had a few drinks at the bar, in company with a dozen boatmen of the "half-horse, half-alligator" breed, then repaired to the gaming room. He returned to the bar a short time later, asserting that one of his companions had seen Rafe Contreras conceal a card in his sleeve. After knocking back a few more drinks, Smedley returned to the back room to play faro.

In a few minutes a shot rang out. The bullet whistled past the ears of the men leaning on the bar, who hurriedly vacated the premises. Juan Contreras, who was tending bar, dashed to the back room to help his brother. From the street, the sound of curses and smashing furniture could be heard, then gun shots, then silence. At last the air was rent by the battlecry of the Mississippi boatmen: "I'm a child of the Snapping Turtle!"

Aleck Masters, a Kentucky flatboatman, witnessed the entire scene. He saw Bill Smedley appear on the front steps, his clothes in tatters and one of his arms, which had been smashed by a bullet, streaming blood. His face was illuminated with satisfaction. Waving his intact arm in the direction of the bar, Smedley shouted: "Boys, serve yourselves! Today the drinks are on the house. The boss has gone on a little trip, and left me in charge of the bar."

Juan Contreras lay on the ground under an armchair, dead; his brother was sprawled over the gaming table with Smedley's knife in his back. The corpses were dragged into a corner and toasts drunk to the health of Bill Smedley, hero of the fray. The victory celebration was in full swing when Mother Colby, alarmed by the uproar, arrived on the scene. She was armed with a pistol and prepared to defend her property, but before she could so much as fire a shot, Aleck Masters hit her over the head with a bottle, bound her hand and foot, and laid her out beside the Contreras brothers.

A little later, news reached the Sure Enuf that friends of the Contreras brothers were grouping for an assault. Finding the surroundings suddenly uncongenial, Bill Smedley disappeared into the night. The avengers patrolled the streets for many months and scoured every building, but Bill Smedley was never seen in the Swamp again.

The reputation of the Sure Enuf was only enhanced by this incident, and business flourished. Mother Colby continued to run the establishment for ten years or so, then sold it to one Frederick Krause, known in the district as "Crazy Bill." Crazy Bill's death was wholly appropriate to his way of life: one night, a practical joker strapped a money belt stuffed with gunpowder around his waist, then struck a match.

Most of the Swamp prostitutes were black slaves who had escaped from their masters or who had been stolen, then sold to pimps or procurers. The white women were vicious, degenerate, and usually drunk. Many of them operated on their own, and those who had no lodgings received their customers in tents set up on the street.

The prostitutes were tough and hard-bitten, and the man who attempted to cheat them was likely to find his eye gouged out, his testicles cut off, or a knife embedded in his belly. They lavished affection, however, on their own boy friends, helped them relieve seamen and riverboatmen of their cash, and tipped them off to other likely prospects while willingly splitting their own earnings with them, thus adding the profits of procuring to those of petty thievery.

The Swamp was a haven for enterprising criminals, especially at night, when activity reached its peak. For the likes of Bill Smedley or Mike Fink, who claimed to have taken in whiskey with their mothers' milk and who could handle a knife or pistol as skillfully and debonairly as any holdup artist, the Swamp held a perennial allure. No other district in America, not even in Natchez, could rival it. Sometimes described as the "citadel of vice," New Orleans owed that reputation to the Swamp.

10

Life on the Plantations

On March 26, 1826, Bernhard de Saxe-Weimar set out for Philadelphia. He embarked on the *Phoenix*, a "not large" steamboat whose boiler was "too powerful" for the boat's frail frame. "This," complains Saxe-Weimar, "communicated to the vessel such a violent shock that it was hardly possible to write." Yet the voyage had its agreeable aspects:

The day was beautiful. The city, as well as the extensive suburb of St. Marie afforded a very picturesque view. It is hard to determine where the extensive suburb of St. Marie ends as the houses gradually stand farther apart until they are confounded with the sugar plantations, of which we observed a good many on both banks of the river. . . . The banks are highly cultivated. Behind the fields, however, the cypress woods are seen to commence. Towards the afternoon something broke in the engine and we had to lie by for repairs for about three hours. We heard music on the plantations as the negroes were allowed to amuse themselves on this first day of the Easter holy-days.

The Mississippi unfolded in all its splendor and mystery, awakening for the onlookers haunting memories of Hernando de Soto, of Marquette and Joliet, of La Salle and the chevalier de Tonti, of the le Moyne brothers, of Juchereau de St. Denis, of cruel Périer and the elegant marquis de Vaudreuil, and, finally, of the countless Indians who in the days of their freedom, before the arrival of the white man, had furrowed the reddish waters of the river in their slender canoes.

Overlooking the riverbanks stood the great plantations of Louisiana. In the north of the state, their owners were Anglo-Saxon and the principal crop was cotton; in the south, they belonged to Creole

252

planters and were mainly given over to sugarcane. Just outside New Orleans—an area that today would lie well within the city limits—were the plantations of the Creole aristocracy. These wealthy sugarcane growers played a prominent role in the political, administrative, and social life of Louisiana.

From the river, the lovely, fertile land stretched out as far as the eye could see, continuing unbroken all the way to the horizon. In the forefront of this flat landscape rose the levee, with its growth of poplars, palm trees, willows, and tall wild grasses. Beyond the levee stretched sweeping green lawns planted with orange trees, magnolias, and huge oaks festooned with Spanish moss. Further back lay the main house and its outbuildings: kitchen, bachelor apartments, dovecote, stable, greenhouse. Behind the main house were the slave quarters, a cluster of buildings forming a kind of miniature village with its "main street" and its bell tower. Beyond the slave quarters rose the sugar mill, a large brick structure with a tall chimney. Beyond the mill lay the vast fields of sugarcane, while far in the distance a dense, swampy forest formed a backdrop to the scene. Arching over the whole was the huge, luminous Louisiana sky, often lit up in the evening by spectacular sunsets.

THE MASTER'S HOUSE

The homes of the Creole planters may have lacked the majesty of houses built of stone, but they charmed the eye with their simplicity of design and harmonious proportions. In the early 1820s, when the Greek Revival style was coming into vogue in the North, and Doric columns, Corinthian capitals, and marble staircases were all the rage, the Creoles remained faithful to the West Indian style: long, low-slung houses with wood and brick frames, stuccoed in white or pale yellow, and topped by a long sloping roof. C. C. Robin has left a detailed description:

All of them have covered balconies, some stretching all the way around the house, others confined to the front and back facades. The balconies are roofed by extensions of the main roof, which goes straight up to a point, rather than flattening out like our mansards. These roofs are supported by small wooden columns, most attractive to the eye. The balconies are generally some eight or nine feet deep.

Hope Estate Plantation, Baton Rouge. The house, built in 1798, was typical of the plantation architecture of the region. The octagonal dovecotes are a distinctly French touch. From a gouache on paper by Marie Adrien Persac, *ca.* 1857.

The balconies prevented the sun's rays from striking the surface of the house and assured that the interior would stay reasonably cool. In the daytime, the inhabitants stepped out on the balconies to take the air; in the evening, they dined on them and enjoyed the evening breeze from the river.

Harmonious in its proportions and appropriate to the climate, this style enjoyed enduring popularity. Twenty years later, in the 1840s, the people around New Orleans were still erecting the same type of house—with the added refinement of columns built of brick and surfaced, like the rest of the structure, in stucco.

The plantation houses were never more than two stories high, and the balconies were constructed around the second story. The rooms were large, with lofty ceilings and tall windows flanked on the outside by dark green shutters. To promote air circulation, the rooms were lavishly fenestrated; the dining room generally obtained cross ventilation from facing sets of windows. The furnishings here, as in the owner's New Orleans townhouse, were simple but elegant. The Creole planter's home was designed not for public display but for the felicities of family life. Rather than obtruding from the landscape, the house seemed to blend into it.

In fact, the facade of the house was often partially obscured by trees and flowering bushes that both sheltered the building from the summer sun and surrounded it with pleasant smells. Turning off the River Road—a route that left the traveler covered with dust during the dry spells and spattered with mud in the rainy season—one entered the estate by way of an avenue bordered with oaks, magnolias, orange and lemon trees. Another tree-lined thoroughfare led to the sugar mill. On every side, the visitor encountered nature in all its abundance: lush vegetation, either running wild or precariously held in check by man.

The plantation owners often took great care in laying out their gardens. Valcourt Aime, descendant of an ancient Breton family that had emigrated to Louisiana when the territory was still under French dominion, imported a French gardener who had earned a diploma from the Paris Botanical Gardens and placed a dozen slaves under his direction. Then Aime proceeded to bring in plants from every corner of the globe: Korea, Madagascar, India, Japan, Europe, Central

America. His gardens became so renowned that his fellow Creoles, always prone to hyperbole, nicknamed him the Louis XIV of Louisiana.

THE SLAVE QUARTERS

A planting of cypresses separated the master's domain from the slave quarters. A typical slave dwelling was built of wood; it had two, three, and sometimes four rooms and housed two families. The windows had no glass panes but were equipped with wooden shutters to keep out the cold. The furniture was sparse: rudimentary beds whose tickings were stuffed with dried Spanish moss (no different, in this respect, from the mattresses of the masters), a table; in the room that served as a kitchen, there were a few crude chairs and a worktable. There were no closets or armoires; a few nails or pegs driven into the wall accommodated the slaves' modest wardrobes. On most plantations, the slave cabins were lined up on either side of a long street; occasionally, they were grouped around a small square or open area, rather like a tiny European village. Joseph Holt Ingraham, a Yankee traveling by steamboat to New Orleans, glimpsed the slave quarters of a sugarcane plantation from the deck: "some forty snow white cottages built around a pleasant square, in the center of which was a grove or cluster of magnificent sycamores."

After visiting New Orleans, Ingraham paid a call on a friend who owned an estate a few miles outside the city. He noted that the slaves' cottages were laid out "with great regularity" on either side of a long street and that each cottage had "an enclosed piece of ground, apparently for a vegetable garden." The slaves' quarters teemed with activity: "Decrepit negroes were basking in the sun, mothers were nursing babies, one or two old blind negresses were spinning in their doors. . . . At the foot (of a tower with a belfry) half a score of naked kids were frolicking or sleeping in the warm sun, under the surveillance of an old matron who sat knitting upon a camp-stool in the midst of them."

Every plantation had its bell tower, which roused the slaves at daybreak, called them to breakfast (depending on the season, at around seven or eight in the morning), summoned them to dinner at noon, and sounded for the last time at sunset to announce the end of the working day. At that time, the slaves returned to their cottages, where they could tend to their own little garden plots, if they were not too exhausted from the day's labor, or indulge in a bit of fishing. Some considerate masters gave the slaves Saturday afternoons to work in their own vegetable gardens, and on certain plantations slaves were permitted to raise their own pigs and chickens.

Much has been written about the slaves' diet, with Americans and Creoles each accusing the other of providing the slaves with inadequate nourishment. Karl Pöstl, always a stickler for detail, has left us a precise account of a typical daily menu. Breakfast for the slaves, he informs us, consisted of a soup cooked with a strip of bacon or salted meat. For the midday meal, there was cornbread, salted or fresh meat, and a corn pudding. The evening meal consisted of cornbread and soup, but no meat. Pöstl emphasizes that the slaves were regularly supplied with meat "to keep them in good condition"; it is clear, however, that their diet was not properly balanced. The slaves rarely ate green vegetables; even those who cultivated small gardens generally sold their greens for pocket money, just as they more often than not sold any fish that they caught.

Food management varied from plantation to plantation. On some, the master distributed the provisions and the slaves took charge of preparing their own meals; on others, the meals were delivered to the fields on carts, fully cooked.

On the smaller estates, the masters usually took a keen interest in the day-to-day management of affairs and watched over the well-being of their slaves. On the larger plantations, particularly those of the Creole sugarcane growers, the supervision of the slaves as a rule was left to appointed overseers, who were generally white men but sometimes free blacks.

A Sugar Plantation

Etienne de Boré, the first planter to succeed in granulating cane sugar, owned one of the finest sugarcane plantations on the lower Mississippi. His estate, only six miles from New Orleans' Vieux Carré, comprised a model farm as well as a sugar plantation. The enterprise was administered by two of the old man's grandsons, Jean-Baptiste and Deschapelles Lebreton, as well as by two other young

Frenchmen of good family who, having suffered financial reverses, were obliged to earn their own living as overseers. Despite his advanced age, Monsieur de Boré was deeply involved in the running of the estate, and nothing was done without his advice and approval. Every evening, the supervisory staff met with him to receive their orders for the next day's program.

The farm was so productive that every day a wagonload of vegetables, fruit, and poultry was driven to market by some of Monsieur de Boré's slaves. The wagon returned to the plantation later in the morning, bringing the mail, the master's newspaper, and a fresh supply of local gossip.

The plantation had extensive gardens, and visitors were always impressed by the beauty of their layout and the marvelous variety of trees and shrubs. The paths were bordered by orange, lemon, and pecan trees; laurels and crepe myrtles surrounded the house. Virtually every variety of fruit or flower able to grow in that subtropical climate was represented on the plantation. As for the sugarcane, the plantation operated so efficiently that the yield varied very little from year to year, despite the caprices of the weather.

The overseer had no easy job. It was his responsibility to assemble the slaves every morning and assign them their daily tasks. He had to see to it that their cottages were kept clean and in a decent state of repair, as well as supervising their personal hygiene and arranging for the care of the sick. The overseer was expected to maintain order and discipline among the slaves and to make sure that their work was up to standard. He was required to exercise authority and command respect—but if he showed himself too harsh, too rigidly authoritarian in his responses, he risked inciting the slaves to run away from the plantation or even to rise in open revolt. Whether he erred on the side of strictness or laxity, the overseer was certain of incurring the wrath of his employer.

Nineteenth-century attitudes toward corporal punishment obviously differed greatly from ours, and it is sometimes difficult to assess where, in the eyes of the slave owners, discipline ended and intimidation or brutality began. Every overseer was equipped with a whip, which he cracked at regular intervals to "encourage" the workers at their tasks—rather like an animal tamer in the circus. Under the administration of Governor André Roman, a public servant whose moral stature was admired by all, overseers were forbidden to administer more than ten lashes to a slave without first procuring the master's permission. Charles Gayarré, another grandson of Etienne de Boré, records: "I do not remember having seen a negro whipped, but I remember having been present when occasionally one of them, for some delinquency, was put in the stocks for the night or during a whole Sunday."

The slave always had the right to appeal to his master if he believed that he was being bullied or brutalized by the overseer, and there is evidence that the masters often intervened on the slave's behalf.

The overseer lived in a small cottage separate from the main building and was treated by the master and his family with a courtesy not unmixed with condescension. The slaves generally looked upon him with something close to contempt.

The overseer was assisted by a driver, or head slave, chosen for his intelligence and authority. He too carried a whip and supervised the work details in the fields or in the refinery during the processing of the sugar crop. He also took charge of the slaves during their Saturday night expeditions to the "bambousses" or dances at neighboring plantations. According to Audubon, some of these drivers attained considerable rank in the plantation hierarchy. On the estate of Monsieur St. Amand, Audubon met a "good looking black man" who had been in his master's employ "for eight years, and had obtained so much of his master's confidence, as to have the entire care of the plantation." The man combined severity with kindliness: "He spoke roughly to his underservants but had a good indulgent eye, and no doubt does what he can to accommodate master and all."

Like most large plantations in the South, the de Boré plantation was an almost self-sufficient community. The estate produced an abundance of eggs, milk, butter, meat, poultry, vegetables, and fruit. The storehouses were piled high with corn, rice, and hay. The stables housed both draft and saddle horses, as well as mules for heavy labor; they also contained innumerable carts, carriages, and buggies. Wool and leather came from the sheep and cattle on the estate, honey from the plantation's own hives. Game was plentiful in the neighboring forests; the Mississippi yielded fish and shrimp, and crabs could be found in nearby lakes and ponds. As for skilled labor, the slave population included carpenters, masons, blacksmiths, wheelwrights, and sometimes, according to Gayarré, "an excellent shoemaker."

The planters were also fortunate in the materials available to them. At the beginning of the century, Berquin-Duvallon remarked:

The Louisiana sugarcane grower can count among his additional advantages (besides that of having the Mississippi riverway outside his front door) ready access to three commodities essential to the running of his estate: brick, which can be manufactured from the alluvial soil; wood for construction, barrelmaking and fuel, which is available in the forests that stretch for twenty-five or thirty acres at the end of his land; and shells (which are used in place of limestone in this region for making whitewash), which are found in abundance in nearby lakes and transported in great quantities by means of a canal that cuts through the intervening stretches of forest.

Monsieur de Boré even grew his own grapes, but he imported his wine from France, for nothing but the best would do for his table. The self-sufficiency of his estate was by no means unique. The plantations of the Destrehans, the Fortiers, the Duplantiers, the Bringiers, the Lacadières, the Aimes, the McCutcheons (Americans who had purchased the old Trépagnier estate on the banks of the Mississippi and adopted the Creole style of living), and, of course, the Marignys all enjoyed the status of small principalities. As the American traveler William Sparks recalled, these families lived "surrounded by wealth, tangible and substantial, descending from generation to generation, affording to each all the blessings wealth can give."

Generous and hospitable by temperament, the great plantation owners seemed eager to share their abundance with others. The hunting parties at the Marigny or de Boré estates were lovingly remembered by many. Halfway between the river and the cypress grove on the de Boré estate was situated a lake, a favorite rendezvous for wild ducks, moor hens, snipes, corncrakes, and plovers. The lake was also a well-known gathering place for the élite of New Orleans—bankers, merchants, lawyers, doctors, and brokers—who assembled there every Saturday, rifles in hand. They came uninvited, for Boré Lake, as it was popularly known, had come to be regarded as public domain, and the owners took no offense at the encroachment. Some of the sportsmen set up tents along the lake, in order to get in a bit of shooting before dawn. Bonfires were lit, and the campers caroused late into the night. Occasionally, Charles Gayarré reports, disputes broke out—culminating, in proper Creole style, with a duel.

Amidst the luxuriant undergrowth, where land and water intermingled, game was in good supply, and the sportsmen often transformed their hunting parties into bloody massacres. Audubon reports that at a hunting expedition he attended near Bayou St. John, more than 48,000 plovers were shot in a single day. "A single individual occupying a place near me, claimed sixty-three dozen."

Monsieur de Boré at Home

Etienne de Boré had been a cavalry captain in the army of Louis XV, and he was thoroughly "old regime" in his attitudes and habits. His passion for all things military had, however, won him over to the Bonapartist cause. An engraving of the Battle of Austerlitz held a place of honor on his drawing room wall: the picture depicted the moment when General Rapp, bareheaded and out of breath, had galloped up to the Emperor and gasped out "Victory! Victory! The enemy is annihilated!" To which Napoleon reportedly replied: "I never saw thee, Rapp, looking so handsome." This engraving was a constant source of irritation to Boré's son-in-law, the elder Gayarré, whose father was a Spanish grandee. Though born in Louisiana, Don Carlos Gayarré remained strongly attached to his father's homeland, and he had little love for the man who had so brutally conquered Spain. He refrained from voicing his sentiments in his father-in-law's presence, but whenever a French victory was announced, he would promptly retire to his bedchamber. Snatching up his guitar, he would then give full vent to his patriotic ardor, bellowing out bloodthirsty battle hymns at the top of his voice. The defeat, exile, and death of Napoleon afforded Gayarré deep satisfaction. The same was true for Pierre Foucher, another of de Boré's sons-in-law, who had a propensity for republicanism and disliked kings and priests as much as emperors.

With these three opinionated gentlemen all living under the same roof, one would have expected the atmosphere of the de Boré home to be somewhat tense and acrimonious. "And yet," says Charles Ga-

yarré, "they all lived in perfect harmony, which shows that they possessed at least a large fund of good-breeding and forbearance."

Life on the plantation was strictly regulated by routine, imposing
a quasi-military discipline on all the inhabitants, both black and
white. A bell sounded at dawn, awakening the slaves and summon-
ing them to assemble in front of the master's house, where they all
knelt for prayers before departing for the fields. A male member of
the de Boré family was always in attendance at these morning prayer
meetings and again in the evening, at sundown, when the slaves re-
assembled for prayers. Charles Gayarré was hardly more than eight
years old when he was called on to preside over the prayers of the
"dark assemblage."

After the evening meals, guards armed with heavy clubs were
posted two by two at various points around the estate. Their tour of
duty lasted until midnight, at which time it was the overseer's responsibility to assure that everyone was in his proper place.

The master's meals followed a relentlessly rigid schedule: breakfast at eight, lunch at two in the afternoon, dinner at seven. Monsieur de Boré kept an open table, and it was a rare meal that did not
include several guests—family friends from New Orleans or neighboring estates, travelers passing through the area, or itinerant peddlers. At this period, a steady stream of peddlers plied the route between Baton Rouge and New Orleans, traveling overland by foot or
wagon or descending the river by canoe. The peddlers often arranged
to pass by the de Boré estate, where they knew they would be welcomed at the family table and later provided with a comfortable bed
for the night. That a former officer of Louis XV—albeit a converted
Bonapartist—would receive such miscellaneous company into his
home might seem cause for surprise. Gayarré explains: "They belonged by virtue of their white skin to the aristocratic class, and it
was the prevailing feeling not to degrade the poorest and humblest
of the Caucasian race by lowering him to the level of the servile
blacks."

A bell summoned the members of the household to meals. Monsieur de Boré, punctual to the minute, immediately repaired to the
dining room. He would remain standing at his place—he had a large
chair in the middle of the long table—for two or three minutes, giv-

ing the rest of the diners time to assemble, and then, with a wave of his hand, would invite everyone to be seated. Those who arrived after the others had sat down seldom attempted to join the company, for Monsieur de Boré subjected all latecomers to a stare of furious disdain.

Like the French nobles of the pre-Revolutionary era, the wealthy Creoles made it a point of honor to spread a lavish table. On Sundays, the family was often joined at dinner by several dozen guests. The quality of the food was generally very high, and the wines were never less than reputable; for though the Creoles were not, as a group, much given to drunkenness or gluttony, they had a fine appreciation for the pleasures of the table. A Creole banquet typically featured a great variety of carefully prepared dishes, each of which the guest was expected to sample.

CREOLE COOKING

Creole cooking was both inventive and refined; but it was not to everyone's taste. Pierre de Laussat, Napoleon's administrator in the Louisiana colony, found the food far too spicy: "Such an abundance of spices! Such overpowering seasoning! Creole cooking is calculated to burn the palate!"

To be sure, Creole cooks have always made generous use of herbs and spices in preparing food. The Creole cuisine combines French, Spanish, African, and Indian elements: the spices, herbs, and garlic may come from one tradition, the sauces and pastries from another. Conforming to the French model with such classic dishes as charlotte russe, beignets, pain perdu, daubes, timbales, roasted meats, and fish filets covered with delicate sauces, Creole cooking also featured dishes of local origin, which gave the ingenious cook a chance to display his individual flair. Gayarré comments: "The negroes are born cooks, as other less favored beings are born poets. The African brute, guided by the superior intelligence of his Caucasian master . . . gradually evolved into an artist of the highest degree of excellence, and had from natural impulses and affinities, without any conscious analysis of principles, created an art of cooking for which he would deserve to be immortalized." The slaves did not draw their knowledge from cookbooks, for few of them could read. They relied on experience, memory, and sheer intuition. "Their inspiration," says Gayarré, "came directly from the deity of the pots and pans." And he imagines "with what supreme, indescribable contempt would Aunt Henriette or Uncle Frontin have looked down upon the best French *cordon bleu* that had presumed to teach her or him!"

Gumbos were the most original creation of Creole cuisine. Gumbo was soup—but soup with a difference. A Creole lady, Hélène Allain, wrote: "You start by making a hearty stew of ham, oyster and chicken; you then add a quantity of water, generously seasoned, to a *roux*, and, just before serving, add a shower of the aromatic powder that will make the soup thicken. . . . The gumbo is served along with rice and seasonings." The aromatic powder was filé—powdered sassafras leaf—"a greenish powder generally prepared by the Indians, impoverished and debilitated descendants of the once-proud Choctaw tribe." Okra could also be used to thicken the gumbo. A great favorite was *gombo z'herbes*, or herb gumbo, made with bacon, a large variety of greens and aromatic herbs, okra, ham, and crabmeat. But every Creole cook had his own "secret" recipe for gumbo, and no dish offered so bold a challenge to the cook's creative talents.

Gumbos were served at every occasion, at the homes of rich and poor alike. In high society, a gumbo was traditionally offered, along with a ham, a roast, and pastries, at the close of an evening's entertainment. Sometimes the meal would be served at dawn, accompanied by a good deal of strong, hot coffee, just before the guests took their departure.

Creole cooking abounded with regional specialties: turtle soup, oyster paté, bouillabaisse, shellfish stews, crayfish bisque, and jambalaya—a dish more commonly associated with the people of the Delta than with the Creole aristocrats of New Orleans or the lower Mississippi. Jambalaya was, in fact, the favorite dish of the Delta people, and in almost every kitchen of the region a pot regularly hung suspended over the fireplace, giving off a savory aroma of smoked bacon, shrimp, crabs, onions, ham, tomatoes, rice, and red peppers.

The black kitchen help were not only brilliant cooks; they also understood the art of laying an attractive table. On festive occasions, a vast array of dishes—meat, fish, numerous sundries—presented a gustatory display of awesome proportions and admirable ingenuity.

Etienne de Boré had two chefs, one black and one mulatto, and numerous assistant cooks. The kitchen was a small brick structure situated some distance from the master's house. This arrangement was common to most plantations. It greatly reduced the risk of a serious fire and insulated the family dwelling both from the cooking smells and from the incessant noise—laughter, disputes, singing—of the kitchen crew. On rainy days, however (and in Louisiana the rains can be torrential), transporting the food from the kitchen to the master's table presented a problem. In such weather, the atmosphere in the kitchen grew anxious and stormy.

At this era, the cooking was generally done over a large fireplace, which was fueled with thick tree trunks. The meat was prepared on a spit, and cakes and breads were baked in iron ovens placed over the hot embers. The chimney was festooned with pots, pans, and kitchen utensils, all hanging from iron hooks. A large worktable occupied the center of the room.

For the plantation master's children, the kitchen was a wondrous domain full of warmth, delicious smells, and the cheerful hum of conversation. The cooks and kitchen help who presided over this realm often treated the children to songs and stories, as well as hot morsels of whatever was cooking. The memory of these visits to the kitchen was one of the enduring treasures of a plantation childhood.

New Year Festivities

For children and slaves, the New Year was the most festive holiday of the Creole calendar, for the Creoles had not yet adopted the Anglo-Saxon custom of exchanging gifts at Christmas. New Year's Day was a holiday for all. The night before, the whole plantation celebrated. In the master's house, an elaborate supper was served, complete with fine wines, and the arrival of the New Year was toasted in both punch and champagne. In the slaves' quarters, a great feast was also set out, and the slaves, dressed in their Sunday finery, danced and sang and drank tafia until dawn.

The last to go to bed, the slaves were also the first to rise, for it was their duty to wake their masters, bring them their breakfast, and wish them a Happy New Year. Alcée Fortier reports that the black mammies traditionally greeted their boy charges with the wish that they be good, rich, and happy, and their girl charges with the hope that they would behave, get a rich husband, and have many children.

Later in the day, the field laborers came to the big house to pay their respects to the planter and his family. Even the very elderly and infirm among the slaves, who generally left their cabins only to warm themselves in the sun, joined the procession to the big house. A good master never failed to give each of his slaves a present on New Year's Day. Generally the men received a pair of trousers, the women a dress and a brightly colored kerchief. The slaves also traditionally were given a sack of flour, some household utensil, or a blanket. There was no field work that day, and the laborers were free to dance and make music.

For Creole families, Epiphany was a day for exchanging visits. In the afternoon, the young people set off to pay their respects to their elders, and the roads between New Orleans and the outlying plantations were crowded with traffic. In New Orleans itself, the day was a particularly noisy one. In spite of the mayor's formal ban on fireworks, the sky was crisscrossed with rockets, and firecrackers exploded in every back street and alley. Groups of blacks wandered through the city, pausing to sing under promising windows in the hope of receiving a few coins. The children of the town added to the ruckus, parading by with their new drums and trumpets.

A well-bred young man never made a New Year's call without bringing a gift for the mistress of the house—generally candy or flowers, for a more elaborate gift would be interpreted as a declaration of interest, if there were a marriageable daughter in the house, or resented as an affront if there were not. On New Year's Day, the dining room table in many Creole homes was covered with a profusion of cut flowers, sweets, and pastries, all surrounding a huge bowl of steaming punch. Toasts were exchanged, along with compliments and best wishes for the coming year. The day concluded with a light supper—though it is hard to believe that at this point anyone had much appetite left.

HARVEST TIME

Another occasion greatly looked forward to by the people along the river was the sugar harvest, though it was also a period of intense work for all those concerned with the crop. As Joseph Holt Ingraham observed, "The making of sugar and the making of love are two of the sweetest occupations of this world." In any case, even the slaves, on whom the greatest burden of labor fell, regarded harvest time as a season of festivity.

As Berquin-Duvallon explains, the sugarcane is planted during the period from January to March.

It takes root in early spring, is dormant during the dry months of May and June, begins to gather strength in July, and during the next three months, stimulated by the rains and by the humid heat, it expands and thickens at a great rate until, by the end of October, it forms a towering growth some eight or nine feet tall, and is ready to be cut and processed.

From the moment of planting until the last cane has fallen to the ground, the work is unremitting. Constant hoeing is required, and before the frosts (which in Louisiana often occur in February) the old stalks must be cut down and used to mulch the seedlings. "Few agricultural regions require so much meticulous attention in order to yield a profitable return," comments Berquin-Duvallon. Part of the difficulty lay in the timing: "For a period of six months, from early October until the end of March, the sugar grower is caught up in a round of work, harvesting grains, fodder, and sugar crop, as well as overseeing the running of his estate."

The master or overseer was in the fields at dawn, both summer and winter, to supervise the slaves. In summer, the whites wore shirts and trousers of thin cotton, with straw hats to keep off the sun. In winter, they wore thicker clothes and, like their slaves, often donned hoods. Throughout the year, they wore soft black boots. As for the blacks, for many years they went virtually naked during the summer months. "Only their privates were covered by a strip of cloth attached to a waistband in front and behind," noted Perrin du Lac in 1804. C. C. Robin reports that "the women worked the fields in rags, with their breasts exposed."

Slave owners were obligated by law to distribute clothing to their slaves at least twice a year. According to V. Alton Moody, the slaves' wardrobe was similar to the one provided by the state to prisoners. The precise terms of the law were that slaves who did not have their own vegetable garden had the right to a cloth shirt and trousers for summer use, and a cloth shirt and woolen trousers and hood for the winter. All the slaves, even the household servants, went barefoot in the summer, but in the winter wore a sort of primitive moccasin. The women dressed in makeshift garments for working in the field, but on Sundays, Robin recalls, "they decked themselves out like ladies," or at any rate attired themselves in dresses that made up in colorfulness for what they lacked in elegance.

During the summer months, the sugarcane required little attention beyond periodic hoeing, and the field hands were employed elsewhere. The slaves harvested the corn, brought in the hay, cut wood, planted vegetables, cleaned gutters, repaired the levee, and checked the machinery in the sugar refinery to assure that it was in good operating order.

During the actual period of the sugar harvest, everyone—blacks and whites, masters and slaves—worked very hard. On some plantations, the work crews were divided into three shifts, working six hours apiece; on others, the shifts were eight hours long, and at still others the slaves worked twelve or even fifteen hours at a stretch, Sundays and holidays included. We are assured, however, that the slaves were very well fed and put on weight during the harvest, for the masters supplemented their diet in order to keep up their morale.

For those in charge—the master, the estate manager, or some outside expert (generally a former sugar refiner from Santo Domingo brought in by an inexperienced planter to oversee the manufacturing of the sugar)—the work was equally demanding. Some of them put in eighteen hours at a stretch for weeks on end. But as the sugar piled up in the storehouse—the sugar sap being first converted to syrup, then into solid granules—a corresponding pile of dollars took glistening shape in the supervisors' imaginations and provided an incentive for renewed labor.

Whereas the planters in Santo Domingo could recycle the crushed sugar stalks or "bagasse" as fuel during the refining process, the

Louisianians were obliged to use wood, for their humid climate rendered the canes too moist to burn. The narrow stalks were harvested first, the thicker ones later. The plantation owner often lent a hand himself in cutting the canes, which were carried off to the presses as fast as they fell. Once the fragrant juice had been extracted, the process of crystallization began.

The planter used four or even five different kettles for the refining process. Each had a distinctive name and function. There was the "grand," in which the juice, freshly extracted from the cane, was initially boiled; the "cleanser," in which it received a second boiling; the "torch," in which the owner watched for the first signs of purification and thickening; the "syrup," in which the juice was supposed to obtain a syrupy consistency (although, according to Pierre de Laussat, that "never quite happened"); and the "battery," in which the final cooking took place.

Visitors to a plantation during harvest season were often taken on a tour of the refinery. One such visitor, Joseph Holt Ingraham, recorded his impressions: "As we entered (in the boiling-house), the slaves, who were dressed in coarse trousers, some with, others without shirts, were engaged in the several departments of their sweet employment whose fatigues some African Orpheus was lightening with a loud chorus which was instantly hushed, on our entrance, to a half-assured whistling." The slaves worked under the watchful eye of a white overseer "with a very unpleasant physiognomy." The man was leaning casually against one of the brick pillars. When the party of visitors entered, he "raised his hat respectfully . . . but did not change his position." He carried "a short-handled whip loaded in the butt, which had a lash four or five times the length of the staff." Although he answered his master when spoken to, he said not a word to the visitors and kept his eyes fixed continually on the slaves.

The cutting of the last row of sugarcanes was the occasion for a piece of ritual. The driver selected the tallest of the canes and the "best knife" or best worker in his crew. When the other canes had been felled, everyone gathered around the single remaining stalk, which the driver had tied with a blue ribbon. The chosen field hand circled the stalk, chanting a song in its praise, and brandishing a knife. After the stalk had been cut, it was borne in triumph to the master's house. All the slaves, men, women, and children, joined the joyful procession, waving bright bandanas and singing songs in honor of the cane. The master greeted each adult black with a glass of hard liquor, and the day culminated in a harvest ball.

The harvest season generally lasted from two to three months, depending on the plantation. Several days of holiday followed, which the slaves filled with dancing and festivity. The song of the sugarcane, "improvised by one of the gang, the rest all joining in a prolonged and unintelligible chorus," could be heard far into the night. The voices struck Ingraham as "most musical, most melancholy."

WORK SONGS

Singing was an integral accompaniment to the slaves' work, a vital and distinctive form of expression. Many planters recognized the role that music played in alleviating the field laborers' tasks and not only allowed singing but even encouraged it. On some plantations, one especially gifted singer was assigned the job of leading the music for his fellow slaves. Clearly, singing served as a greater stimulus for production than did the threat of the lash.

These work songs—a few phrases improvised by a "leader," then elaborated by the work crew—were a typically African mode of expression, forming part of the blacks' cultural heritage. The blacks of West Africa, for instance, were generally either farm workers or fishermen, and they had songs for all their daily activities: songs for planting grain, for netting fish, for hunting, weaving, tanning skins, bringing in the harvest. As Leroi Jones reminds us, on the plantations of Georgia and Louisiana, these old songs had lost their meaning. The innumerable occupations of the African day were now reduced to a handful: working in the fields among sugarcane, rice, cotton, or tobacco. In Africa, the black had worked his own field; in his new life, he worked for a master. No longer could he sing: "After the planting / if the gods bring rain / my family, my ancestors / will be as rich as they are beautiful."

The transplanted African had to adapt his old work songs to the altered conditions of his new life, and the once vigorous rhythms were gradually transformed into soulful laments wrung from the depths of the singer's soul. No longer did the slaves implore the gods for abundant rainfall, rich harvests, good hunting or fishing; now they asked only to be eased of their pains and solaced in their sufferings. Yet in spite of their hardships they managed to retain a sense of joy, which manifested itself in dance and festivity. The sugarcane rituals perhaps preserved the African musical tradition in its purest form.

The African heritage seemed to survive longest on the large plantations, where the slaves formed self-sustaining communities on the estate. Even there, however, Creole and English words crept into the songs. They were needed to describe those aspects of daily life that had no equivalent in the old culture; and inevitably, with time, fewer and fewer slaves could speak or understand the African dialects.

The American writer Lafcadio Hearn wrote down a song overheard on a Louisiana plantation, in which Creole French mingles strangely but characteristically with African dialect:

Ouendé, ouendé macaya!
Mo pas barassé, macaya!
Ouendé, ouendé macaya!
Mo bois bon divin, macaya!
Ouendé, ouendé macaya!
Mo mangé bon poulet, macaya!
Ouendé, ouendé macaya!

As Hearn translates:

Go on! go on! eat enormously!
I ain't one bit ashamed—eat outrageously!
Go on! go on! eat prodigiously!
I drink good wine!—eat ferociously!
Go on! go on! eat unceasingly!
I eat good chicken—gorging myself!
Go on! go on! etc. . . .

The song is a call to feast; the African words invite the diners to "stuff themselves," while the *gombo* French drops polite references to the "good wine" and "good chicken" that the guests may consume without being "ashamed." Leroi Jones interprets the song as representing, in its two languages, a split personality in the slaves: the language of the masters expresses the slaves' naïve aspirations to white refinement and restraint, while the African dialect gives vent to a natural tendency to exuberance and excess. In his interpretation, the song reveals the unconscious guilt of a people born in servitude, who seek to identify themselves with those who enslave them. It reflects two different and opposing worlds that occasionally intermingle and overlap, as when the white festivities spread to the slave quarters on the plantation.

The beauty and complexity of African music was lost on the planters. They found the slave songs meaningless or incomprehensible, even when they were sung in Creole dialect. The melodies they considered barbarous, the dances childish or improper. The blacks, for their part, were scandalized by the spectacle of their masters dancing the waltz, with their arms wound around the waists of their partners.

From the moment of birth to the moment of death, the masters and slaves on a plantation shared in a common fund of daily experience that built up an intimacy, a personal closeness and warmth that was seldom found in the city. But no matter how affectionate a master the Creole planter might be, he never concerned himself with the slaves' education or their psychological well-being. He was content if he knew that they were adequately fed, properly dressed, and enjoying general good health. Even the best master tended to regard all blacks as "barbarians" (the term is Charles Gayarré's) and to treat them like feckless, ignorant children who had to be kept in line with the whip, just like the white children up in the main house. Because the masters harbored no ill will toward their slaves and indeed looked on them with a degree of affection—caring for them if they fell ill, granting them permission to hold dances, supplying liquor and molasses on the occasion of a feast day or a birth in the family— they concluded that the slaves were happy. Habit inspired complacency, and the slave owners seemed insensitive to the indignities inherent in their peculiar institution as were the northerners to the misery of their growing industrial populations or the frontiersmen to the merciless decimation of the Indians.

There were some planters, however, who ventured to express doubt as to the validity of the institution. Most prominent was Julien Poydras, a French-born plantation owner of enormous wealth. He had begun his career as a traveling salesman who cut a conspicuous figure in the streets of New Orleans: up to his deth in 1824, he remained faithful to the buckled shoes and silk stockings of the ancien régime. In his will, Poydras provided for the freeing of all 1,200 of his slaves over a period of twenty-five years. Slaves aged sixty or over were to be given food and shelter for the remainder of their lives, along with an annual allowance of twenty-five dollars. Poydras bequeathed five hundred dollars apiece to certain household servants, and ten dollars apiece to all others. A short time later, two other wealthy landowners, Alexander Milne and John McDonogh left wills granting freedom to certain of their slaves. McDonogh's will also specified that the overseers were "to continue to bring the negroes together for morning and evening prayers . . . and [were] to establish (law permitting) a Sunday school and a building for the worship of God on each of my estates."

11

The World of Bayous and Prairies

Vast fields of cotton stretched along the banks of the Mississippi above Baton Rouge, extending along the Bayou Boeuf and the Bayou Lafourche, through the foothills of Natchitoches and Opelousas, and all the way to Attakapas and to the parishes of Pointe Coupée and Feliciana. The daily life of the cotton planter was similar enough to that of the sugar planter (though the former was generally Anglo-Saxon and Protestant rather than Creole and Catholic) that we can dispense with a detailed description. Like the sugar planter, the cotton planter usually lived in a handsome house surrounded by oaks and magnolias. He ruled his estate like a feudal overlord, kept an open table, and was fond of hunting, horseback riding, and vigorous exercise. The slaves on the cotton plantations labored long hours in the fields under the watchful eyes of overseers, just like the slaves who tended the sugarcane. The more pious among their masters found occasions to remind them that the institution of slavery was condoned, even approved, by the Holy Bible—for had not Noah himself condemned the sons of Canaan to perpetual bondage? And were not the blacks clearly placed on earth to serve white masters? Many conscientious slave owners regarded it as their duty to preach the Gospel to their blacks, and, as we have seen, some undertook to construct churches on their estates for the especial use of the slaves.

Where the cotton and the sugar plantations differed was in the rhythm of the work. Cotton seeds were sown in early April, and in less than two weeks the young plants broke through the surface of the soil. They flowered in June, and in August the capsules burst open, revealing the beautiful, silky tufts within. The harvest took place in mid-September. From dawn to dusk, virtually the entire slave population on the estate, men, women, and children, could be seen moving slowly through the cotton fields, hauling huge baskets or sacks that they stuffed methodically with cotton, keeping time to the rhythm of a plaintive work song. When the sacks and baskets were filled, their contents were emptied into a wagon and transported to the cotton gin. Every large plantation possessed one or more gins, and when the harvest on the estate was completed, the gins were rented out to the owners of smaller plantations.

When the harvest was in, the celebrations began—a hectic series of balls, feasts, picnics. After this pause, everyone turned to the business of processing the cotton.

ORDINARY PEOPLE

It is well to keep in mind that the great cotton magnates, those aristocrats who figure so prominently in the folk history of Louisiana, were actually few in number. The vast majority of the rural white population lived on small or modest-sized holdings; many had no more than two or three slaves, with whom they worked side by side in the fields. The relationship between master and slave was often close: they took meals together and lived in adjacent quarters. Their intimacy was sometimes attested by the mulatto children who lived and played about the estate.

But perhaps the most important point to remember is that most of the landowners in Louisiana, as elsewhere in the South, owned no slaves at all. The landowners who fit this category were generally referred to as "poor whites," though the term did not always fit the reality. Some of them tilled their fields themselves with hoe and spade, but others could afford to hire field laborers, and some of them lived in a style that would have aroused the envy of more than a few small plantation owners. The "poor whites" fell into three groups: the Acadians, known as the "little people," who were the most numerous; the Germans, the most prosperous; and the Americans, the poorest.

Another class of property owners, while possessing land and even wealth, was condemned to live on the margins of society as only semicitizens: the free blacks. Some were simple farmers, working small holdings; a few owned cotton or sugar plantations. In the western parishes, they constituted a sizable portion of the population, and a number of them owned dozens of slaves. According to H. E. Sterkx, the total property value of the free blacks far exceeded that of the Acadians.

The Acadians, for their part, seemed to be resigned to a primitive and poverty-ridden existence. A few Acadian families did indeed prosper: they sent their sons to college and managed to cut a figure in Louisiana society. But the vast majority of Acadians seemed devoid of any other ambition but to live "just like their *popas* and their *grand-popas* before them."

In 1803, Perrin du Lac characterized the Acadians as follows:

They are lethargic by temperament, and seem little inclined to extricate themselves from the poverty that has oppressed them since their arrival in the territory. Lacking either vigor or ambition, they live on the very brink of destitution, scratching a meager living from the soil, which they till themselves with no outside help. These people have no sense of personal cleanliness; their houses seem more suitable for rearing livestock than human beings, and their children appear to receive little in the way of parental attention.

In the 1820s, a number of wealthy Americans, slaveowners on a large scale, moved into the traditionally Acadian territory along Bayou Lafourche and established sugarcane plantations. The proximity of these energetic neighbors in no way troubled the serenity of the old inhabitants. As a contemporary, William Sparks, reported:

The enterprise of the new-comers did not stimulate to emulation the action of these people. They were content and unenvious, and when kindly received and respectfully treated, were social and generous in their intercourse with their American neighbors. They were confiding and trustful; but once deceived, they were not to be won back, but only manifested their resentment by withdrawing from communicating with the deceiver, and ever after distrusting, and refusing him their confidence.

Gradually the Americans expanded their holdings in the region; as the Acadians retreated inland, the Americans bought them out. Some of the old settlers established themselves on previously uninhabited bayous; others withdrew deep into the cypress forests. They put up new homes on the high ground that rose from the swamps, "from the products of which, and the trophies of the gun and fishing line and hook, and an occasional frog, and the abundance of crawfish, they contrive to eke out a miserable livelihood, and afford the fullest illustration of the adage, 'Where ignorance is bliss, it is folly to be wise.'"

Sparks was conscious of the vast social and economic gulf separating the Acadians and the newcomers:

The contrast between these princely estates, and the palatial mansions which adorn them, and make a home of luxuriant beauty, and the little log huts, their immediate neighbors, tells at once that the population is either very rich or very poor, and that under such circumstances the communication must be extremely limited; for the ignorance of the poor unfits them for social and intelligent intercourse with their more wealthy and more cultivated neighbors. This is true whether the planter is French or American.

The Acadians peopled the parishes of Avoyelles, Lafayette, St. Martin, St. John the Baptist, St. Charles, and St. James. They were also to be found around Natchitoches and Opelousas and along Bayou Lafourche all the way down to the Gulf of Mexico. They became in time the indigenous population of the bayou regions, which seemed to suit their needs perfectly. Modest and easily satisfied, they lived off whatever bounty Nature could provide: they could always be sure of plenty of children, plenty of corn, rice, game, fish.

BAYOU LAFOURCHE

When, in the early 1820s, W. W. Pugh settled his family in the Lafourche region, he noted that both banks of the bayou were lined with small farm holdings, so closely crammed together that the bayou seemed to form a sort of village main street over a hundred miles long.

The Acadians were a prolific race, and families of a dozen or more children were the rule rather than the exception. When the father of a family died, his land was divided among the sons in narrow strips running from the bayou to the outlying cypress swamps. In time, houses proliferated: small, squat dwellings of rustic appearance, with walls made of adobe mixed with Spanish moss, roughly hewed cypress beams, and cypress plank roofs. A covered porch ran along the front of every house, which was placed so as to overlook the bayou—or rather the levee, for Bayou Lafourche, which caught the overflow of the Mississippi, was susceptible to flooding, and the people who inhabited its banks had been compelled to build a dike to protect themselves. The levee became the main thoroughfare for the inhabitants, for much of their activity centered on the water. When the waters were high, steamboats, brigs, and schooners passed up and down, carrying three or four hundred tons of freight each at a time. But the Acadians' preferred boat was the pirogue, a small, lithe craft made from a hollowed-out cypress log—a technique they had learned from the Indians.

Life on an Acadian farm followed a simple routine, which William Sparks described in detail. The women, along with their daughters, spun and sewed; washed the laundry in the bayou, their skirts tucked up around their legs; and combed and wove the cotton raised on the farm. The little ones, "half naked children with little, black piercing eyes, and dishevelled uncombed hair," played about the yard in the midst of the pigs, cows, dogs, and chickens. The wealthier Acadians had a horse and carriage; the poorer ones made do with a pirogue.

The menfolk worked in the fields, fished, or hunted for game. Both men and women were generally dressed in cotton clothing with red and blue stripes; the men wore broad-brimmed hats fashioned of palmetto leaves to protect themselves from the sun. In their kitchen gardens, they grew a little cotton, some rice, and corn, and reserved space for sweet potatoes and sometimes for sugarcane or tobacco. "Their wants were few," wrote William Sparks, "and were all supplied at home. Save a little flour, powder and shot, they purchase nothing." He omitted, however, to mention coffee, a drink beloved of the Acadians.

The Acadians built their own houses, made their own furniture, manufactured mattresses, dishware, shoes, cotton goods, clothing, sheets, bread—in short, virtually all their household needs. Frugal though they were, they knew how to enjoy themselves and avoided putting themselves to unnecessary labor. Their favorite pastimes were exchanging gossip with neighbors, dancing, and taking afternoon siestas.

"The population," notes W. W. Pugh, "was fond of amusements. Balls were of weekly occurrence, given at small cost, and the young

and middle-aged enjoyed themselves to their heart's content." The invitations were easily conveyed. William Sparks recalled that "a youth on his pony would take a small wand, and tie to its top end a red or white flag, and ride up and down the bayou, from the house where the ball was intended, for two or three miles; returning, tie the wand and flag to flaunt above the gate, informing all—'This is the place.'"

A more direct method of attracting the neighbors' attention, described by W. W. Pugh, was to dispatch a messenger "who fired a gun before the door of each dwelling . . . and announced in a loud voice: 'Bal ce soir chez . . . .'" The most popular dance at these occasions was the rigodon, whose rhythm was so infectious that the very musicians laid their violins aside to join the dancers. Refreshments usually consisted of a steaming pot of gumbo, washed down with tafia diluted with water.

The education of the male children in Acadian families was generally consigned to the fathers, that of the females to the mothers. Boys were taught to set traps, till the soil, hunt, and fish; girls learned to spin, sew, weave, and milk the cows. Like their parents, most of the children were illiterate. As good Catholics, they learned to say their prayers—a litany that served as the sum total of their cultural and spiritual resources.

The evening, after dinner, was the time for exchanging visits, gossip, and conversation. While the women sat at their looms, the men busied themselves repairing household tools or utensils, and the talk ran on until late into the night. Jay Karl Ditchy, a modern writer on the Acadians, describes a typical evening:

The conversation had less to do with agricultural matters than with the stuff of superstition. One could discover which of the old women in the community was most adept at foretelling the future; which of the old men could cure eye infections with a fragment of consecrated wafer; who could stop bleeding or heal scabies. One gained insight into the precise nature of the torments that awaited sinners in Hell, and the joys awaiting the godly in Paradise; and came to appreciate the prevalence and power of witches and sorcerers.

The old folk told anecdotes of their youth, when the region was still haunted by sinister old crones, mysterious strangers, and dissipated young people who took part in curious sabbath rites. Some of the elders attested to "aetherial music or strange, plaintive cries, mixed with bursts of strident music, which could sometimes be heard on foggy nights, especially in winter." If one of the Acadians could read, the rest listened with rapt attention as he read aloud the weather forecasts and recipes from the almanac. Werewolves were, of course, an inexhaustible topic of discussion, as were will-o'-the-wisps, which many people, in this region of swamps, attributed to the presence of lost souls.

Marriage Rites and Customs

Marriages—arranged, anticipated, presumptive—were another favorite topic of conversation at the Acadians' evening gatherings. The inhabitants of the Delta were a hot-blooded breed, and the mothers were anxious to marry off their daughters before the girls emerged from adolescence. The marriages were generally arranged by the families, though the parents did not entirely disregard their offsprings' preferences. The girl's family was in the market for a solid young Acadian who displayed ability in farming and raising livestock; the boy's family hoped for an industrious housekeeper, skilled at sewing, weaving, and spinning. The marriage negotiations were usually initiated by a relative or friend on the young man's side. The phrase for getting married, in the colorful Acadian dialect, was "boiling the pot together."

In the remoter regions of the Delta, where neither church nor priest was to be found, marriages were solemnized by a distinctive ritual. Before a gathering of relatives and neighbors, the young couple joined hands and jumped over a broomstick, which was held a foot off the ground. This rite completed, they were saluted as man and wife by the assembled witnesses.

Whenever possible, however, the marriage ceremony was held in church. According to William Sparks,

It was the custom for the bride and groom, with a party of friends, all on horseback, to repair without ceremony to the church, where they were united in matrimony by the good priest, who kissed the bride, a privilege he never failed to put into execution when he blessed the couple, received his fee, and sent them away rejoicing. The ceremony was short, and without ostentation; and then the happy and expectant pair, often on the same horse, would return with the party as they had come, with two or three musicians playing the violin in merry tunes on horseback, as they joyfully galloped home, where a ball awaited them at night, and all went merry with the married belle.

Sometimes the ceremony included a charivari—a gay, burlesque procession accompanied by a good deal of noise. The custom was an old one and was particularly popular in New Orleans, until the authorities suppressed it as a public nuisance. But the institution survived among the French-speaking population in the rural areas. The charivari was reserved for marriages between people of widely disparate ages and for the remarriages of widows and widowers. A band of revelers assembled at nightfall outside the house of the newlyweds and proceeded to serenade the couple by banging on pots, pans, and other metal utensils. This cacophony was accompanied by impromptu dancing and shouts of "Charivari! Charivari!" The racket was traditionally brought to an end by the appearance of the bride and groom, who invited their obstreperous well-wishers to have some refreshment and promised to schedule a marriage ball in the near future.

No sooner was an Acadian woman married than she became pregnant. She dispensed with the services of doctor or midwife when the time came to give birth; a friendly female neighbor provided her with all the help she needed. The babies were welcomed with joy, whatever their sex; and though the hygienic conditions were probably by no means ideal, the mortality rate was surprisingly low, for both mother and child received excellent nourishment.

Because Acadian families tended to run large, there was often a shortage of names for the latecomers—which may explain why some of the infants sported such unusual ones. Alcée Fortier reports that a boy named Duradon had five sisters answering to the names of Elfigé, Enyoné, Méridié, Ozéna, and Fronie; and that one father named his five sons Valmir, Valmor, Valsin, Valcourt, and Valérien, while another had a son called Deus and a daughter called Déussa. In practice, however, these fancy names were seldom used, for the

Acadians delighted in diminutives, and every family had its share of Dédés, Babas, Tatas, Vavas, Sasas, Lalas, Titis, Nonos, Bobos, Vévés.

THE DELTA

In the Delta, submerged forests and marshy flatlands alternated with patches of dry terrain overgrown with diverse vegetation. Cypress trees covered with Spanish moss, looking something like monstrous spiderwebs, filtered out the overhead light and gave a dreamlike cast to the landscape. The lakes and bayous teemed with alligators, tortoises, otters, muskrats. The Delta was a sanctuary for birds and a refuge for Indians, outlaws, and backwoodsmen with no other fortune than their strong arms and indomitable spirits.

The French were the first to settle in the Delta. They were followed by Spaniards, Italians, Irish, Chinese, Portuguese, Danes, Greeks, Swedes, Eastern Europeans—peasants driven from their native lands by poverty or repression, sailors who had jumped ship, adventurers of every kind. Most of the newcomers took to fishing or trapping and adapted so well to their environment that one visitor described them as "aquatic men with fins like fishes, noses like alligators, feet like ducks." A variety of languages flourished in the Delta (though, here as elsewhere in Louisiana, French remained dominant), and each community clung jealously to its own customs and way of life.

The Isleños, Spaniards from the Canary Islands, inhabited the Terre-aux-Boeufs ("Land of the Cattle"), a narrow strip between Lakes Lery and Borgne. Tradition had it that this region had once been overrun with bison; whence its name. The Isleños cultivated rice and some corn; they hunted, fished, and tended abundant household gardens. By all accounts, the soil was exceptionally fertile, but the Isleños were convinced *"que serve mas para los bueyes que para los cristianos"* ("that it was more suitable for cattle than for Christians").

The Isleños brought their game and garden produce to New Orleans in large carts drawn by cattle and harnessed, Spanish-style, to the beasts' horns. They would take a quick meal at some wayside inn, spend nine hours or so at the French Market, and then head directly home without ever allowing themselves to be distracted by the pleasures of the metropolis. The journey home was a long one, and since the cattle knew the way, their masters often stretched out on the straw strewn inside the carts and took a well-earned nap, lulled to sleep by the ponderous, methodical rhythm of the cattle's gait.

The Isleños tended to be somber, taciturn, and suspicious of strangers, even of their French neighbors with whom they shared the same religion. They kept to themselves and married among their own kind. They were devout Catholics, and the religious holidays, which they observed with fervor, seem to have provided the only break in their workaday routine.

Another ethnic group, the Tockos, based their economy on gathering oysters. Even at this period, small communities of fishermen had long been established in the Delta, where shellfish and crustaceans could be found in abundance. Oysters were the craze of the day: they were in great demand in New Orleans, where rich and poor alike devoured them at all hours of the day or night. Oysters were served raw, fried, or boiled; in stews or chowders; with coffee, tafia, or whiskey. The best were to be found in "Mussel Valley," a broad expanse of flatland between La Balize and Fort Plaquemine, whence they were transported to New Orleans. According to the Baron de Montlezun, "pirogues loaded with forty thousand oysters were sold for a total of forty gourdes,[1] and sometimes more."

Sometime around 1825 a group of sailors from the Dalmatian coast jumped ship and sought refuge in the swampy southern reaches of the Mississippi. Some of their compatriots eventually managed to join them, becoming in time the principal purveyors of oysters to the city of New Orleans. The Creoles called these people "Tockos"—a term whose etymology remains obscure.

The Tockos were migratory laborers who set up huts on stilts wherever the oyster beds were richest. They prized their pirogues above all their other possessions. Tockos were solitary, introverted, melancholy individuals who seemed to be congenitally afflicted with a sort of metaphysical anguish. Occasionally they came together for an evening to sing and drink wine; from time to time, one of them,

---

1. One gourde was the equivalent of one piastre.

overcome by loneliness, the dreariness of the surroundings consisting largely of marshy landscape and brackish water, or the appalling silence of the swamps, would put an end to himself.

To these people the Acadians formed a strong contrast. One cannot but admire the ease and good humor with which these displaced northerners adapted themselves to a new environment. In Canada, their chief enemies had been cold, hunger, and Indians; in Louisiana, they had to contend with heat, humidity, and insects. According to Berquin-Duvallon, few countries of the world surpassed Louisiana for the prevalence of insects. The worst was the mosquito, "a diabolical creature that harasses, infuriates, and torments you day and night." A century earlier, a French missionary remarked that "this little insect has provoked more curses since the French arrived on the Mississippi than all the curses that had previously been uttered in the world."

The Acadians managed to adapt even to the mosquitoes, and they developed into skilled hunters and trappers of otter, muskrat, raccoons, and alligators. While the men trapped and hunted, the women processed the skins and pelts, tended the vegetable gardens, and looked after the domestic animals: several scrawny hens, sometimes a cow or two, and invariably a number of pigs who lolled in the mud and were fed on small crabs, fish, and crawfish. The pigs had virtually evolved into amphibians.

The Acadians themselves ate crabs, fish, and crawfish as staples of their diet, along with shrimp and frogs' legs. They also feasted off the wild fowl that abounded in the region: ducks, quail, snipe, pheasants, wild geese. And the countryside yielded honey, grapes, currants, blackberries, and strawberries.

Their way of life was simple, devoid of luxuries, and marked by friendly sociability. Not only did the Acadians exchange visits with their neighbors, they often worked in common and shared each other's joys and sorrows. Families took turns in arranging dances, which offered the women an occasion to display their finery and men and women alike the chance for social intercourse in a cheerful, unconstrained setting.

From time to time, the trappers loaded their pirogues with a full cargo of furs and made their way to town. They returned with a load of household provisions, tools, and utensils. Properly handled, a pirogue could travel some fifteen miles a day downstream, but it was slow, painful going to travel home against the current. Even slower and more painful were the portages: the pirogue had to be unloaded, and goods and boat alike carried to the next waterway—lake, river, or bayou—on the route home.

In the Delta, the pirogue was the principal means of transportation: it was used by the priest making his calls, the dentist visiting his patients, the traveling salesman hawking his wares. At this period, most commerce was carried on by itinerant peddlers. Some specialized in the commodities they offered; others had a traveling emporium of merchandise, including dress hooks, thread, scissors, combs, ribbons, kitchen utensils, cotton goods, mirrors, books, cloves, coffee, salves, and potions. The peddlers traveled from house to house, farm to farm; they were assured of a warm welcome, for along with their merchandise they brought news of the outside world. Most of them were Frenchmen, though there were also a few Central European Jews, whom the Acadians called "Arabs." In the Delta, much of their business was carried on by barter: the peddlers exchanged their goods for rice, furs, or alligator skins.

MOORING THE HORSES, NAVIGATING THE PRAIRIE

The Attakapas prairie region was affectionately described by a mid-nineteenth-century inhabitant, Alexandre Barde:

It may be that some rhapsodic souls have abused poetic license in portraying these savannas as flowery expanses shimmering with golden-winged butterflies and crystalline lakes; but the realists are no closer to the truth with their talk of snakes and briar patches. The fields of tall grasses, billowing like waves in the breeze, present an image of indescribable beauty.

Early on, according to Barde, members of the French aristocracy established themselves in the Attakapas. They implanted there "the virtues and vices of their class; sparkling virtues, and vices hardly less attractive in their very brilliance." Then came the Spaniards, for whom the region was merely a way station en route from their new settlement at Pensacola, Florida, to San Antonio, Texas. They built a fort in the region, and Governor O'Reilly offered tracts of land to settlers possessing a hundred head of cattle, two slaves, and a number of horses and sheep. The Spanish tended to congregate around the Bayou Tèche, while the French settled for the most part in the western reaches of the area. Although St. Martinville, a modest hamlet that its inhabitants grandiloquently nicknamed "Little Paris," remained a French enclave, in New Iberia, the atmosphere was decidedly *latino*: the streets swarmed with dashing horsemen and swirling fandango dancers, sombreros, and mantillas. In character, the settlers were indolent and easygoing. A number of landowners possessed enormous herds of cattle, and hired Indian *vaqueros* to look after them. The cattle were maintained in a semiwild state: "From time to time," recalled C. C. Robin, "they were driven into a wide enclosure called a corral to accustom them to the sight of humans; this was referred to as 'domestication.'"

When the Acadians arrived, the Spanish authorities made them small grants of land, along with some tools and livestock, and "ambition, honesty, and honor took root in the region." According to the same commentator, Alexandre Barde, the Attakapas now experienced its "Golden Age." For "thievery was unknown, even among the Negroes," and the "farflung parishes of the region formed a single large family."

The Acadians penetrated deep into the region, built their homes near water, cleared pasture land that they surrounded with wooden fencing, and began to enlarge their modest herds. The Acadians called their ranchhouses *vacheries* and referred to themselves as cowboys or *vaqueros*. Although they never acquired the skill and style of the Texan or Mexican cowboys, they developed into creditable horsemen. In this part of Louisiana, the horse replaced the pirogue as the principal mode of transport, though for particularly heavy loads the inhabitants resorted to carts drawn by oxen.

Whereas most American backwoodsmen built their houses of logs, the Acadians utilized mud and moss. The chimneys too were made of dried mud, and when the houses were more than one story high, a small staircase led from the front porch to the upper loft. Inside, the furniture was of the simplest, with the loom and the spinning wheel occupying the places of honor. Alexandre Barde describes an Acadian interior in his usual effusive terms: "The decor is not sumptuous, but as bright and sparkling as a looking-glass. The women are hard at work, their cheerful countenances, framed by brunette hair, bent over the loom from Monday morn until Saturday noon, for all the world like fine ladies bent over the piano."

From a distance, the tall grasses waving in the wind resembled the billows of the ocean, and the Acadians frequently described the features of the region in nautical terms. The scattered clusters of tall timber forest were called "isles," or, if they projected into the prairie, "headlands." If the trees formed a curve, the configuration was a "cove" or "bay." To cross the prairie was to "navigate" it; to make the return trip was to "tack about." The Acadian "moored" his horse at the hitching post; when he started off in ox cart or buggy, he "set sail" or "put out to sea." When he furnished his home, he "rigged it out."

On the edge of the great prairie lay the market town of Lafayette (formerly Vermillonville), where the Acadians flocked every Saturday to make their purchases. The town was a station for the stagecoach and mailcoach; it was the nerve center for news and gossip, as well as a place to go for necessities of every kind. There you could find a priest, a doctor, a wheelwright, an officer of the law, and of course there was a tavern as well.

Every parish had its own sheriff—a typically American institution, whose importance was not lost on French visitors to the region. C. C. Robin observed:

The law seems to have been formed to multiply his functions. He is mandated to assure the public peace and safety; any man must lend him assistance if he requests it; all prisoners are under his care; he convenes the elections and makes certain they are honestly conducted; he draws up the list of jurors in both civil and criminal cases, and delivers the summons. . . . In the courtroom, he remains standing, not as a sign of inferiority but to represent the vigilance of the law.

The period from 1815 to 1830 saw change and growth in the Attakapas as in all of western Louisiana. The sheriffs must have been very busy. The "Golden Age" apparently came to an end when the Americans grew conscious of the potentialities of Texas. In 1820, the population of the vast Texas territory was barely three thousand people and the Spaniards needed only a few scattered garrisons to maintain order throughout the region. Freebooters and adventurers had been drifting into Texas since the beginning of the century, and in 1824, when the Mexican government passed a law allowing general colonization of the province, land-hungry Americans began to arrive in droves. The majority of the new settlers were sober and hard-working, of decent character and honorable intentions. Inevitably, however, among their number were a contingent of hardened criminals. The initials G.T.T. ("Gone to Texas") became, in the neighboring states, a shorthand for "fugitive from justice." In order to reach Texas, these outlaws had to pass through the neighboring territories, and many of them traversed the Attakapas, stealing livestock and even, on occasion, slaves. They also organized raids into the neighboring regions from Texas. The atmosphere came to resemble that of the Wild West rather than the Deep South. Gunfire crackled along the Sabine River, and the inhabitants of the region were forced to form vigilante committees to protect their property and their lives.

The rallying point for the lawless elements in the Attakapas was the home of a former *vaquero* named Gudbeer, reputed to be the son of a gypsy. According to Alexandre Barde, Gudbeer's tavern was frequented by "blacks, whites of dubious character, and a goodly number of night owls." There the visitors drank bad whiskey and played cards, "with the women cutting the deck."

Another disreputable Attakapas institution was the brothel opened about 1820 in a location "luxuriantly overgrown with vegetation" and known as Runaway Prairie because, located as it was in the midst of an all-but-impenetrable forest, it was a natural refuge for escaped slaves. The owner of the brothel was a free black named Coco. According to Alexandre Barde, Coco did not belong to that breed of black who seemed destined for the brute work of slavery; he was "one of the more handsome examples of the African race" and was universally respected. Coco had two mistresses, two white sisters, the daughters of a blacksmith, whom he had seduced with his mesmerizing charm. By these two women he had nineteen children, every one of them a thief or a hussy.

SQUATTERS

During the early years of the nineteenth century, there began to arrive in Louisiana wandering bands of Scotch and Irish farm laborers who, for want of money to buy land, settled as squatters in the pine forests of the interior. So poverty-stricken was their existence that a contemporary was prompted to exclaim: "A noble race of people! reduced to a condition but little above the wild Indian of the forest, or the European gypsy."

These Celtic immigrants were too proud to hire themselves out to other whites or to compete with the blacks for their simplest needs. Nor were the whites overeager to seek their services, for they were not easily assimilated into the existing strata, whether urban or rural, of Louisiana society. They were accused of committing thefts on the plantations and of selling whiskey to the slaves. On the whole, they were regarded by the other whites as exerting a demoralizing influence on the blacks.

Many Scots were distinguished for their piety. Those who knew how to read invariably read the Bible; neighbors gathered of an evening to listen with reverential attention to the Word of God. From time to time, an itinerant preacher, Baptist or Methodist, would venture into the wilderness to spread the Gospel; he could be sure of a warm welcome. Dressed in somber black, lank hair flowing down to his shoulders, the traveling minister often arrived at the cabin door toward nightfall after a long journey on horseback through wild forests and desolate prairies. He shared the evening meal with his hosts, then bedded down in a corner of the cabin. The next day, he would deliver a fiery sermon describing in terrifyingly graphic detail the torments of the damned, to the edification of the neighbors who had gathered from miles around. These "camp meetings," which began at dawn and lasted late into the night, were sometimes accompanied by barbecues at which whiskey flowed in profusion. The mixture of revivalist preaching and strong liquor often produced a kind of mass hysteria among the congregation. The air was rent with shouts of "Halleluia!" and whole families publicly confessed to the most frightful sins, meanwhile imploring divine forgiveness. Young girls rolled on the ground in a frenzy of possession, tearing at the bodices of their dresses, and frothing at the mouth. This period of evangelical fervor came to be known as the Second Great Awakening.

THE REDSKINS

The poor whites' nearest neighbors were the Indians, who still inhabited the north and northwest portions of the state. The Choctaws lived in Ouachita Parish, the Avoyelles in Avoyelles Parish, and the Caddos in Natchitoches. The Choctaws, by far the largest of these tribes, inhabited forest villages surrounded by palisades. They roofed their dwellings with palmetto leaves, raised corn and a few vegetables, kept some chickens and dogs, and cooked with iron, copper, or handmade clay pots.

Primarily, however, these Indians were hunters. For several centuries, they had engaged in the fur trade, catching the animals in traps or killing them with arrows. Hunting had evolved into a communal activity that required elaborate preparations, careful coordination of movements, and an accepted system for distributing the fruits of the hunt. All this meant that innumerable meetings and discussions were held before, during, and after the hunt; there were also feasts and dances at the outset of the hunt to encourage the hunters. If the venture proved successful, lengthier and even more elaborate celebrations were in order. The community sang the praises of those men who had distinguished themselves during the hunt and invoked by name, to the accompaniment of mournful chanting and moaning, those hunters who had recently died. In this way, the participants in the hunt received public recognition.

Now, however, the rifle had replaced the bow and arrow; a single individual or a small group of hunters could easily pursue game, and hunting had ceased to be a public enterprise for the Indians. The bonds of tribal unity, accordingly, began to grow slack—tightening again only when one tribe infringed on another's territorial rights. But since the whites had swallowed up so much of the traditional Indian hunting grounds of the Mississippi Valley, there was little occasion for the time-honored pursuit of intertribal warfare. With the passing years, the Indians lived increasingly within the family unit or in small, steadily shrinking groups. Their ancestral traditions grew dimmer, and their feasts and ceremonies gradually lost their meaning.

The search for food had become less of an ordeal. C. C. Robin reports on the new hunting methods: "The natives often go out in pairs. One of them carries a stuffed deer's head and, concealing his body behind a tree, thrusts forth the head so as to attract the notice of any passing deer. While the animal's attention is thus distracted, the other native takes aim and fires." To kill birds, rabbits, and squirrels, the Choctaw Indians used a seven-foot-long blowpipe fashioned from a reed.

The Indians traded their pelts and furs for firearms, gunpowder, blankets, handkerchiefs, and a variety of trinkets and household utensils. Their pirogues, laden with deer and bear skins, were a common sight on every river and waterway. They also used bear fat as an item of exchange. C. C. Robin remarks that a single bear could yield as many as eighty pots of fat.

The women did the domestic chores, wove baskets, and looked after the children. Robin, who spent some time among the Choctaws, reports that "they are extremely indulgent with their children, never thwart them, never ill-treat them." They took especial pleasure in dancing, singing, and public ceremonies of every kind. The most important annual event was the corn feast, celebrated with fasting, dances, and ritual ablutions. The Indians, both men and women, wore their long hair tied in two braids. They decorated themselves with feathers, and on festive occasions painted their faces in bright colors.

The Indian male was forbidden to marry a woman from his own *ogla* or tribal group, and custom demanded that his mother or another female from his *ogla* be dispatched to the *ogla* of the prospective bride to ask her hand in marriage. The Choctaw kinship structure was based on the female line; the request, therefore, was first addressed to the girl's mother or nearest female relative. If consent was granted, the two women then applied to the chiefs of their respective *oglas* for permission for the young couple to marry.

These formalities completed and the marriage date fixed, all the friends and relatives of the young man set off for the future wife's village, where the ceremony would be performed. Custom demanded that just before the marriage took place the groom, accompanied by his friends, should attempt to carry off the bride, who was protected by the young men of her own village. A mock combat was staged, in the course of which the girl pretended to flee, only to be overtaken and captured by her fiancé. After this ritual reenactment, the actual marriage ceremony was performed. The chiefs of the two tribal groups presided, and it was the occasion for much feasting and dancing.

As the Indian territory was infiltrated by European settlers, such tribal traditions gradually lost their hold. Little by little the Indian nations were destroyed by the march of white civilization. Many natives fell victim to alcoholism; many were reduced to a state of servile dependence on the white invaders. Deprived of their land, the Indians were also progressively deprived of their culture, their customs, their beliefs. Without the support of their age-old tribal traditions, they were virtually powerless to resist either the influence of white values or the attack of white diseases. Though some individuals survived, the Indian nations perished. And even though there still existed in the early years of the twentieth century a small band of Choctaws residing in St. Tammany Parish, who practiced their ancestral occupations of tanning and pottery-making and on certain nights of the year danced the sacred Snake Dance, these Choctaws were nothing more than the shadow of a lost civilization, the fossil remains of the great Indian tribes of Louisiana.

Conclusion

As the century took its course, Louisiana was increasingly caught up in the dynamic evolution of the United States of America—that country of boundless vitality, with its passionate love of innovation, its bewildering blend of warmhearted generosity and cruel indifference, of hardheaded pragmatism and lofty idealism. A visitor returning to New Orleans after a dozen years' absence might have had difficulty in recognizing the quaint provincial town of his former visit in this vibrant new metropolis. The 1830s saw widespread changes in the face of the city. The streets were entirely repaved; gas lights were installed; imposing new structures, both private and public, rose on every side. Magnificent Greek Revival banks stood forth, nineteenth-century temples of mercantilism. Two new hotels, the St. Charles and the St. Louis, were considered the finest examples of hotel architecture in the nation. The city was now divided into three districts and boasted a new canal and two railroad lines. New Orleans had become the richest city in the Union and the capital of the South.

From the privacy of their townhouses, the old Creole inhabitants looked out on the teeming new city with a mixture of bewilderment and disdain. They made it a point of honor to keep aloof from the American influences that pervaded New Orleans. But their children could not help learning English; and in the rural areas, neighboring families naturally came together, and a Creole father seldom refused his daughter's hand to the son of a prosperous American landowner.

In time, there emerged from the fusion of Creole and American elements a new breed of American, the southerner. The southerner spoke, lived, and acted differently from the Yankee. For him, it was

293

the South that mattered, not the Union; and in asserting their independence from northern styles and ideals, the Americans in Louisiana drew imperceptibly closer to their Creole neighbors. Thus Americans and Creoles, though they shared neither the same culture, the same language, or the same religion, came together through a mutual love of their native soil and a common vision of Louisiana as a traditional, conservative society—a last bastion of chivalry and honor against the encroachments of Yankee "barbarism." From 1830 on, the question of slavery and of tariff restrictions would dominate the history of the South, and Creoles and Americans alike would follow with passionate interest the electoral campaign that pitted President Andrew Jackson against John C. Calhoun, the man from South Carolina who was already speaking out for a confederation of southern states.

The Louisianians, whether Creole or American, countered the northerners' attacks with a fervent defense of slavery, the peculiar institution that many of them had previously, in fact, only tolerated as a necessary evil. But now even those southerners who secretly regarded slavery as a repugnant and inequitable practice were reluctant to voice their opinions for fear of being accused of disloyalty to the South. Though they might on occasion, in the company of non-southerners, concede that the institution was morally reprehensible, they were quick to add that the blacks fared better as slaves than they did as free men and women.

In response to an influx of northern abolitionists who were distributing tracts and holding meetings throughout the state and "inciting the Negroes to rebellion," the Louisiana legislature in 1830 voted a series of laws placing severe restrictions on the rights of all blacks, whether free or slave. The process of emancipation was made more difficult, and freed slaves were required to leave the state. Moreover, imprisonment was the penalty for teaching a slave to read or write. In 1831, Nat Turner's revolt in Virginia, in the course of which fifty-seven whites were killed, prompted further restrictive measures. Throughout the 1830s, rumors of slave uprisings were rife, and the blacks were subjected to continual surveillance and harassment.

But the year 1830 was even grimmer for the Indian population. In

January, the Congress of the United States, after a long debate, ratified the Indian Removal Act, which directed the five great Indian nations—the Creek, Cherokee, Chickasaw, Choctaw, and Seminole—be deported to Indian Territory in Oklahoma. Stripped of their land by the "Great White Father in Washington," the Choctaw people (with the exception of a few *oglas*) stoically took up their burdens and started out on the long trek to their new federally appointed homes. Their old domains were quickly overrun by squatters and homesteaders. Little now remained of Louisiana's ancient Indian heritage except for a haunting litany of place names: Atchafalaya, Natchitoches, Catahoula, Attakapas, Opelousas, Tchoupitoulas, Tangipahoa, Cabahanoose, Cataouatche.

A chapter in the history of Louisiana had come to a close.

Bibliography

Books and Articles

Allain, Hélène d'Aquin. *Souvenirs d'Amérique et de France, par une Créole.* Paris: Bourguet-Calas, 1883.

Alliot, Paul. "Memoir Sent to Washington." In *Louisiana Under the Rule of Spain, France, and the U.S.A., 1785–1807: Social, Economic, and Political Conditions of the Territory Represented in the Louisiana Purchase, as Portrayed in Hitherto Unpublished Contemporary Accounts by Dr. Paul Alliot and Various Spanish, French, English, and American Officials.* 2 vols. Cleveland: Arthur H. Clark Company, 1911.

Arsenault, Bona. *Histoire et généalogie des Acadiens.* 2 vols. Québec: Le Conseil de la Vie française en Amérique, 1965.

Asbury, Herbert. *The French Quarter: An Informal History of the New Orleans Underworld.* New York: A. A. Knopf, 1936.

Audubon, John James. *Journal of John James Audubon Made During His Trip to New Orleans in 1820–1821.* Edited by Howard Corning. Boston: The Club of Odd Volumes, 1929.

———. *Scènes de la nature dans les Etats-Unis et le Nord de l'Amérique.* Translated by Eugène Bazin. 2 vols. Paris: P. Bertrand, 1857.

Bancroft, Frederic. *Slave Trading in the Old South.* New York: Ungar, 1959.

Barbé-Marbois, François. *Histoire de la Louisiane et de la Cession de cette colonie par la France aux Etats-Unis de l'Amérique septentrionale.* Paris: Firmin-Didot, 1829.

Barde, Alexandre. *Histoire des comités de vigilance aux Attakapas.* Saint-Jean-Baptiste, La.: Imprimerie de Meschacébé et de l'Avant-Coureur, 1861.

Baudier, Roger. *The Catholic Church in Louisiana.* New Orleans: A. W. Hyatt, 1936.

Baudry des Lozières, Louis Narcisse. *Voyage à la Louisiane, et sur le continent de l'Amérique septentrionale, fait dans les années 1794 à 1798.* Paris: Dentu, 1802.

Bernhard, Karl, Duke of Saxe-Weimar-Eisenach. *Travels Through North America, During the Years 1825 and 1826.* 2 vols. Philadelphia: Carey, Lea, and Carey, 1828.

Berquin-Duvallon. *Vue de la colonie espagnole du Mississippi, ou des provinces de Louisiane et Floride Occidentale, en l'année 1802, par un observateur résident sur les lieux.* Paris: Imprimerie Expéditive, 1803.

Blair, Walter, and Franklin J. Meine. *Mike Fink, King of Mississippi Keelboatmen.* New York: H. Holt and Company, 1933.

Bushnell, David I., Jr. *The Choctaw of Bayou Lacomb, St. Tammany Parish, Louisiana.* Washington, D.C.: Government Printing Office, 1909.

Cable, George Washington. *The Creoles of Louisiana.* London: J. C. Nimmo, 1885.

————. "Creole Slave Songs." *Century Magazine,* XXXI (1886).

————. "The Dance of Congo Square." *Century Magazine,* XXXI (1886).

Caldwell, Stephen A. *A Banking History of Louisiana.* Baton Rouge: Louisiana State University Press, 1935.

Carter, Hodding. *Lower Mississippi.* New York: Farrar & Rinehart, 1942.

Castellanos, Henry C. *New Orleans As It Was: Episodes of Louisiana Life.* New Orleans: L. Graham & Sons, 1895.

Chambon, Celestin M. *In and Around the Old St. Louis Cathedral of New Orleans.* New Orleans: Philippe's Printery, 1908.

Charlevoix, Pierre François Xavier de. *History and General Description of New France.* Translated and edited by John Gilmary Shea. 6 vols. New York: F. P. Harper, 1900.

Chase, John Churchill. *Frenchmen, Desire, Good Children, and Other Streets of New Orleans.* New Orleans: R. L. Crager, 1949.

Clapp, Theodore. *Autobiographical Sketches and Recollections During a Thirty-Five Years' Residence in New Orleans.* Boston: Phillips, Sampson, and Company, 1857.

Condon, John Francis. *Annals of Louisiana, from the Close of Martin's History, 1815, to the Commencement of the Civil War, 1861.* New Orleans: J. A. Gresham, 1882.

Cramer, Zadok. *The Navigator, Containing Directions for Navigating the Monongahela, Allegheny, Ohio, and Mississippi Rivers with an Ample Account of These Much Admired Waters . . . and a Concise Description of Their Towns, Villages, Harbors, Settlements, &c.* Pittsburgh: Cramer & Spear, 1818.

Cruchet, René. *En Louisiane: Légendes et Réalités.* Bordeaux: Editions Delmas, 1937.

Darby, William. *A Geographical Description of the State of Louisiana, the Southern Part of the State of Mississippi, and Territory of Alabama.* New York: James Olmstead, 1817.

Deiler, John Hanno. *The Settlement of the German Coast of Louisiana and the Creoles of German Descent.* Philadelphia: Americana Germanica Press, 1909.

Ditchy, Jay Karl. *Les Acadiens louisianais et leur parler.* Paris: E. Droz, 1932.

Dubroca, Isabelle Christina. "A Study of Negro Emancipation in Louisiana, 1803–1865." M.A. thesis, Tulane University, 1924.

Dubroca, Louis. *L'Itinéraire des Français dans la Louisiane, contenant l'histoire de cette colonie française, sa description, le tableau des moeurs des peuples qui l'habitent, l'état de son commerce au moment de sa cession à l'Espagne, et le degré de prospérité dont elle est susceptible, d'après les renseignments et les relations les plus authentiques.* Paris: Dubroca, 1802.

Duffy, John. "Slavery and Slave Health in Louisiana 1766–1825." *Bulletin of the Tulane University Medical Faculty,* XXVI (February, 1967), 1–6.

Everett, Donald. "Free Persons of Color in New Orleans, 1803–1865." Ph.D. dissertation, Tulane University, 1952.

Fay, Edwin Whitfield. *The History of Education in Louisiana.* Washington, D.C.: Government Printing Office, 1898.

Ficatier, Marc. "Les Louisianais français, créoles et acadiens." *Revue de Psychologie des Peuples* (3rd trimester, 1957).

Fortier, Alcée. *A History of Louisiana.* 4 vols. New York: Goupil and Company of Paris, 1904.

———. *Louisiana Folk-Tales, in French Dialect and English Translation.* Boston: Houghton, Mifflin, 1895.

———. *Louisiana Studies: Literature, Customs and Dialects, History and Education.* New Orleans: F. F. Hansell and Brother, 1894.

———. "Les Planteurs sucriers de l'ancien régime en Louisiane." *Revue de Synthèse historique* (1906).

Fossier, Albert. *New Orleans: The Glamour Period, 1800–1840. A History of the Conflicts of Nationalities, Languages, Religion, Morals, Cultures, Laws, Politics, and Economics During the Formative Period of New Orleans.* New Orleans: Pelican Publishing Company, 1957.

Gayarré, Charles. *History of Louisiana.* 4 vols. New Orleans: Armand Hawkins, 1885.

———. *Histoire de la Louisiane.* 2 vols. New Orleans: Magne et Weisse, 1846–47.

———. *Fernanda de Lemos.* New York: G. W. Carleton, 1872.

———. "A Sugar Plantation of the Old Regime." *Harper's Magazine,* March, 1887.

Gould, Emerson W. *Fifty Years on the Mississippi: or, Gould's History of River Navigation.* St. Louis: Nixon-Jones Printing Company, 1889.

Griffin, Harry Lewis. *The Attakapas Country: A History of Lafayette Parish.* New Orleans: Pelican Publishing Company, 1959.

Hall, Basil. *Travels in North America in the Years 1827 and 1828.* 2 vols. Philadelphia: Carey, Lea & Carey, 1829.

Herrin, M. H. *The Creole Aristocracy: A Study of the Creole of Southern Louisiana, His Origin, His Accomplishments, His Contribution to the American Way of Life.* New York: Exposition Press, 1952.

Herskovits, Melville Jean. *The Myth of the Negro Past*. Boston: Beacon Press, 1958.

――――. *The New World Negro: Selected Papers in Afroamerican Studies*. Edited by Frances S. Herskovits. Bloomington: Indiana University Press, 1966.

Howe, William Wirt. *Memoirs of François-Xavier Martin*. Preface to François-Xavier Martin, *History of Louisiana from the Earliest Period*. New Orleans: J. A. Gresham, 1882.

――――. *Municipal History of New Orleans*. Johns Hopkins University Studies in Historical and Political Science, Series 1, Vol. 7, No. 4. Baltimore: Johns Hopkins Press, 1889.

Huber, Leonard V., and Samuel Wilson, Jr. *The Saint Louis Cemeteries of New Orleans*. New Orleans: St. Louis Cathedral, 1963.

Ingraham, Joseph Holt. *The South-west: By a Yankee*. 2 vols. New York: Harper & Brothers, 1835.

Jackson, John Robert. "The Poor Whites of Ante-bellum Louisiana." M.A. thesis, Tulane University, 1935.

Jones, Leroi. *Black Music*. New York: William Morrow, 1967.

――――. *Blues People: Negro Music in White America*. New York: William Morrow, 1963.

Kane, Harnett T. *Deep Delta Country*. New York: Duell, Sloan & Pearce, 1944.

――――. *Plantation Parade*. New York: William Morrow, 1945.

――――. *Gone Are the Days: An Illustrated History of the Old South*. New York: Dutton, 1960.

――――. *The Bayous of Louisiana*. New York: W. Morrow & Company, 1943.

Kennedy, Robert Emmet. *Mellows: A Chronicle of Unknown Singers*. New York: A. and C. Boni, 1925.

King, Grace. *Creole Families in New Orleans*. New York: Macmillan, 1921.

――――. *New Orleans, the Place and the People*. New York: Macmillan, 1895.

Kmen, Henry A. *Music in New Orleans: The Formative Years, 1791–1841*. Baton Rouge: Louisiana State University Press, 1966.

Korn, Bertram Wallace. *The Early Jews of New Orleans*. Waltham, Mass.: American Jewish Historical Society, 1969.

Krehbiel, Henry Edward. *Afro-American Folksongs: A Study in Racial and National Music*. New York: G. Schirmer, 1914.

Lacour, Arthur Burton, with Stuart Omer Landry. *New Orleans Masquerade: Chronicles of Carnival*. New Orleans: Pelican Publishing Company, 1952.

Latrobe, Benjamin H. *Impressions Respecting New Orleans: Diary and Sketches, 1818–1820*. Edited by Samuel Wilson, Jr. New York: Columbia University Press, 1951.

Laussat, Pierre Clément de. *Memoirs of My Life*. Translated by Agnes-

Josephine Pastwa. Edited by Robert D. Bush. Baton Rouge: Louisiana State University Press, 1977.

Lauvrière, Emile. *Histoire de la Louisiane française, 1673–1939.* Baton Rouge: Louisiana State University Press, 1940.

Lavisse, Ernest. *Histoire générale du IVe siècle à nos jours.* 12 vols. Paris: A. Colin, 1893–1901.

LeBlanc, Dudley. *The True Story of the Acadians.* Lafayette, La.: Louisiana Tribune, 1932.

Le Page du Pratz, Antoine Simon. *The History of Louisiana.* Edited by Joseph G. Tregle, Jr. Baton Rouge: Louisiana State University Press, 1975.

Levasseur, Auguste. *Lafayette en Amérique, en 1824 et 1825, ou Journal d'un voyage aux Etats-Unis.* 2 vols. Paris: Baudouin, 1829.

Lockwood, Luke Vincent. *Colonial Furniture in America.* 2 vols. New York: C. Scribner's Sons, 1926.

McConnell, Roland Calhoun. *Negro Troops in Antebellum Louisiana: A History of the Battalion of Free Men of Color.* Baton Rouge: Louisiana State University Press, 1968.

McIlhenny, Edward Avery, comp. *Befo' de War Spirituals: Words and Melodies.* Boston: Christopher Publishing House, 1933.

Mallard, Robert Q. *Plantation Life Before Emancipation.* Richmond, Va.: Whittel & Shepperson, 1892.

Marquette, Jacques. *Récit des voyages et des découverts du P. Jacques Marquette, de la Compagnie de Jésus, en l'année 1673 et aux suivantes.* Albany, N.Y.: Weed, Parson & Company, 1855.

Martin, François Xavier. *The History of Louisiana, from the Earliest Period.* New Orleans: J. A. Gresham, 1882.

Martineau, Harriet. *Retrospect of Western Travel.* 2 vols. London: Saunders and Otley, 1838.

———. *Society in America.* 2 vols. in 1. New York: Saunders and Otley, 1837.

Matas, Rudolph. *The History of Medicine in Louisiana.* Edited by John Duffy. 2 vols. Baton Rouge: Louisiana State University Press, 1958–62.

Metraux, Alfred. *Le Vaudou haïtien.* Paris: Gallimard, 1958.

Monette, John Wesley. *History of the Discovery and Settlement of the Valley of the Mississippi, by the Three Great European Powers, Spain, France, and Great Britain, and the Subsequent Occupation, Settlement, and Extension of Civil Government by the United States Until the Year 1846.* 2 vols. New York: Harper & Brothers, 1846.

Montlezun, Baron de. *Voyage fait dans les années 1816 et 1817, de New-Yorck à la Nouvelle-Orléans, et de l'Orénoque au Mississipi, par les Petites et les Grandes-Antilles, contenant des détails absolument nouveaux sur ces contrées, des portraits de personnages influant dans les Etats-Unis, et des anecdotes sur les réfugiés qui y sont établis.* 2 vols. Paris: Gide Fils, 1818.

Moody, Vernie Alton. *Slavery on Louisiana Plantations.* New Orleans: Cabildo, 1924.

Moreau de Saint-Méry, Médéric Louis Elie. *Description topographique, physique, civile, politique et historique de la partie française de l'isle Saint-Domingue. Avec des observations générales sur sa population, sur le caractère & les moeurs de ses divers habitans; sur son climat, sa culture, ses productions, son administration.* 2 vols. Paris: Dupont, 1797–98.

Nardini, Louis Raphael. *My Historic Natchitoches, Louisiana, and Its Environment: A History of Natchitoches, Louisiana, and the Neutral Strip Area of the State of Louisiana and Its Inhabitants.* Natchitoches: Nardini Publishing Company, 1963.

Niehaus, Earl F. *The Irish in New Orleans, 1800–1860.* Baton Rouge: Louisiana State University Press, 1965.

Nolte, Vincent Otto. *Fifty Years in Both Hemispheres: or, Reminiscences of the Life of a Former Merchant.* New York: Redfield, 1854.

O'Connor, Thomas. *History of the Fire Department of New Orleans from the Earliest Days to the Present Time, including the Original Volunteer Department, the Firemen's Charitable Association, and the Department Down to 1895.* New Orleans: n.p., 1895.

Olmsted, Frederick Law. *A Journey in the Seaboard Slave States in the Years 1853–1854, with Remarks on Their Economy.* 2 vols. New York: Putnam's Sons, 1904.

Pasquet, D. *Histoire politique et sociale du peuple américain.* 2 vols. in 3. Paris: A. Picard, 1924–31. Volume I.

Paxton, John Adem. *The New Orleans Directory and Register.* New Orleans: Printed for the author, 1822.

Perrin du Lac, François Marie. *Voyage dans les deux Louisianes, et chez les nations sauvages du Missouri, par les Etats-Unis, l'Ohio et les provinces qui le bordent, en 1801, 1802 et 1803; avec un aperçu des moeurs, des usages, du caractère et des coutumes religieuses et civiles des peuples de ces diverses contrées.* Lyon: Druyset ainé et Buynand, 1805.

Phillips, Ulrich Bonnell. *Life and Labor in the Old South.* Boston: Little, Brown, and Company, 1929.

Picornell, J. M. *Considérations hygiéniques sur la Nouvelle Orléans.* New Orleans: n.p., 1823.

Portré-Bobinski, Germaine. *Natchitoches, the Up-to-Date Oldest Town in Louisiana.* New Orleans: Dameron-Pierson Co., 1936.

Post, Lauren C. *Cajun Sketches from the Prairie of Southwest Louisiana.* Baton Rouge: Louisiana State University Press, 1962.

Pöstl, Karl Anton [Charles Sealsfield]. *The Americans as They Are, Described in a Tour Through the Valley of the Mississippi.* London: Hurst, Chance, 1828.

Pugh, W. W. "Bayou Lafourche from 1820 to 1825." *Louisiana Planter and Sugar Manufacturer,* September 29, 1888.

Quick, Herbert, and Edward Quick. *Mississippi Steamboatin': A History of Steamboating on the Mississippi and Its Tributaries.* New York: Henry Holt, 1926.

Richards, Addison. "Rice Land of the South." *Harper's New Monthly Magazine,* November, 1859.

Richardson, William. *Journal from Boston to the Western Country and Down the Ohio and Mississippi Rivers to New Orleans (1815–1816).* New York: Valve Pilot Corporation, 1940.

Roberts, Walter Adolphe. *Lake Pontchartrain.* Indianapolis: Bobbs-Merrill, 1946.

Robin, Claude C. *Voyages dans l'intérieur de la Louisiane, de la Floride occidentale, et dans les isles de la Martinique et de Saint-Domingue, pendant les années 1802, 1803, 1804, 1805, et 1806.* 3 vols. Paris: F. Buisson, 1807.

Roussève, Charles Barthelemy. *The Negro in Louisiana: Aspects of His History and His Literature.* New Orleans: Xavier University Press, 1937.

Saxon, Lyle. *Fabulous New Orleans.* New York: D. Appleton-Century, 1928.

———. *Old Louisiana.* New York: Century Company, 1929.

———. *Father Mississippi.* New York: Century, 1927.

Saxon, Lyle, Edward Dreyer, and Robert Tallant, comp. *Gumba Ya Ya.* Boston: Houghton-Mifflin, 1945.

Searight, Sarah. *New Orleans.* New York: Stein and Day, 1973.

Sparks, William Henry. *The Memories of Fifty Years: Containing Brief Biographical Notices of Distinguished Americans, and Anecdotes of Remarkable Men, Interspersed with Scenes and Incidents Occurring During a Long Life of Observation Chiefly Spent in the Southwest.* Macon, Ga.: J. W. Burke, 1882.

Spencer, Robert F., and Jesse D. Jennings, *et al. The Native Americans: Ethnology and Backgrounds of the North American Indians.* New York: Harper & Row, 1965.

Sterkx, Henry Eugene. *The Free Negro in Ante-Bellum Louisiana.* Rutherford, N.J.: Fairleigh Dickinson University Press, 1972.

Tallant, Robert. *Mardi Gras.* Garden City, N.Y.: Doubleday, 1948.

———. *The Romantic New Orleanians.* New York: Dutton, 1950.

———. *Voodoo in New Orleans.* New York: Macmillan, 1946.

Taylor, Joe Gray. *Negro Slavery in Louisiana.* Baton Rouge: Louisiana Historical Association, 1963.

Thomas, Pierre Frédéric. *Essai sur la fièvre jaune d'Amérique . . . précédé de Considérations hygiéniques sur la Nouvelle Orléans.* New Orleans: n.p., 1823.

Tinker, Edward Laroque. *Les écrits de langue française en Louisiane aux*

XIXe siècle: Essais biographiques et bibliographiques. Paris: Champion, 1932.

———. *Creole City: Its Past and Its People.* New York: Longmans, Green, 1953.

———. *Gombo, the Creole Dialect of Louisiana.* Worcester, Mass.: American Antiquarian Society, 1936.

———. *The Palingenesis of Craps.* New York: The Press of the Woolly Whale, 1933.

———. *Pen, Pills & Pistols: A Louisiana Chronicle.* New York: American Society of the French Legion of Honor, 1934.

Tocqueville, Alexis de. *Democracy in America.* Translated by Henry Reeve. Edited by Francis Bowen and Phillips Bradley. 2 vols. New York: Vintage Books, 1945.

Trollope, Frances. *Domestic Manners of the Americans.* 2 vols. New York: Dodd, Mead, 1832.

Vergennes, Charles Gravier, Comte de. *Mémoire historique et politique sur la Louisiane.* Paris: Le petit Jeune, 1802.

Vetter, Ernest G. *Fabulous Frenchtown: The Story of the Famous French Quarter of New Orleans.* Washington, D.C.: Coronet Press, 1955.

Wilcox, Ruth Turner. *Five Centuries of American Costume.* New York: Scribner, 1963.

Williamson, Frederick W. *Yesterday and Today in Louisiana Agriculture: How Twenty-Five Years of Extension Service Changed the Pattern of Farming and Rural Life.* Baton Rouge: Louisiana State University Division of Agricultural Extension, 1940.

Wilson, Samuel Jr., et al. *New Orleans Architecture: The American Sector.* New Orleans: Pelican Publishing Company, 1972.

Wilson, Samuel Jr., and Leonard V. Huber. *The Cabildo on Jackson Square.* New Orleans: Friends of the Cabildo, 1970.

Young, Perry. *The Mistick Krewe: Chronicles of Comus and His Kin.* New Orleans: Heritage Press, 1969.

NEWSPAPERS

New Orleans *Abeille*
New Orleans *Argus*
New Orleans *Courrier de la Louisiane*
New Orleans *Louisianais et l'Ami des Lois*
New Orleans *Louisiana Gazette*

PRINTED DOCUMENTS

Le Code noir, ou, Edit du Roy, servant de règlement, pour le gouvernement & l'administration de la justice, police, discipline & le commerce des esclaves nègres, dans la province & colonie de la Louisianne. Donné à

Versailles au mois de Mars 1724. Paris: Saugrain et Pierre Prault, 1728.

A Digest of the Ordinances, Resolutions, By-Laws, and Regulations of the Corporation of New Orleans, and a Collection of the Laws of the Legislature Relative to the Said City. New Orleans: G. Brusle, 1836.

MANUSCRIPTS

Special Collections Division, Tulane University
 De La Vergne Family Papers
 David Reer Papers
 Roman Family Papers
 Acklen Family Papers
 John McDonogh Papers
 Farrar Papers
 Valcourt Aime Plantation Diary
City of New Orleans
 Municipal Archives
 Notarial Archives
Ascension Parish Archives
Iberville Parish Archives
St. Charles Parish Archives

Index